"Landon Dowden may be the most gift⌐
the privilege of knowing. His solid and skillful exposition, flavored by
a natural and delightful wit, is a combination that few preachers can
feature with integrity. Landon gives the ancient text a pair of tennis
shoes and makes it walk where we walk. Now God's grace in his life is
in print to our benefit through his volume on Esther. He shows us how
God demonstrates His heart for the salvation of His people through
the actions of this familiar, heroic, and beloved Old Testament woman.
Furthermore, he shows us the full realization of her courage and sacrifice in Christ Jesus. Use this volume as you study, teach, and preach
Esther's beautiful picture of love and redemption."

Jim Shaddix, D.Min., Ph.D., W. A. Criswell Chair of Expository
Preaching, and director, Center for Preaching and Pastoral Leadership,
Southeastern Baptist Theological Seminary, Wake Forest, NC

"Landon Dowden is one of the finest expositors alive. He is warm, witty,
and most of all, thoroughly biblical and relentlessly Christ-exalting. In
this volume on Esther, he not only helps the reader understand the
details of each passage but also magnifies the glory of our Sovereign
God in each exposition, thus helping the reader cultivate a deeper trust
in God and a greater appreciation for the outworking of His purposes in
redemptive history, which culminate in Christ. I will certainly be using
this commentary when I preach Esther, and this commentary has made
me want to preach it soon!"

Tony Merida

"Can Christ be preached from Esther in an expository manner that
is hermeneutically authentic? Absolutely! And this commentary by
Landon Dowden shows us how in a masterful display of faithful, text-
driven preaching. This is Christ-centered preaching at its best. I was
blessed by reading it, and you will be too."

Daniel L. Akin

"Landon Dowden is a clear thinking pastor-theologian and a master
communicator, and his exceptional gifts are put to full use in his work
on Esther. Pastors who are expository preachers know it is rare to find
a commentary that is exegetically careful, theologically sound, and
homiletically helpful. Dowden's work is such a find. Somehow he has

produced a book that is both theologically substantive and entertaining to read. Plus, it is Christ-centered from beginning to end. So, whether readers want simply to learn more about Esther or to learn how this part of the Old Testament finds fulfillment in Christ, they need look no further than this book."

Allan Moseley, professor of Old Testament and Hebrew, Southeastern Baptist Theological Seminary, Wake Forest, North Carolina

"Dr. Landon Dowden is a scholar who has both feet firmly planted in the church. As a pastor-scholar, he has done an excellent job with the next installment of the Christ-Centered Exposition Commentary. While the book of Esther is not explicitly theological in many places, Dr. Dowden illustrates the many ways we can see God's hand at work in this text. Dr. Dowden not only explains the meaning of the text, but he also relates it to today in a format that every preacher will find useful."

Norris Grubs, provost, New Orleans Baptist Theological Seminary

"In this commentary, Landon shows that it is not only possible but necessary to see and preach Christ in Esther. His exposition is biblically sound and practical. Anybody wanting to faithfully preach and teach the book of Esther in a Christ-centered way should pick up this valuable resource."

Robby Gallaty, senior pastor, Long Hollow Baptist Church, Hendersonville, Tennessee

AUTHOR Landon Dowden

SERIES EDITORS David Platt, Daniel L. Akin, and Tony Merida

CHRIST-CENTERED

Exposition

EXALTING JESUS IN

ESTHER

HOLMAN®

REFERENCE

NASHVILLE, TENNESSEE

B&H Publishing Group
Nashville, Tennessee
All rights reserved.

ISBN: 978-1-4336-0995-4

Dewey Decimal Classification: 220.7
Subject Heading: BIBLE. O.T. Esther—
COMMENTARIES\JESUS CHRIST

Printed in the United States of America

2 3 4 5 6 7 8 9 10 • 26 25 24 23 22

BP

SERIES DEDICATION

Dedicated to Adrian Rogers and John Piper. They have taught us to love the gospel of Jesus Christ, to preach the Bible as the inerrant Word of God, to pastor the church for which our Savior died, and to have a passion to see all nations gladly worship the Lamb.

—David Platt, Tony Merida, and Danny Akin
March 2013

AUTHOR'S DEDICATION

To Tara, Arabella, Adalaide, Adoniram, and Alastair.
Even when you cannot see him, hear him, or feel him,
God is alive, awake, and accomplishing his purposes
for your good and for his glory!

"That night sleep escaped the king . . ." (Esth 6:1)

TABLE OF CONTENTS

Esther

ACKNOWLEDGMENTS

As I prepare to submit this volume, my beautiful bride, Tara, and I will soon celebrate our fifteenth wedding anniversary.

Tara, my expression of gratitude first extends to the Lord for giving you to me and for his grace to make each of these years sweeter. When your father entrusted me with your care at the altar, he said to me, "She is such a joy!" He was right. You fill our home with warmth and love. Your laughter is my favorite sound in the entire world. Thank you for putting up with my craziness and quirks. Thank you for bringing needed balance to my life. Thank you for always believing in me even when I do not. Any good that comes from this commentary will be because of your sacrifices and the Lord's grace. I love you. MTML.

I could not have finished this work if not for the support and sacrifices of my children as well. Thank you, Arabella, for letting me borrow your headphones so I could bring the decibels down to a working level in the loud house! Thank you, Arabella and Adalaide, for checking on my progress and for helping with different responsibilities so I could keep writing. I am thankful for the evidences of the Lord's grace in your lives. Thank you also to Adoniram and Alastair for sacrificing extra batting-practice time and for praying for Daddy to finish his book! I love all four of you and am grateful the Lord placed you in our quiver.

We are blessed to be so close to so many family members. Thank you to my godly mother, Barbara, my sacrificial sister, Larilyn, my generous and wonderful in-laws, TK and Rita, and our amazing Aunt Frances. Thank you all for loving our children so well and for helping Tara and me in countless ways. I love each of you and thank the Lord for you. Though she is with Christ now, I also remain thankful for my grandmother, Mary Graham, for all the love and prayers she lavished on her little preacher man.

Should the Lord give us this August, I will have served as the lead pastor at The Church at Trace Crossing for seven years. I continue to be blessed to shepherd a faith family who longs for the whole counsel of God's Word. By God's grace I am thankful to say, "My brothers and sisters, I myself am convinced about you that you also are full of goodness, filled with all knowledge, and able to instruct one another" (Rom 15:14). May the Lord continue to advance his gospel in and through us for the good of our city and for his glory.

I am blessed to serve alongside some of the greatest brothers; they constitute our pastoral staff and elders. Mitchell, Mathew, Kevin, Jim, Tommy, Matt, and Rob—thank you for your support, your prayers, your encouragement, your sacrifices, and your faithfulness. Mathew and Kevin, in particular, thank you for always striving to rightly divide God's Word and feed the Lord's sheep well. Thank you, Mitchell, for making sure we sing the Word. For all of you, I thank the Lord often. Serving with you is one of my greatest joys.

Thank you to David Platt, Tony Merida, and Danny Akin for entrusting me with another volume in the Christ-Centered Exposition series. To be given the opportunity to write about Ezekiel was a grace, but now with Esther I have received grace upon grace. I am thankful for how the Lord has used each of you in my life through these years of friendship.

And now, Father, to the one whom I owe the greatest gratitude: you sought me when I was far away. You gave me ears to hear the gospel and grace to respond. You have been so faithful when I have not. Your goodness to me overflows, and I deserve none of it. Father, I pray you would use this book to make much of Jesus. I love you and say thank you for so many evidences of your grace.

Landon Dowden
April 30, 2018

SERIES INTRODUCTION

Augustine said, "Where Scripture speaks, God speaks." The editors of the Christ-Centered Exposition Commentary series believe that where God speaks, the pastor must speak. God speaks through his written Word. We must speak from that Word. We believe the Bible is God breathed, authoritative, inerrant, sufficient, understandable, necessary, and timeless. We also affirm that the Bible is a Christ-centered book; that is, it contains a unified story of redemptive history of which Jesus is the hero. Because of this Christ-centered trajectory that runs from Genesis 1 through Revelation 22, we believe the Bible has a corresponding global-missions thrust. From beginning to end, we see God's mission as one of making worshipers of Christ from every tribe and tongue worked out through this redemptive drama in Scripture. To that end we must preach the Word.

In addition to these distinct convictions, the Christ-Centered Exposition Commentary series has some distinguishing characteristics. First, this series seeks to display exegetical accuracy. What the Bible says is what we want to say. While not every volume in the series will be a verse-by-verse commentary, we nevertheless desire to handle the text carefully and explain it rightly. Those who teach and preach bear the heavy responsibility of saying what God has said in his Word and declaring what God has done in Christ. We desire to handle God's Word faithfully, knowing that we must give an account for how we have fulfilled this holy calling (Jas 3:1).

Second, the Christ-Centered Exposition Commentary series has pastors in view. While we hope others will read this series, such as parents, teachers, small-group leaders, and student ministers, we desire to provide a commentary busy pastors will use for weekly preparation of biblically faithful and gospel-saturated sermons. This series is not academic in nature. Our aim is to present a readable and pastoral style of commentaries. We believe this aim will serve the church of the Lord Jesus Christ.

Third, we want the Christ-Centered Exposition Commentary series to be known for the inclusion of helpful illustrations and theologically driven applications. Many commentaries offer no help in illustrations, and few offer any kind of help in application. Often those that do offer illustrative material and application unfortunately give little serious attention to the text. While giving ourselves primarily to explanation, we also hope to serve readers by providing inspiring and illuminating illustrations coupled with timely and timeless application.

Finally, as the name suggests, the editors seek to exalt Jesus from every book of the Bible. In saying this, we are not commending wild allegory or fanciful typology. We certainly believe we must be constrained to the meaning intended by the divine Author himself, the Holy Spirit of God. However, we also believe the Bible has a messianic focus, and our hope is that the individual authors will exalt Christ from particular texts. Luke 24:25-27,44-47 and John 5:39,46 inform both our hermeneutics and our homiletics. Not every author will do this the same way or have the same degree of Christ-centered emphasis. That is fine with us. We believe faithful exposition that is Christ centered is not monolithic. We do believe, however, that we must read the whole Bible as Christian Scripture. Therefore, our aim is both to honor the historical particularity of each biblical passage and to highlight its intrinsic connection to the Redeemer.

The editors are indebted to the contributors of each volume. The reader will detect a unique style from each writer, and we celebrate these unique gifts and traits. While distinctive in their approaches, the authors share a common characteristic in that they are pastoral theologians. They love the church, and they regularly preach and teach God's Word to God's people. Further, many of these contributors are younger voices. We think these new, fresh voices can serve the church well, especially among a rising generation that has the task of proclaiming the Word of Christ and the Christ of the Word to the lost world.

We hope and pray this series will serve the body of Christ well in these ways until our Savior returns in glory. If it does, we will have succeeded in our assignment.

David Platt
Daniel L. Akin
Tony Merida
Series Editors
February 2013

Esther

Introduction
Can Christ Be Preached from Esther?

Exalting Christ . . . in Esther? This is the second question I asked myself when I was contacted about writing this commentary. The first question was, What did I do to Akin, Platt, and Merida? They initially asked me to write on Ezekiel, which I did, and it is not exactly full of kicks and giggles. Now they want me to write a Christ-exalting commentary on the only book in the Bible that has no mention of God. *Not one single reference!* There is not a "Most High," a "Holy One," a "Sovereign One," an "Almighty," a "Great I Am," an "Elohim," or an "Adonai" in Esther. Despite the best efforts of some to find it acrostically using the first letters of a phrase in 5:4 or backwards using the last letters of another phrase in 5:13, there is not even a mention of Yahweh anywhere in the book (Firth, *The Message of Esther*, 11). There is also no word given to a prophet, no vision or dream through which God speaks, and as a matter of fact, not even a single prayer is mentioned in any of the ten chapters (Jenkins, "Esther and the Silent Sovereignty of God"). There is no comment on the Torah or the temple. So, in the book of Esther, there is certainly not a specific mention of Jesus. Can Christ be preached from Esther?

Honestly, I hesitated to respond positively to an opportunity to write this commentary. Though I have seen the Veggie Tales version of Esther numerous times (I have four children), none of the churches of which I have been a member ever offered a chapter-by-chapter, in-depth study of the book, much less a sermon series. Moreover, none of the exegesis classes I took in seminary covered Esther. In my research I found several pastors who preached a multipart sermon series on Esther in which they either combined large portions of Esther's ten chapters or they skipped some of them entirely, such as Tim Keller's "Esther and the Hiddenness of God." Also through my search, though, I am happy to share I found at least two pastors who offered a chapter-by-chapter sermon series, but those who shepherd their people through Esther on a verse-by-verse basis seem to be few and far between. Of those who have preached through Esther, whether in part or in total, one wonders how many did so with a Christocentric lens.

My main hesitation in responding positively to an opportunity to write this commentary, however, was that as a committed practitioner and adjunct professor of expository preaching, I needed to make sure I could actually do what I was being asked to do. Can sermons that exalt Christ be preached from Esther? Maybe you have purchased this book because you were wondering the same thing. Can sermons that exalt Christ be preached from Esther that are not full of eisegesis (i.e., putting something into the text that was not true for its original audience, or making the text say something that in reality the text is not saying)? Graeme Goldsworthy offers some helpful wisdom here:

> We do not start at Genesis 1 and work our way forward until we discover where it is all leading. Rather we first come to Christ, and he directs us to study the Old Testament in the light of the gospel. The gospel will interpret the Old Testament by showing us its goal and meaning. (*According to Plan*, 55)

Because it is helpful when an author admits his biases up front (though I would say mine is more a biblical/theological conviction than a bias), you should know the default hermeneutic I use to fuel my homiletic on these matters is that Jesus believes Christ-centered preaching can occur from the Old Testament (see Luke 24:25-26,44-48) and the apostles practiced it (Acts 2:14-36). Finding consensus on how Christ should be preached from the Old Testament, however, is about as easy as finding a leprechaun at the end of a rainbow. Some like Richard Longenecker believe "our commitment as Christians is to the reproduction of the apostolic faith and doctrine, and not necessarily to the specific apostolic exegetical practices" (*Biblical Exegesis in the Apostolic Period*, 219). Likewise, Abraham Kuruvilla cautions against "creating a comprehensive apostolic hermeneutical model out of" what he calls "scant data" (*Privilege the Text!*, 246). He contends that important questions need to be asked when considering Luke's use of "in all the Scriptures" (Luke 24:27). He asks,

> Is it every portion of Scripture, or every book, or every pericope, or every paragraph, or every verse, or every jot and tittle?
> The subsequent statements by Jesus to the Emmaus disciples suggest that what is meant is every *portion* of Scripture—a broad reference to its various parts, primarily the major divisions: Law, Prophets, and Psalms (writings). (Ibid., 248)

An important question, then, is, Can *each* text in the Old Testament teach us something about Christ? Or, with our task in mind, can each text in Esther be used to teach us something about Christ? Tim Keller contends that redemptive-historical preaching

> reads the Bible in a way that stresses the organic unity between unfolding historical stages of God's redemption in Christ. This approach is careful to "preach Christ" and his salvation from every passage of the Bible, whether he is overtly referred to or not. ("Preaching the Gospel in a Post-Modern World")

Consider also these words from Al Mohler:

> Every single text of Scripture points to Christ. He is the Lord of all, and therefore He is the Lord of the Scriptures too. From Moses to the prophets, He is the focus of every single word of the Bible. Every verse of Scripture finds its fulfillment in Him, and every story in the Bible ends with Him. (*He Is Not Silent*, 96)

In considering these different views, I find the words of my mentor, Jim Shaddix, particularly helpful. He writes,

> While some texts have Christ as their center (christocentric), and others have Christ as their intended realization (christotelic), some texts simply reflect the character and image of Christ into which God is re-creating us (christiconic). (Vines and Shaddix, *Progress in the Pulpit*, 119)

He goes on to add,

> Whether the best line to the cross is a beeline, or whether you and I need to take a few side roads in order to preserve hermeneutical integrity, we must make sure we reach the cross in every message. And when we do, we must make sure to unpack the good news enough that people have the whole story. (Ibid., 124)

Where you land in hermeneutical and homiletical camps I will leave you to discern, but the most important question we need to answer is, How can we rightly divide God's Word so that when we give an account to the chief Shepherd we will not need to hang our heads in shame? Faithfully proclaiming "Thus says the Lord" is a massive responsibility that should never be entered into lightly or without diligent preparation. Proclaiming Christ-exalting expositions from Esther is indeed possible. Let's consider now some (hopefully) helpful information as we get started.

Where Does the Book of Esther Fit in Redemptive History?

What is really going on in this book? Or to ask it better, What role does this book play in the overarching story of God redeeming a people for his name's sake? To grasp what is really happening in Esther, we have to go all the way back to Genesis 3:15. From that moment in the garden, Satan has wanted to destroy the offspring who would eventually crush his head. We see him attempt this in Exodus with backbreaking work for God's people in slavery, with newborn males being tossed into the Nile, and with Pharaoh's desire to crush the Israelites by the Red Sea—and yet all of these attempts failed. We see it again in the New Testament, after the incarnation of Christ in Bethlehem, with Herod having all males two years old and younger killed. Both attempts to destroy God's people failed, and so did one that occurred between them, which is recorded for us in Esther (3:8-15). Haman, in fact, is just another pawn under the influence of Satan to try to annihilate God's people and prevent any possibility of the Messiah. This gets us to a good, one-sentence summary of Esther: **Through his providence and in keeping with his promises, God places Esther and Mordecai in positions of power to preserve his people and punish his enemies.**

Somehow I made it through eight years of seminary without fully grasping the big picture of the Bible. It was not until I discovered Graeme Goldsworthy's work, *Gospel and Kingdom*, and his contention that the overall focus of the Bible is the kingdom of God that the picture began to become a little clearer. By "the kingdom of God," Goldsworthy means God's people in God's place under God's rule (*Gospel and Kingdom*, 54). In his book *God's Big Picture*, Vaughn Roberts adds one more phrase to Goldsworthy's definition: "The kingdom of God is God's people in God's place under God's rule *and blessing*" (*God's Big Picture*, 21; emphasis added). I have found Roberts's work to be so helpful that I have not only led my congregation through it but also made it required reading for each of my doctoral students.

Using Goldsworthy's and Roberts's terms to place Esther in the overall redemptive story of the Bible, God's people (most of them) had been removed from God's place (the promised land) because they refused to submit to God's rule. According to his own faithfulness, God did not destroy the Israelites but disciplined them with exile. Specifically, the events in Esther occur during the third (Esth 1:3), seventh (2:16), and twelfth (3:7) years of Ahasuerus's reign (486–465 BC), and most likely between what is recorded in the sixth and seventh chapters of Ezra. In Ezra 1:1-4 we are informed that Cyrus let some of the exiles return to Jerusalem (539 BC), and 42,360 Jews chose to do so, bringing 7,337 of their servants with them (Ezra 2:64-65). The families of Mordecai and Esther, however, were not among those who returned to Jerusalem, and "sixty years later large numbers of Jews remained in the eastern half of the Persian empire, many in the great imperial cities of Persia itself" (Baldwin, *Esther*, 17). As we will see, Mordecai and Esther are in Susa (Esth 2:5), Persia's winter capital (LaSor, Hubbard, and Bush, *Old Testament Survey*, 532).

In the last chapters of Genesis and the beginning of Exodus, God is growing a people from one man to many. In the second half of Exodus and all of Leviticus, God is giving his people his instructions. In Joshua God is moving his people into the place he has for them. In Esther we can see that even after Israel has been unfaithful to him, God remains faithful and is preserving a people for his name's sake. Haman (who is a real piece of work if you have not read about him yet) wants to destroy not just Mordecai but every Jew living within Ahasuerus's realm of power. God, however, made promises to Abraham (Gen 12:1-3; 17:7) that include his descendants, and God intends to keep all of his promises. In redemptive history the book of Esther is not only about God's continuing to have a people but also about his preservation of his people from extinction. Somewhere in Ahasuerus's realm were those through whom the Messiah would eventually be sent, and nothing Haman (or Satan) attempted would be able to overcome God's protective hand.

What Can We Learn about God in the Book of Esther?

One of the most important questions we can ask when studying the Bible is, What does this text teach/reveal about God? We may often be prone to read each text through a self-centered lens, but the Bible's main focus is revealing who God is and what he is doing. God, however, is not mentioned specifically in the book of Esther. Nevertheless, Mark Dever contends that Esther "is one of the longest sustained meditations on the sovereignty and providence of God in the whole Bible. It is really just one long narrative illustration of Romans 8:28" (*The Message of the*

Old Testament, 454). Similarly, Gary Smith says, "The story of Esther is a case study for the truth that 'for those who love God *all things* work together for good, for those who are called according to his purpose' (Rom. 8:28)" ("Esther," 426). Esther, then, reminds us that even when circumstances may appear contrary to the fact, God is both watching and working for our good. He is advancing his purposes despite making no appearances (Jenkins, "Esther and the Silent Sovereignty of God").

Many years ago I was leading a Disciple Now weekend in Tupelo, Mississippi, when another leader shared an illustration I have never forgotten and have used countless times since. He asked for a volunteer. Once the teenager was at the front of the room, the leader pulled a set of keys from his pocket and told the youth, "No matter what, these keys will always be in front of you." He then asked the teenager, "Where are the keys?" And the teen responded, "In front of me." The leader asked, "How do you know?" The youth answered, "Because I can see them."

The leader next pulled out a scarf and blindfolded the youth. He began to shake the keys and asked, "Where are the keys?" The student responded, "In front of me." The leader then followed up: "How do you know?" To this the teen said, "I can hear them."

Next the leader stopped moving the keys and asked, "Where are the keys now?" The student, not being able to see them or hear them, instinctively reached in front of him until he grabbed the keys and said, "They are in front of me." The leader then asked, "How do you know?" and the student responded, "Because I can feel them."

In the final phase of his illustration the leader took one step back just out of arm's reach from the student and asked one final time, "Where are the keys?" The student could not see them, could not hear them, and as he reached out frantically in front of him and grasped nothing but air, he could not feel them. The leader asked again, "Where are the keys?" While still trying to find the keys, the student's new response was, "I don't know." The leader then asked, "Where did I tell you the keys would always be?" The youth answered, "In front of me." So the leader followed up with, "So, where do you think the keys are?" The frustrated teen responded, "I guess in front of me!"

The leader then had the student remove his blindfold, and when he knew the student could see the keys just out of arm's reach but still in front of him, the leader asked, "So, where are the keys?" The teen responded, "In front of me." The leader then explained all the mystery around the keys, the blindfold, and the questions: "There are times in our lives when we do not see God. There are times in our lives when we do not hear God. There are times in our lives when we do not feel God. But he has promised never to leave us nor forsake us. Our trust in his presence is not based on our feelings but on his faithfulness."

I did not know it when I saw this illustration unfold, but God would use it later in my life. When I was a senior in college, my father passed away unexpectedly. His funeral was the first funeral I ever preached. Later in the evening of the day we buried him, I was sitting on a swing in our front yard. On that swing I did not see God. On that swing I did not hear God. And on that swing I did not feel God. But I knew God was with me because of his promise and not because of an overwhelming sense of his presence.

Has there ever been some event or some blessing or some comfort or some guidance that you know was God's work, but he did not audibly speak to you or perform a miracle to accomplish whatever it was? Maybe you said something like, "God did this," or, "God provided that." Perhaps he even used the ordinary means of an encouraging word from a friend rather than writing the message in the sky for all to see. There are things in all our lives that we attribute to God without his directly saying, "You know I'm doing this, right? You know this is my work, right?" We often refer to his providence even though we may not visibly see his presence. This is true for the book of Esther. In this book God's name is not mentioned once, but his work is seen in every chapter. As LaSor, Hubbard, and Bush write, "Coincidences in Esther are the fingerprints of God's hands at work" (*Old Testament Survey*, 538).

Here are some of those "coincidences" or "stuff" Dever says "just seems to happen" in Esther:

- Esther just *happens* to be Jewish, and she just *happens* to be beautiful.
- Esther just *happens* to be favored by the king.
- Mordecai just *happens* to overhear the plot against the king's life.
- A report of this just *happens* to be written in the king's chronicles.
- Haman just *happens* to notice that Mordecai does not kneel down before him, and he just *happens* to find out that Mordecai is a Jew.
- When Haman plots his revenge, the dice just *happen* to indicate that the date for exacting revenge is put off for almost a year!

(What does Prov 16:33 say? "The lot is cast into the lap, but its every decision is from the Lord.")

- Esther just *happens* to get the king's approval to speak, but then she *happens* to put off her request for another day.
- Her deferral just *happens* to send Haman out by Mordecai one more time, . . .
- . . . which just *happens* to cause him to recount it to his friends.
- They, in turn, just *happen* to encourage him to build a scaffold immediately!
- So Haman just *happens* to be excited to approach the king early the next morning.
- It just so *happens* that the previous night, the mighty king could not command a moment's sleep, . . .
- . . . and he just *happened* to have had a book brought to him that recounted Mordecai's deed.
- He then *happened* to ask whether Mordecai had been rewarded, to which his attendants *happened* to know the answer. Simply consider for a moment the fact that Mordecai *happened* not to have been rewarded for having saved the king's life. How unusual this must have been! Someone who saved the king's life never rewarded? I wonder if Mordecai ever chafed under that: "Doesn't he realize what I did for him?" Well, it all just *happened*.
- Haman *happens* to approach the king just when the king is wondering how Mordecai should be honored.
- Later on the king *happens* to return to the queen just when Haman *happens* to be pleading with Esther in a way that can be misconstrued.
- The gallows Haman built for Mordecai just *happens* to be ready when King Xerxes wants to hang Haman (Dever, *The Message of the Old Testament*, 455–56; emphasis original).

All of these "coincidences" show that the events in Esther are not determined by chance but by control, not by luck but by the Lord. To see it any other way is dangerous. As Dever warns,

> Apart from believing that God actively and sovereignly
> rules over our world, the book of Esther becomes a mere
> celebration of Mordecai's wisdom, Esther's courage, and, most
> of all, simple chance and luck. . . . This book was written to

show that God himself acts to achieve the total defeat of his foes and the safety of his people. (Ibid., 456)

Similarly, Elyse Fitzpatrick writes,

The book of Esther is not simply a morality tale about a few faithful Jewish people who stand up for God in the midst of a pagan land. More fundamentally and splendidly, it is the story of God's desire to glorify himself and make his Son beautiful in the lives of alienated, weak exiles from covenant faithfulness—like us. ("Introduction to Esther," 599)

Who Wrote the Book of Esther?

We know the book of Esther is inspired by God (2 Tim 3:16), but who was its human author? A lot of ink has been used by commentary writers espousing their views, but we do not know who wrote this book. The two most common guesses are the people who know the events best—Mordecai and Esther. Some scholars lean toward Mordecai as the author because of Esther 9:20: "Mordecai recorded these events and sent letters to all the Jews in all of King Ahaseurus's provinces, both near and far." Not satisfied with this explanation, however, some church fathers thought Ezra may have written the book (Smith, "Esther," 420). Whoever the author is, he or she recorded how God preserved his people and also how the feast of Purim was established. Not knowing who the human author is, however, does not make this book any less "profitable for teaching, for rebuking, for correcting, for training in righteousness" (2 Tim 3:16).

Some Suggestions, Surprises, and Possible Frustrations in Preaching through Esther

First, you will most likely not surprise anyone with how Esther ends, but what may be surprising to them is how many details about the story they have wrong. "I know Mordecai entered Esther in a beauty contest." That comment is what someone shared with me when I told them I was planning on preaching through Esther. That person is a believer and a member of a church. And also wrong. And he (or she—I'm protecting the guilty) is not the only one who holds views of the details of Esther that are incorrect. In preaching through the book, I found that the overall highlights of the story didn't surprise anyone, but what was surprising was the number of details in the story that they had either missed or misinterpreted. If you preach through this book, it may not be the first time your people have heard of the story, but it may be the first time they study it and get the details straight!

Second, the imperfections of Esther and Mordecai may resonate with your people more than you imagine. As I prepared to preach through Esther, I was worried about how our people would respond to what seemed to be moments of compromise with the world in both Esther's and Mordecai's actions. I was worried that, since they seemed less consistent than Daniel or Joseph when striving to live faithfully in a foreign land, our people would not be able to relate to them. I was wrong. In my first meeting with our LifeGroup leaders, one of them expressed his appreciation for Esther's and Mordecai's imperfections but God's still using them in his plans. His sentiment was echoed in my own LifeGroup later that night and throughout the semester. I found that at least in the case of the people I shepherd, Esther and Mordecai are far more relatable than I ever imagined.

Third, in Esther we have all the information we need but not all the information we want. Was Esther taken into custody against her will, or did she and Mordecai accept the situation? Why doesn't Mordecai honor Haman? Mordecai tells others it is because he is a Jew, but even with that explanation the dots are not connected for us. Did Esther, Mordecai, and all the Jews pray when they fasted, or did they just fast? Was Esther right or wrong when she asked Ahasuerus for the Jews in Susa to have one more day to kill their enemies? The biblical author neither condemns nor vindicates her actions, which gets us to another possible frustration when preaching through the book of Esther.

Fourth, we may not be able to make as many definite calls as we would like. You will be tempted to say, Esther was wrong when she _____, or Mordecai was right when he _____, but because we do not have the information we would like, we can't always be definitive. You will also find that the biblical author records actions made by the characters but does not comment on their morality or spirituality. As an example, let's consider Mordecai's lack of honoring of Haman but from a different angle this time. We are told Mordecai does not honor Haman, and when asked about it, the other gatekeepers discern it has something to do with Mordecai's being a Jew. But nowhere along the way does the biblical author affirm Mordecai's actions. The author neither supports nor dissents from the actions but just records them. As preachers of the text, then, we cannot add what is not supplied. We may be tempted to either vindicate or condemn Mordecai, but unfortunately we do not possess all the material to make such a call. Therefore, our aim (and responsibility) is to preach what is clearest from the text. And though we may not be able to say with complete certainty that Mordecai did the right or wrong thing, we can say in full confidence that God used Mordecai's actions to advance his providential plan of preserving his people.

Fifth, God delivers his people through ordinary means. In the book of Esther, no sea is split for God's people to walk across on dry land. In the book of Esther, no manna appears on the ground to sustain God's people for forty years. In the book of Esther, no lions' jaws are held shut by angels, and no young Jews walk around in and then out of a fiery furnace. No, in the book of Esther, God will not deliver his people through magnificent displays of his power. Instead, God delivers his people through the ordinary decisions and actions of Esther, Mordecai, and the others in the text. Perhaps this is another reason this portion of Scripture resonates so deeply with so many believers in our day, who have never walked on water or been used to raise the dead but who are striving to obey the Lord. God does significant work through what often seems like insignificant events in our lives.

Sixth, a lot of interesting names are listed in Esther, so take the time to make sure you can pronounce them clearly and correctly. Besides meeting Ahasuerus in the opening phrase of the book, you will eventually be introduced to Mehuman, Biztha, Harbona, Bigtha, Parshandatha, Parmashta, and others. The feast of Purim may be new to you as well. While some may advise, "If you say the names of people and places in the Bible confidently, no one will know the difference," for one of my seminary professors such lack of linguistic precision would never suffice. We should strive to both read and preach the Word faithfully. If you are unsure how best to discern the pronunciations, multiple Bible software programs as well as some helpful internet sources, such as www.blueletterbible.org, offer recordings of pronunciations for you.

A Brief Note on Starting Your Sermon Series

In sermon preparation, knowing the meaning of a biblical text is only the first half of sermon groundwork. The next half is how to communicate that information, in the power of the Spirit, to the people God has entrusted to you. I am always excited when I believe the Lord has helped me, through my study, to understand the main point of a Scripture passage. But then a little apprehension creeps in as I am reminded I have to continue praying and discerning how to arrange and proclaim what I have learned in a way that will allow the truth to be communicated clearly. I often jokingly say sermon prep is a lot of agony and a little joy. It is actually all joy: joyful toiling to present ourselves "to God as one approved, a worker who doesn't need to be ashamed, correctly teaching the word of truth" (2 Tim 2:15).

In the first sermon of the Esther series I preached for those I shepherd, I spent half of my time with introductory matters and then half of it examining Esther 1:1-9. Since some of the important details such as when, where, and two important whos (Ahasuerus and Vashti) are addressed in the first nine verses, that approach flowed well. You may, however, craft an introductory or overview sermon of Esther with key background and big picture information and then prepare a sermon on 1:1-9 or even 1:1-22 as a second sermon. You know the people you shepherd best, so do what will help them grasp Scripture best. For this commentary, however, I will treat the material in 1:1-9 as a single sermon. For a list of the remaining passages and how they are considered, please refer to the table of contents in this volume.

With these introductory matters considered and concluded, we will now focus on our responsibility and privilege of exalting Jesus in Esther! May the Lord use his Spirit and his Word in and through you, and may it be for your good, for the good of your faith family, for the good of your city, and, above all, for the glory of God.

Only God Is Awesome

ESTHER 1:1-9

Main Idea: No matter how pagan or how powerful a ruler seems to be, he or she can never thwart God's providence.

I. Exiles Do Not Adore Worldly Arrogance (1:1-4).
II. Exiles Are Not in Awe of Worldly Abundance (1:5-7).
III. Exiles Are Not Afraid of Worldly Authority (1:8-9).
IV. Exiles Are Not Surprised by No Worldly Acknowledgment of God.
V. Exiles Do Not Adopt a Worldly Agenda but Adore the Only Awesome God.

The first verse of the Bible informs us that "God created the heavens and the earth" (Gen 1:1). The initial verses of Exodus list the names of Jacob's sons and relate Israel's great multiplication (Exod 1:1-7). The opening verses of Joshua state that God's plan to give his people the promised land will move forward through Joshua's leadership despite Moses's death (Josh 1:1-2). In the beginning verses of Ezekiel, God reminds his people, who are in exile, of his purpose, provision, and presence in their discipline (Dowden, *Exalting Jesus in Ezekiel*, 3). There is no indication that Ezekiel was seeking a word from the Lord, but in what seemed like an ordinary day, God did something extraordinary and provided Ezekiel with a breathtaking vision. In these examples we see mentions of God, his people, his plans, and even one of his prophets.

In the opening verses of Esther, however, there is no prophet of the Lord, no extraordinary vision, no mention of God's people, and maybe most surprising, no mention of God. Instead, 1:1-9 reveals a pompous pagan throwing an extended party to display his wealth and power. The author notes the vast expanse of Ahasuerus's empire (1:1) and his expensive décor and serving pieces (1:6-7). This pagan is consumed with his own (perceived) greatness and concerned that others acknowledge it (1:4). He's portrayed as the kind of guy who would ask, "You can see how awesome I am, right?" But what he will learn soon enough and what we need to be constantly reminded of is that only God is awesome.

Several years ago I had the habit of saying many things or situations were awesome. Did you see that game? It was awesome. I saw a raccoon run across the road. That's awesome! The new toothpaste we bought is awesome. You get the gist. I probably would have continued with such overuse if it had not been for one of our elders. Hearing me respond, "That's awesome," to something that was at best mediocre prompted him to say, "No, only God is awesome." I accepted his reproof and almost as quickly affirmed his conviction. If anything, or more accurately anyone, is the definition of *awesome*, it is God alone. There are some words that we should use only in reference to him because of his greatness and goodness.

If you were a Jew living in Susa (1:2) during the exile, you may have heard that God is awesome because of what you were taught growing up, but experience might leave you struggling with the concept. Despite not being mentioned in 1:1-9, God's people are in Susa (see 2:5), and they are a "religious minority living in a dominant culture with completely different views from [them] on almost everything" (Jenkins, "Esther and the Silent Sovereignty of God").

In our world today, many Christian brothers and sisters face severe persecution as they live under the reign of pagan political leaders. What Esther's first readers needed to be reminded of, as do many in our day, is no matter how pagan or powerful a ruler seems to be, he or she can never thwart God's providence. God will ultimately use Ahasuerus's narcissism to accomplish his plan of preserving his people. As Isaiah exhorts us,

> God is enthroned above the circle of the earth; its inhabitants are like grasshoppers. He stretches out the heavens like thin cloth and spreads them out like a tent to live in. He reduces princes to nothing and makes judges of the earth like a wasteland. (Isa 40:22-23)

No matter what time or place we as believers find ourselves in, we should always remember two truths. First, God determines our when and our where. Paul says, "From one man he has made every nationality to live over the whole earth and has determined their appointed times and the boundaries of where they live" (Acts 17:26). There was no accident or randomness behind the conception of those who were born during Israel's exile nor to those who were born this week. God makes no mistakes with people he knits together in their mothers' wombs (Ps 139:13), in how he knits them together, in when he knits them together, or in where he determines for them to be born and to live.

The second truth we need to remember is this: no matter where we are on this globe, it is not ultimately our home. Despite the issuing country for our passports, Paul reminds Christians that "our citizenship is in heaven" (Phil 3:20). A new heaven and earth are coming with a new Jerusalem that has been prepared "like a bride adorned for her husband" (Rev 21:2). In the meantime Peter urges us to live as "strangers and exiles" who "abstain from sinful desires that wage war against the soul" and to "conduct [ourselves] honorably among the Gentiles, so that when they slander [us] as evildoers, they will observe [our] good works and will glorify God on the day he visits" (1 Pet 2:11-12).

In the opening verses of Esther, God's people were exiles living under pagan rule. We are exiles as well, and we need not be threatened by worldly pomp, possessions, or power. Nor should we yield to temptations to walk in worldly paths of self-promotion. No matter what circumstances or difficulties we find ourselves in and no matter the practices of those in the culture in which we live, the Lord has tasked us to declare his greatness and not our own. As exiles, let us always adore God, who alone is awesome, and may that worship fuel every step of our obedience. With this in mind, let us now consider Esther 1:1-9.

Exiles Do Not Adore Worldly Arrogance
ESTHER 1:1-4

In the language of the Old Testament, Esther 1:1-4 is actually one sentence. This lengthy sentence reveals important information about the context of Esther. First, what is recorded in Esther occurs during the reign of Ahasuerus and 1:1-20 takes place during the third year of his rule. Now unless you just dominate your family in the advanced levels of *Bible Trivia: Seminary Nerd Edition*, then I am guessing you do not know much about Ahasuerus or when he was a blip on the historical map.

So, who was Ahasuerus and when were his days? Ahasuerus, better known by his Greek name Xerxes, reigned from 486 to 465 BC (Baldwin, *Esther*, 17). He "was the son and successor of Darius I Hystaspes, at the beginning of whose reign the restoration of the Jerusalem Temple took place (Hg. 2:1-9; Zc. 7:1; 8:9)" (Baldwin, *Esther*, 17). Fox notes that some portrayals of Xerxes show "him as an occasionally sagacious and principled, but more often arbitrary, tyrannical, and brutal despot" (*Character*

and Ideology in the Book of Esther, 15). With regard to what we see of Xerxes
in the text, Fox says, "His soul is adequately exposed by simple description of his mental states, which are mostly a collection of impulses"
(ibid., 171). He is consumed with being honored and displaying his
authority. He often wields his incredible power "with . . . little thought
invested in its employment." Rather, it's carried out by the whims of one
who is "erratic, childish, apathetic, and pliable" (ibid., 175–76). Ah! Just
the qualifications one loves to see in his or her political leaders who also
have absolute (or so it is perceived) command.

Second, these verses reveal the boundaries of Ahasuerus's empire.
He ruled 127 provinces that stretched from India to Cush (southern
Pakistan to northern Sudan on our current maps), which was basi-
cally the known world and the "greatest empire ever known" at that
time (Firth, *The Message of Esther*, 38). Strain notes that Ahasuerus was
the "supreme ruler of the world superpower of the day" ("The Lord
Reigns"). The author could have used satrapies (regions composed of
multiple provinces) to describe the realm of Ahasuerus, but that number would have been smaller, and the author clearly wants to introduce
readers to this king by using the grandest means possible. Though letters
will be sent throughout the vast expanse of his territory, the main focus
of events in Esther is the capital city of Susa, where "King Ahasuerus
reigned from his royal throne" (1:2).

In addition to the who, when, and where the author of Esther provides about Ahasuerus, verse 4 records an important what. In the third
year of his reign, he decided to give a feast for Persia's political and
military elites. This is the first reference to a feast in Esther, but it is far
from the last. Dialogue and activities around feasts are found in the
beginning, middle, and conclusion of the book. There are almost more
references to feasts in Esther than in the rest of the Old Testament combined. At these feasts food and drink would have abounded, as well as
time to enjoy both, which is not completely dissimilar from my upbring-
ing in Louisiana (minus the strong-drink part). Few things are better
than an unhurried crawfish boil after spending the day on the water at
Toledo Bend, but I digress.

Ahasuerus's party was not just any feast. It was not a feast to thank
the political and military leaders for their loyalty or service. It was not
a feast to honor them for their sacrifices or to reward specific instances
of merit. No, as the CSB translates so well, it was a feast for Xerxes
to display "the glorious wealth of his kingdom and the magnificent

splendor of his greatness" (1:4). Perhaps the invitations to it said something like this:

Dear Important Person,

Your presence is commanded at the King's Feast,
To give you an opportunity to bask in his glory and greatness,
And to show you what true extravagance and power look like.
What a privilege this will be for you!

Please drop by the palace between noon and midnight any day over
the next six months
Or stay for that entire time.
Also, please do not send your regrets; your absence
will be to *your* everlasting regret.
See you soon!

Who could resist such a tempting invitation? Ahasuerus cared so much about his guests giving considerable thought to his abundance and authority that he extended the party to 180 days. Now that is a party! I am usually exhausted after just a few hours of planning, hosting, and cleaning up for parties my wife and I have at our home. I cannot imagine what it was like for the poor servants who spent six months in nonstop food and drink preparation, caring for guests, and completing their usual responsibilities too.

In light of Esther 1:1-4, let me ask you something: Have you ever been around someone who repeatedly informed you of aspects of his greatness or, similarly, the greatness of his children or pet—and even provided pictures or videos as proof? If I am being honest, I confess to you that I avoid conversations with certain people because I cannot stomach another expounding on the laurels of their offspring. I avoid, even more often, those who have their "toppers" ready so that no matter where you try to steer the conversation they have experienced something, been somewhere, accomplished something, or even suffered something that far exceeds whatever puny thing you were sharing. If you have to tell others about how awesome you are, then you probably are not all that great.

Now let me ask you another question: Have you ever thrown a party to celebrate yourself? Hopefully not. But again, if we are being honest,

I am not unlike Ahasuerus in wanting others to know about my "greatness." I have been guilty of sprinkling my accomplishments into conversations for fear of my self-appraised worth not being recognized or affirmed. Depending on when you are reading this volume, if such a thing as social media still exist with their proliferation of #HumbleBrags and incessant postings of things that are "intended" to give God glory while also providing a little self promotion, then I am sorry my generation blessed you with such a gift.

The author of Esther carefully crafted the opening scene to force us to consider the power and prominence of Ahasuerus. And as much as I recoil at what is recorded, I cannot help but see myself in its reflection. I do not rule a vast empire, nor do I have the resources to provide for a six-month party, but I still often crave to be acknowledged and honored. Even worse, sometimes I am tempted to be angered by others who do not recognize me. That is not the path for the Lord's people, however. As exiles we know better than to place confidence in such fleeting places as worldly wealth, power, and recognition. But if I am not regularly considering the Lord's greatness, then I am prone to consider my own. Reading about his renown in his Word recalibrates my heart and mind and helps me perceive, once again, my proper place in his world. Consider this: Ahasuerus threw a party for 180 days to celebrate his glory, but from the moment he spoke into existence the heavens and the earth, all of creation has never ceased declaring God's. Ahasuerus's party started and finished with a specific duration, but of the celebration of God there will be no end. Now that gives us proper perspective!

One final note for exiles to consider in these opening verses is that a display of evil's power does not mean a diminishing of God's. God has no rival and no equal. He has never been, is not, and will never be threatened or thwarted. To be the leader in Susa is nowhere near being the Sovereign over all. No matter how much power a pagan leader seems to wield, he or she is no threat to God's providence.

Exiles Are Not in Awe of Worldly Abundance
ESTHER 1:5-7

After 180 days of pomp and party, Ahasuerus decided to do what you probably did following your last six-month celebration. He threw another feast. Makes sense. Every good party needs an after-party. But instead of his political and military officials being the guests of honor (Who are we kidding? Ahasuerus is always the guest of honor!), he invited all the citizens of Susa. This second and shorter party (it only lasted seven days) was possibly "a way of thanking them for their involvement in the great feast" (Firth, *The Message of Esther*, 39). I am sure there was no other way those servants would rather be thanked than by having more meals to prepare and cups to clean! And just consider for a moment, when is the last time you noted a seven-day party as "the shorter one"?

While there may have been restraint in the duration, there was certainly none in the display. Continuing to carefully craft a particular image of Ahasuerus, the author of Esther moves from describing the king's provinces to his possessions. Curtains, cords, couches, and cups are all described in detail meant to convey expense and extravagance. Gregory writes,

> This is the only place in the Old Testament where a narrator describes in such detail the background environment of a scene. The reason, presumably, is to give the reader a sense of just how opulent and lavish these feasts are. (*Inconspicuous Providence*, 25)

The mosaic made from marble and mother-of-pearl is meant to say something about the man, Ahasuerus. The cups, which like snowflakes lacked twins and would have made keeping up with your drink a little easier, are meant to communicate something about the one wearing the crown.

One of the lies of identity is that "I am what I have." When trying to discern who we are, some of us are prone to make that decision based on what we possess or what we lack. Having abundant resources or meager resources, however, does not define us. I have known some wonderful and some awful people among both the wealthy and the poor. Having grown up in a double-wide trailer and having driven vehicles that some would call "hoopties," I have often felt insecure and intimidated when defining myself by assets. But of all the treasures Ahasuerus used to impress those who attended his feasts, how many of those items do you think he still possesses today? That's right: none. I am always grieved when I consider the one whom Jesus told to "sell all you have and distribute it to the poor, and you will have treasure in heaven" (Luke 18:22). He refused to do what Jesus said, and instead of embracing the treasure who is Christ, he clung to lesser treasures and walked away to his eternal detriment.

As exiles, we should never place our confidence or our identity in things that are fleeting. As John exhorts,

> For everything in the world—the lust of the flesh, the lust of the eyes, and the pride in one's possessions—is not from the Father, but is from the world. And the world with its lust is passing away, but the one who does the will of God remains forever. (1 John 2:16-17)

The National Corvette Museum in Bowling Green, Kentucky, illustrates this well. On February 12, 2014, a sinkhole opened up under the museum, swallowing eight corvettes. Two years later the directors of the museum opened an exhibit to continually tell the story of what happened. The exhibit is divided into eight sections: The Day, Media Coverage, Pop Culture, Cars Affected, The Recovery, Karst Landscapes, What It Took to Fix the Sinkhole, and the Grand Finale ("Corvette Cave In Exhibit Opens on Two Year Anniversary of Museum Sinkhole"). I think a section is missing. The creators of the exhibit should have added, "The Sinkhole Got Eight of Our Cars but One Day They Will All Be Gone!" Not everyone will grasp this most important lesson from the sinkhole, but as exiles we must beware having "living affections to dying things" ("Of Communion with God the Father, Son, and Holy Ghost," in *The Works of John Owen*, 2:150). The worldly agenda of accumulation and abundance provides no lasting security. One day all those who have placed their confidence in material possessions will be found eternally wanting.

For those who find their identity in possessions, the reality is they can never obtain what they desire. When asked how much money is enough, wealthy American industrialist John D. Rockefeller replied, "Just a little bit more" ("John D. Rockefeller," http://www.newworldencyclopedia.org/entry/John_D._Rockefeller). And indeed, as expensive as his own possessions were and as expansive as was his power, it was not enough for Ahasuerus. Like many of us, he lacked contentment with what he had and was driven by what lacked. He wanted Greece. The king's father

> had struggled against the Greeks during what was known
> as the First Persian War (492–490 B.C.), but it was left to
> Ahasuerus to lead a second invasion of Greece (480–479 B.C.),
> which resulted in the subjugation of several Greek cities
> before a string of costly defeats stopped the Persian advance.
> (Gregory, *Inconspicuous Providence*, 23)

Ahasuerus would never conquer Greece, which Herodotus notes joyfully (*The Histories*, 540–43).

The endless pursuit of accumulation is both dangerous and disappointing and can be destructive. Paul warns Timothy that "the love of money is a root of all kinds of evil, and by craving it, some have wandered away from the faith and pierced themselves with many griefs" (1 Tim 6:10). Moreover, the sum of one's possessions is never the sum of one's person. As exiles we must always remember that who we are is not based on what others say and think about us but on what God says about us in Christ. No matter how others flaunt their worldly accumulations, their cups and curtains and couches cannot compare with the treasure we have in our Christ. As exiles, we should never be in awe of worldly abundance.

Exiles Are Not Afraid of Worldly Authority
ESTHER 1:8-9

Moving from drapes to drinks, the author of Esther informs us a declaration was made to let everyone at the party know they were free to drink as they desired. In other words, despite customary Persian party protocol, just because the king drank, guests would not be forced to drink as well. Consider this for a moment. In order for those he was hosting to know they had freedom to drink or abstain, the king made a royal decree. A royal decree on drinks! Strain comments:

> It's actually hard not to smirk again at the micromanaging, megalomania of the king that needs to legislate for how people drink at his party, which, by the way, is exactly what the author is aiming at. Ahasuerus wants us to bow before him in awe and reverence. He wants to be adored by his subjects, feared by his enemies, obeyed by everyone. He wants total control. ("The Lord Reigns")

The people under Xerxes's reign (Jews included) were living in a place where even the smallest details were regulated by the one in power.

While legislating liquids further revealed Ahasuerus's control, Duguid contends it was not a sign of true power. He writes,

> Real power does not consist in regulating such detailed minutiae. In fact, the tendency to regulate such details

is actually a sign of weakness not power. The stories that
circulate of government regulations requiring bananas to
conform to certain criteria of straightness and size do not
impress us as shining examples of government efficiency but
rather of bureaucrats run amok, compensating for lack of real
significance by inordinate attention to minuscule details. Such
was the empire of Ahasuerus, and as we read its description, it
is hard to resist a chuckle. (*Esther and Ruth*, 9)

Though we can consider Esther 1:8 with some amusement in our
day, God's people living in Susa and throughout the Persian Empire
were probably not doing a lot of laughing. A king who has to announce
to his subjects that they have freedom to drink as they desire, at least at
this one party, is probably not providing a lot of freedoms in his domain,
especially to foreigners.

When we exiles find ourselves under the rule of a tyrant who does
not share our convictions and who seeks to control every aspect of our
lives, we may be tempted both to despair and to acquiesce. Our brothers
and sisters in Christ who live in some of the places most hostile to the
gospel may feel these temptations even today. We should pray for them
now lest they despair because the human whose rule they live under
provides more force than freedom, and nothing appears to be improv-
ing anytime soon. Those living under a tyrant's rule may be tempted to
assimilate fully into the prevailing culture. In order not to stand out from
the crowd, they may choose not to stand up for their convictions. Unlike
Daniel, Shadrach, Meshach, and Abednego, who refused to compromise despite the threat of death, some may be waffling and in need of
"being strengthened with all power, according to his glorious might, so
that [they] may have great endurance and patience" (Col 1:11). If you
did not stop and pray when I suggested it a few sentences ago, maybe
you will do so now.

How can those of us who are not living in the realm of a tyrant apply
this verse to our lives? Well, Ahasuerus wanted to control every aspect
of his people's existence but primarily for his good and not theirs. We
should remember that this is not true of God. God's desire to have every
facet of our lives yielded to him is ultimately for our best. Our seeking
to retain control of any area is not only to the detriment of ourselves but
also hurts our families and faith families.

Second, whether our parents, our bosses, our president, or whomever else may be in a position of authority over us is in view, we should

pray for them frequently (1 Tim 2:2). I regularly pray for our mayor, city council, governor, congress, and president, asking the Lord to provide all they need to serve him faithfully with the stewardship he has entrusted to them. I ask the Lord to give them a sense of the accountability they will have before him one day and ask him to surround them with those who will continually speak his Word into their lives.

Third, no matter who is in charge where we live, may the Spirit always remind us, "The LORD reigns! Let the earth rejoice; let the many coasts and islands be glad" (Ps 97:1). Though I care who wins elections in our country, I ultimately sleep peacefully each night because the Lord reigns! May we be stirred not to "fear those who kill the body but are not able to kill the soul; rather, fear him who is able to destroy both soul and body in hell" (Matt 10:28).

Esther 1:9 introduces Queen Vashti. We will consider her more closely in the next chapter, so I will provide just a few thoughts here. First, the name *Vashti* "has been associated with Persian words meaning 'best' or 'the beloved,' 'the desired one,' a lovely name by which to be known" (Baldwin, *Esther*, 60). Second, after all the details provided in the first eight verses, what is noticeable is the author's minimalist approach to verse 9. In it we are informed a queen is hosting a feast for the women, and the location of the party is somewhere in Ahasuerus's palace but separate from the other feasts. Some speculate that these feasts were part of a wedding celebration, but their thoughts are just that: speculation.

More than anything else, the author uses verse 9 as an important bridge to the material that follows. The one who had great power and possessions, and even decreed how people drank at his party, would soon have one closest to him resist his commands. If 1:1-9 could be considered pomp and trumpets, then what immediately follows in verses 10-12 could be compared to the classy sound of someone blowing raspberries with his mouth! This in itself is a great reminder that, as exiles, we should not be afraid of worldly authority.

Exiles Are Not Surprised by No Worldly Acknowledgment of God

What is clearly missing in Esther 1:1-9 is an acknowledgment of God, and what is present is one who wants to be adored as a god. Gregory notes,

> There is, in all these elaborate descriptions, a characterization
> of the king. He is portrayed as someone who has extravagant
> wealth, unlimited power, and unrivaled pretension.
> Noblemen, military officials, wineries, stone masons, interior
> decorators, and furniture craftsman are under his command.
> The wealth of the kingdom is at his disposal, and he thinks
> nothing of lavishly parading it in front of those under him.
> . . . Clearly, Ahasuerus lacks nothing and spares nothing.
> (*Inconspicuous Providence*, 25–26)

But Ahasuerus is lacking something in 1:1-9. It's the same action and
admission lacking from the rich man in Luke 12:16-21 and from Herod
in Acts 12:20-23. What is lacking is an acknowledgment of God like the
one Paul expresses in Romans 11:36: "For from him and through him
and to him are all things. To him be the glory forever. Amen." Ahasuerus
may feel like he is a god, but he is not. Instead, the prince of Persia will
be a pawn in God's providential plan.

One of my favorite movies is *Gladiator*. In it Russell Crowe plays the
role of a Roman general named Maximus who was betrayed, suffered
the loss of his family, and was sold into slavery. In time he ends up in
the Roman coliseum as a gladiator fighting not just for his freedom but
also for his life. In the first battle all of his training, experience, and
ability prove useful as he leads his band of fellow slaves to victory and
survival. Then, as a means of identifying and celebrating the masked victor, Caesar, who betrayed Maximus, enters the arena and asks the gladiator for his name and to remove his mask. Initially, Maximus refuses the
emperor's request. Enraged by this disrespect, Caesar commands the
gladiator to identify himself. In a powerful moment Maximus reveals
his true identity and then says one of my favorite lines in the film: "The
time for honoring yourself will soon be at an end, Highness." That line
would fit Ahasuerus's situation well. Regardless of the magnificent picture of power and possessions crafted in the opening of Esther, earthly
prominence is no match for heavenly providence.

As exiles, we should not be surprised if there is no worldly acknowledgment of God's greatness, glory, and goodness. Many people think
they have built their own kingdoms and are the masters of their fates
and captains of their souls (William Ernest Henley, "Invictus"). For
them nothing is owed to God. While I am concerned for those who
hold such convictions, I am primarily concerned with those who claim
to know the truth.

How quick are we to credit God for all of his blessings in our lives? When we put away a sin with which we have struggled or if we share the gospel and see someone yield her life to Christ, how much tribute do we offer to God as we share about it with others? We are more prone to acknowledge God if we are more consistent in adoring God.

Exiles Do Not Adopt a Worldly Agenda but Adore the Only Awesome God

Having considered Esther 1:1-9, I want to conclude this chapter with two applications. First, as exiles, we should not adopt a worldly agenda. No spiritual life is to be found in worldly arrogance, worldly abundance, or worldly authority. Eternal life is found only in knowing God and the one he sent—Jesus Christ (see John 17:3). The accumulation of power and possessions is not a worthy end.

As a leader Ahasuerus was concerned with promoting his own glory and greatness. This is not how we as exiles steward positions of authority that God grants to us. Instead, Jesus taught his disciples,

> You know that those who are regarded as rulers of the Gentiles lord it over them, and those in high positions act as tyrants over them. But it is not so among you. On the contrary, whoever wants to become great among you will be your servant, and whoever wants to be first among you will be a slave to all. For even the Son of Man did not come to be served, but to serve, and to give his life as a ransom for many. (Mark 10:42-45)

Greatness in God's kingdom is not found in self-promotion but in self-denial. May it be clear that the only agenda we exiles follow was given to us by the one who has all authority in heaven and on earth.

Second, as exiles, we should keep adoring the only God who is awesome. I often tell our faith family that if we are going to love God passionately and others rightly, then we must consider the cross constantly. When I consider what God has done for us in the cross of Christ, praise for God flows fervently. When I consider Christ's laying down his life to redeem his enemies, loving my neighbor as myself is gospel fueled.

In 1:1-9 there is much fuel for adoration of God when we realize that the king of Persia is no comparison to the King of kings (I am thankful here for Derek Prime's help in considering these truths—*Unspoken Lessons*, 30–32). For example, while all of Persia was subject to Ahasuerus, all of creation is subject to Christ. He reigns . . .

in and over every nation. He is not simply King of the earth, but King of the universe. . . . He rules over the living and the dead. He is ruler over all who exercise rule in the world. He is Lord over all lords, and King over all kings. All powers and beings in the universe must ultimately bow the knee to him. (Prime, *Unspoken Lessons*, 30)

As Abraham Kuyper declares, "There is not a square inch in the whole domain of our human existence over which Christ, who is Sovereign over all, does not cry: 'Mine!'" (Bratt, *Abraham Kuyper*, 488).

There is still more fuel for praise. While Ahasuerus sat on a throne in Susa, Christ has a throne at the right hand of his Father in the heavenly places that is "far above every ruler and authority, power and dominion, and every title given, not only in this age but also in the one to come" (Eph 1:21). There will never be a threat or an end to his reign. While Ahasuerus threw a feast for prominent servants, Christ throws feasts for pardoned sinners. In discussing the Lord's Supper, Prime contends,

There is no banquet on earth to compare with this. It is a love feast for pardoned sinners, whatever their status in human society. . . . This banquet is a foretaste of a far greater banquet to come—the marriage feast of the Lamb. Then we shall sit down and feast with him. (*Unspoken Lessons*, 31)

And last, while Ahasuerus seemed to have unlimited resources, only in Christ do we truly find "incalculable riches" (Eph 3:8). He does not love on a budget but lavishes grace on those whom the Father gives him.

Throughout earth's history there have been powerful pagan leaders. To their rules, however, there have been set periods of time, set boundaries of influence, and limited resources to control. And the one who has set all of those restrictions is God, who still rules and is carrying out his good plan. Their failure to acknowledge him does not mean he did not use them to advance his purposes. As exiles, then, let us continually sing,

This is my Father's world: O let me ne'er forget
That though the wrong seems oft so strong, God is the Ruler
    yet.
This is my Father's world: Why should my heart be sad?

The Lord is King; let the heavens ring! God reigns; let earth
   be glad!
(Babcock, "This Is My Father's World")

Reflect and Discuss

1. Why should we study the book of Esther?
2. Outside of a yearly reading plan, what interaction have you had with
   the book of Esther?
3. Have you ever heard a sermon series that walked through each
   chapter in Esther? If so, how did God use that series in your life?
4. Has there ever been a time when you could not see, hear, or feel
   God? When was that, and how did you eventually come to acknowledge his presence or his promises? When we cannot see, hear, or
   feel God, what should we do?
5. Give an example of how God works in the mundane. Why do we
   tend to acknowledge him more in the miracle than the mundane?
6. How can the book of Esther be an encouragement to us if we are
   concerned by pagan and powerful rulers?
7. Are you, like Ahasuerus, ever tempted to declare your own glory
   and greatness instead of God's? Why is this dangerous?
8. In what area of life are you, like Ahasuerus, failing to acknowledge
   God or his provision?
9. How and why should we put away any temptation we may have
   to want the same abundance and opulence as was on display at
   Ahasuerus's party?
10. In what ways is Jesus a better king than Ahasuerus?

A Drunk King, a Defiant Queen, and a Divine Providence

ESTHER 1:10-22

Main Idea: God will use Ahasuerus's wretchedness and Vashti's rebellion to open the door for Esther's future reign.

I. **What's Happening in the Text (1:10-22)?**
   A. The king's drunken demand (1:10-11)
   B. The queen's definite defiance (1:12)
   C. The counselor's despicable discernment (1:13-20)
   D. The king's dumb decision (1:21)
   E. The king's dishonorable decree (1:22)
II. **Lessons Others Have Taught from This Text**
   A. The dangers of drunkenness and of demeaning women
   B. The better model for the feminist movement
III. **What Can We Learn about God?**
   A. God will use Ahasuerus's wretchedness and Vashti's rebellion to achieve Esther's reign.
   B. God is offended and greatly transgressed by disobedience.
   C. God grants us more grace than Ahasuerus granted Vashti.
IV. **What Can We Learn about Ourselves?**
   A. Without God's grace and intervention, we are all like Ahasuerus.
   B. When accountability is absent, rebellion prevails over repentance.
   C. When boasting, we should not be surprised if God humbles us.
V. **What Can We Learn about Christ?**
   A. Jesus's power is absolute.
   B. Jesus's constant motivation is God's glory and our good.
   C. Jesus is sacrificial.
   D. Jesus deserves all the glory for our beauty.
   E. Jesus deserves honor.

I am grateful for every opportunity I have been given to teach at seminaries or Bible schools in Africa. I love meeting the students, many of whom serve in ministry, and getting to hear their stories and backgrounds. During my first trip to teach at the Uganda Baptist Seminary in Jinja, I had the opportunity to preach to the student body for a spiritual emphasis week and then help teach in their classes. One afternoon I sat in one of the preaching classes as they were sharing prayer requests. One student shared about an internally displaced persons camp in the north where rebel soldiers dressed up like Ugandan soldiers to gain access to the refugees. Those rebels then proceeded to slaughter all of the adults and to take many of the boys captive to fight in their army. The other children were being dispersed, and the one making the request was praying those children would be placed in homes where they would not be further abused or exploited.

I listened to another student who had been in Rwanda during the genocide. I heard how his parents, who had served as professors at the university in Kigali, were participating in a family birthday party when men with guns knocked on their door. The men took the student's parents outside and shot them while he and his siblings fled out the back door of the house. At this point in the telling, another student shook his head and said, "In Africa, you never know who will be in charge when you wake up."

This state of affairs is not just a problem for previous generations or limited to the continent of Africa. Political power grabs through the use of force have occurred in multiple countries. In some places those with the most power are able to take control, and they maintain control for as long as they maintain their power.

Unfortunately, in our world those with the most power are not always the ones with the purest motives. Some wield their power as they wish with primary regard being given to self. Kim Jong Un of North Korea is a contemporary example. I read this week of a high-ranking official who defected from the tyrant's regime to South Korea (Associated Press, "Senior North Korean Defector Says His Sons Were Reason He Fled"). The defector said he was fortunate that both of his sons were already out of the country and in London. When most North Korean officials travel outside of the country, Kim Jong Un keeps at least one of their family members in order to guarantee the diplomat's return. The people of North Korea are currently suffering under an oppressive ruler who does what he wishes to whomever he wishes with no repercussions. And so many in North Korea have known no other life.

Prior to the most recent presidential election in the United States, concerns were expressed over both candidates. For Hillary Clinton there were apprehensions about her trustworthiness. For Donald Trump there was fear of him having the nuclear codes and choosing to use them as a reaction to something someone posted about him on social media. The book of Esther opens on a king who is the most powerful ruler of his day. He wants all to know of his greatness and glory. But as we consider the remainder of chapter 1 in Esther, we will see that the one who has all the power is not a good man who makes decisions for the good of those he leads. Rather, he uses his power for his own agenda, and when drunk, he even uses it against those who are closest to him. He elicits both kinds of concerns mentioned above; he is untrustworthy and impulsive. God, however, will use Ahasuerus's wretchedness and Vashti's rebellion to open the door for Esther's future reign.

What's Happening in the Text?
ESTHER 1:10-22

In this first section of material, I will provide explanation and background for the events recorded in 1:10-22. I will reserve the majority of application, however, for the final three sections of this discussion, where we will examine what we can learn about God, ourselves, and Christ. From time to time, as I preach through books of the Bible, I use this method to vary my delivery style.

The King's Drunken Demand (1:10-11)

I do not know of any good decisions made while someone was intoxicated. I can give you example after example, however, of poor decisions the condition produced. Two illustrations that immediately come to my mind both involve injury, pain, and loss. In the first example, one of my friends in college incurred over $10,000 in medical bills after being punched in the face by a drunk person he did not know. In the second example, I carried a rose and placed it in the chair next to me at my high school graduation where one of my good friends should have been sitting but could not because she was hit and killed by a drunk driver just two weeks prior. My undergraduate degree is in management, and not one single lecture that I heard in four years of study was titled, "Drinking and Decisions: How Intoxication Leads to Wisdom."

The Persians saw drinking and decision-making differently. They believed those who imbibed "spirits" could come into closer contact with the spiritual world and possibly receive helpful counsel. The Persians may have also employed a decision-making strategy that included alternating between drunkenness and sobriety and then deliberating and deciding based on which mental state they were in (Jobes, *Esther*, 67–68).

After 187 days of feasting, apparently not all of Ahasuerus's arteries were clogged; nevertheless, his critical thinking skills were definitely impaired. At the conclusion of the shorter feast, he acted on a drunken whim to show all the other men at the party the beauty of his wife. The author records no one around Ahasuerus trying to dissuade him from his foolishness. No one is chronicled as saying, "This probably won't go well," or asking, "Are you sure about this one, big fella?" Instead the king's eunuchs are commanded to get the queen from the feast she is hosting and to bring her back wearing her crown or headdress. The eunuchs will comply. Vashti, however, will not.

The Queen's Definite Defiance (1:12)

Before considering the queen's rebellion, let us first consider her reputation. Who was Vashti? As previously noted, the name *Vashti* means "the best" or "desired," which leads some to believe *Vashti* may be "an honorary title for the favored wife rather than her actual name" (Smith, *Ezra, Nehemiah, Esther*, 231). Others contend she was also known by her Greek name, Amestris, and that she was "ruthless, powerful, and influential, once taking horrible revenge on a woman with whom her husband had been in love" (Prime, *Unspoken Lessons*, 32).

Based on what is revealed in the Bible, Vashti was beautiful and bold but (spoiler alert) would be banished. Beyond her refusal to obey the king's command, she has no other actions recorded in Esther. Readers are not privy to any of her conversations, not even the one she had with the likes of Biztha and Bigtha and the rest of the eunuch envoys. Bush notes that "non-speech narration carries the primary freight in [Esther] in both plot development and characterization" (*Ruth/Esther*, 311). Instead of revealing dialogue made with her, the author of Esther only provides dialogue about her in the remainder of the first chapter.

Beyond the second chapter Vashti is not mentioned again in the text. From the biblical perspective then, we know Ahasuerus had a queen named Vashti, she was beautiful, she refused his drunken command, a decree would be made banishing her from his presence, and all of this would provide an opportunity for a new queen to be crowned. While minimal content is devoted to Vashti in the text, her refusal to appear before the king is a major facet in God's preservation of his people.

But what led her to refuse to go before the king and those gathered with him? An answer to this question is not provided in the text. Here, then, is a good point at which to remind ourselves of something important regarding the study of Esther: unknowns are OK. Though we do not have all the information we may want in the Bible, we have all the information the Lord wants us to have for now and all the information we need.

The lack of a reason for Vashti's rebellion being recorded in the text has not stopped some from seeking to provide their own. Some think the king intended her crown or headdress to be her only article of clothing. Another thought is that she was embarrassed by some blemish and did not want to appear in the royal court in such a state. Of course, there is another reasonable possibility, which many have noted, and that is that she did not want to be paraded in front of the king's frat party to be, at a minimum, heckled, or worse, harmed by men who had been drinking for seven days. Whatever the reason, Baldwin notes the absence of an explanation in the text "strengthens the tension of the story by implying that Vashti had no rights in relation to her husband, and therefore reasons were irrelevant" (*Esther*, 60–61). Vashti's concerns were not important, only Ahasuerus's commands were.

Though readers are not provided a reason for Vashti's rebellion, the author does note the king's reaction. He is not a happy camper. Nor would the reader expect him to be. After the author has labored in describing Ahasuerus's power and possessions and greatness and glory, one would expect all to obey any command he made with the utmost expediency. But the first slash in the façade of the king's "absolute" power is seen in his inability to command either his queen or his own emotions. As Matthew Henry notes, "He that had rule over 127 provinces had no rule over his own spirit" (*Commentary on the Whole Bible*, 505). Internally he was a burning rage that would "kindle" or "ignite" his subsequent actions (Wakely, "רעב," 1:683).

Why was the king so mad? The answer is not simply because she disobeyed but because she would not participate in what he wanted displayed. Over the two feasts Ahasuerus had been showing off all his treasures and resources, and for the grand finale he wanted to show everyone his beautiful queen. Of course, displaying her beauty was not really about her but about him. Her beauty was to be a means to the end of furthering his boasting in his glory and greatness. But as Firth says, "The balloon of his prestige which had been so carefully established is pricked by a woman who will not come to his party" (*The Message of Esther*, 40). The question thus becomes, What should be done with Vashti?

The Counselor's Despicable Discernment (1:13-20)

On January 28, 1986, the space shuttle *Challenger* exploded seventy-three seconds after liftoff. The entire crew of seven perished, including Christa McAuliffe, a schoolteacher chosen to participate in NASA's Teacher in Space program. A presidential commission was formed to help discern what went wrong. Teitel says, "The Commission ultimately flagged the root cause of the accident as 'a serious flaw in the decision-making process leading up to the launch'" ("How Groupthink Led to 7 Lives Lost in the Challenger Explosion").

The NASA employees in charge of decision-making for *Challenger*'s launch failed to let voices outside of the group influence their assessments. Considering this thirty years after the *Challenger* explosion, Schwartz and Wald note that "a body of research that is getting more and more attention points to the ways that smart people working collectively can be dumber than the sum of their brains" ("The Nation: NASA's Curse?; 'Groupthink' Is 30 Years Old and Still Going Strong"). What happens in Esther 1:13-20 could certainly be described as "a serious flaw in the decision-making process," and it is clear the group of wise men from whom Ahasuerus seeks counsel in dealing with Vashti seem none the smarter for working collectively.

After the queen defied the king's command, Ahasuerus turned to a group of seven men—close advisors—to see what, if anything, should be done with Vashti according to the law. Often a wife for the king would be selected from among the families of a group like this seven, so it made sense for him to seek their discernment on the issue. Memucan's anxiety and Ahasuerus's anger, however, end up leading to a fabricated law based on fear and fickleness instead of foresight. Cooler heads, if they were even present, definitely did not prevail in the group's predictions of empire-wide revolts by wives inspired by Vashti's defiance.

For her great offense not only against the king but to all under his reign, Memucan proposed Vashti never be allowed again in Ahasuerus's presence and the forfeit of her royal position. Little imagination is required to discern what Memucan means when he says someone "more worthy" should be queen. His ideal woman would obey the king the first time a command was given, every time a command was given, and with a happy heart. In his eyes the kingdom would be better served if a woman like this was queen.

The "wise men" hoped a decree from the emperor and his strict discipline toward Vashti would discourage the other wives in the realm from disrespecting their husbands. Ironically, Fox notes that Memucan's "advice creates the very hullabaloo he had wanted to squelch and prevents Vashti from doing precisely what she had refused to do" (*Character and Ideology*, 168). In worrying that word would get out to all the realm regarding the queen's actions, the king and his most trusted ones would actually be the cause of it.

The King's Dumb Decision (1:21)

The psalmist says, "How happy is the one who does not walk in the advice of the wicked or stand in the pathway with sinners or sit in the company of mockers" (Ps 1:1). Based on those criteria, Ahasuerus was neither happy nor blessed. He needed a father like the one in Proverbs, one who counsels, "My son, if sinners entice you, don't be persuaded" (Prov 1:10). Sadly, Ahasuerus and the officials around him thought Memucan's proposal was a great idea. The king accepted and then acted on the bad advice.

Though we will consider more in-depth application in a moment, I want to note a few observations here. Ahasuerus had been drinking and then made a demeaning demand of his wife. In the progression of events, he went from wanting everyone to see her to never wanting to see her again. In colloquial terms we might ask, "React much?" And in light of his counselors, "Influenced much?" After the decision and the decree, there is no record of his offering or seeking reconciliation, and there is certainly no grace extended to his bride.

So, what happened to Vashti? Fox says she was "made the victim of Xerxes' instability and the princes' insecurity" (*Character and Ideology*, 167). The Bible, however, does not tell us anything else about her story. One is inclined to think, though, of the story of Brer Rabbit. If we strain to listen, we might just hear this plea in a feminine, Persian dialect: "Please don't throw me into the briar patch!" (Joel Chandler Harris, "Brer Rabbit and the Tar Baby"). In other words, she may well have ended up exactly where she preferred to be.

The King's Dishonorable Decree (1:22)

Fox pulls no punches when he writes,

> Xerxes, as we quickly learn, is weak-willed, fickle, and self-centered. He and his advisers are a twittery, silly-headed, cowardly lot who need to hide behind a law to reinforce their status in their homes. (*Character and Ideology*, 168)

When I was a freshman in high school, our varsity football team won no games. When I was a sophomore, we won two. One day at practice, one of our players complained to our coach that hardly anyone was attending our games. Our coach replied with something I have never forgotten: "Respect is earned, not given." For Ahasuerus and his boys, though, it seems respect is demanded even where it is not deserved. To his shame the king dispatches his decree in every language in his realm.

After commenting on the decree being disseminated throughout the empire, Duguid asks some thoughtful questions:

> What was actually achieved by all this huffing and puffing?
> Was the social order of Persia really threatened by this one
> woman's resistance? Even if it were, can such a principle
> of male authority in the household really be imposed by
> governmental decree? Are all men to exercise power in such
> a self-centered way as Ahasuerus did, and then expect instant
> obedience? Is every man supposed to banish his wife if she
> fails to submit to his will? (*Esther and Ruth*, 12)

Duguid concludes that all the decree demonstrates in every language of the empire is that the one, who in Esther 1:1-10 seemed to possess incredible power, actually lacks "authority in his own household" (ibid.). Whether the decree actually had any impact on the homes in the empire is not recorded. So, will one "more worthy" than Vashti be found to serve as queen? Time will tell.

Lessons Others Have Taught from This Text

In one of the doctoral seminars I taught a few years ago, a young gifted pastor shared a video of one of his sermons. Afterward I allowed the other students to provide feedback. They offered him many positive comments. But when it was my turn to share, I asked the student one question: What was the main point of that biblical text? He could not provide it to me, nor had he proclaimed it in his sermon. I then evaluated what he had shared and pointed out that though he considered a passage of Scripture and had great skills in communication, he had failed to preach the main idea the biblical author was addressing. In God's grace this student accepted my reproof and has since made it his goal to make sure the main idea of each biblical text is the main idea of his sermon. He also encourages the other pastors he serves with and those he mentors to adopt the same practice.

One of the elders with whom I served in Baton Rouge used to caution those he taught how to study the Bible to be careful about "getting off in the broccoli." What he meant was that we need to be careful about making side issues main issues or wading off into peripheral issues to the detriment of the primary concern. In my observations of commentaries and sermons on Esther, those preaching through 1:10-22 tend to "get off in the broccoli" with two issues in particular. Issue 1 is the danger of drunkenness that leads to the demeaning of women. Issue 2 is debating whether Vashti or Esther is the better representative of the modern feminist movement. I will address both issues now, but neither should be the main point when you're preaching through this passage.

The Dangers of Drunkenness and of Demeaning Women

"Do not get drunk" and "Treat women better" are both good advice, but neither statement reflects the main point of 1:10-22. Before you accuse me of being a drunk who affirms disrespecting women, let me say this: while I consider drunkenness and misogyny horrific, neither topic can be identified as the main lesson of the author's communication. With that being said, I do think Prime asks two good questions about the influence alcohol had on Ahasuerus:

> First, would Xerxes have commanded Vashti to be brought before his guests—rather like a piece of furniture—if he had been completely sober? Secondly, if he had been sober, would he have become so angry? (*Unspoken Lessons*, 33)

Sin often leads to more sin.

As you teach through 1:10-22 then, it would be fine to affirm Paul's imperative, "Don't get drunk with wine, which leads to reckless living, but be filled by the Spirit" (Eph 5:18). Ahasuerus's actions are certainly an illustration of the dangers of alcohol. But if you are planning to use Esther as your focal text and your main point is prohibition rather than providence, then you will have made a side (but important) issue the main issue.

The Better Model for the Feminist Movement

When studying Esther, I was surprised to find so much discussion about whether Vashti or Esther served the cause of feminine advancement in a more helpful way. For instance, some contend that "Vashti is a counterpart of Esther. Vashti's recalcitrance contrasts with Esther's docility" and that "Esther is contraposed to Vashti not only in her initial obedience and ductility but also in the subtlety of her later efforts to sway the king to her will" (Fox, *Character and Ideology*, 169). Some writers like Vashti's brashness and refusal to play by the rules of the boys in the boardroom. But Esther's approaching the king while seated on his throne would require no less courage than Vashti's refusal to do so.

With regard to standing up for causes, it should be noted that Vashti's decision was about herself and resulted in her being banned from further influence, while Esther's advocacy was about more than herself and she maintained a position of influence. More could be said here, but neither time nor space permits. Just remember, the modern feminist movement was not the original author's concern, nor should it be the main focus of a sermon.

What Can We Learn about God?

*God Will Use Ahasuerus's Wretchedness and
Vashti's Rebellion to Achieve Esther's Reign*

The psalmist declares, "The LORD is a great God, a great King above all gods" (Ps 95:3). In Psalms we are also told to "say among the nations: 'The LORD reigns'" (Ps 96:10). Why would we be instructed to say this in every nation? Have all voted for God to reign? Have their legislative bodies passed bills affirming God's leadership? Of course not, but God is sovereign regardless and does not rule over just a small group of earnest believers.

One of the great mysteries is how someone can do evil toward another, and yet God can simultaneously work whatever it is for the good of his providential plan. One of the clearest examples of this is found in the actions of Joseph's brothers (Gen 37). When Joseph considered what his brothers did and God's use of their betrayal, he said, "You planned evil against me; God planned it for good to bring about the present result—the survival of many people" (Gen 50:20). God did not put an evil plan into the hearts of Joseph's brothers, but he used their choices to accomplish his purposes.

In Esther 1:10-22 God uses a series of decisions made by Vashti and Ahasuerus that he neither initiated nor prevented. He did not cause or stop Ahasuerus's drunkenness, which led to the king's desire not to honor his wife. God did not cause or stop Ahasuerus's angry reaction, which led to his seeking bad counsel. God did not cause or stop the king's decision based on foolish counsel or his disastrous decree. But a drunk king and a defiant queen would be used in the Lord's definite providence. Neither the good nor the bad actions of pagans prevent God from accomplishing his plan.

What seemed insignificant for the Jews—a pagan party, a marital spat between two Persian royals, and a decision to replace the queen— actually had a lot of significance for God's people. Before we are even aware there is a problem, then, God's providence is already at work. If Haman had risen to power without Esther's being in place, it could have been disastrous for God's people. But the Lord oversaw Ahasuerus's drunkenness and Vashti's defiance without violating their wills or wants and used all of it to accomplish what he wanted.

God Is Offended and Greatly Transgressed by Disobedience

God has every right to be offended by our disobedience, and he is more transgressed than we will ever be. Ahasuerus's pride was wounded by Vashti's refusal to come to his feast, and his anger was kindled. There is no record of him seeking to find out if something was wrong with her; there's just a revealing of his wrath. He was embarrassed, offended, and indignant. Memucan's declaration that Vashti's rebellion was not just against the emperor but the entire empire did not aid the cause of reconciliation but of reckoning. It implied, This needs to be made right!

Fortunately, when people sin against us, we do not react anything like Ahasuerus or Memucan, right? We are never prone to want vengeance, are we? When someone posts something on social media about us that is false or negative, we are never inclined to respond in the same manner, are we? Interestingly, Ahasuerus got all bent out of shape, but his command for Vashti was not with holy intentions, nor was her refusal a sin.

As noted earlier, there is no documented offer of reconciliation from the king toward his queen. Forgiveness was certainly not in the proposal from the group of "wise men." But we are nothing like Ahasuerus, right? We quickly, totally, and lavishly forgive those who do wrong against us, right? We never hold a grudge or keep a record of wrongs, do we?

With regard to sin, no one is more offended, more transgressed, and more grieved than God. Every sin is a rejection of his reign and an assertion of ours. Every sin is a choice to disbelieve and disobey the good words of our good King. He has every right to be offended and to enact swift justice. The Lord, however, is "a compassionate and gracious God, slow to anger and abounding in faithful love and truth" (Exod 34:6). He also forgives iniquity (Exod 34:7). When we refuse to forgive fully and freely, we are not imaging God faithfully.

God Grants Us More Grace Than Ahasuerus Granted Vashti

For one rejection of Ahasuerus's authority, Vashti was banished from his presence forever, but God atones for our sin and brings us into his presence. James informs us that "whoever keeps the entire law, and yet stumbles at one point, is guilty of breaking it all" (Jas 2:10). One transgression against God's good precepts is the same as if we have rebelled against the sum of them. Paul lets us know that we are all guilty of this: "For all have sinned and fall short of the glory of God" (Rom 3:23). For choosing just one sin, we deserve the full brunt of holy, eternal wrath. If you disagree and think this sounds too drastic, then you have a diminished and insufficient view both of your sin and of God's holiness. For one refusal to obey his command, God could punish us forever. And in doing so, he would still be right and good and holy.

I, however, am not guilty of breaking just one of God's commands one time in my life. I consider it a good start to the day if I have not chosen sin before my feet hit the floor each morning (because temptations like selfishness and slothfulness start nagging as soon as I wake). Yet, despite my sins being too numerous to count, God has chosen to enact reconciliation and not ruin (see 2 Cor 5:18-21). He says to his people, "Though your sins are scarlet, they will be as white as snow; though they are crimson red, they will be like wool" (Isa 1:18). Indeed, even when it seems certain God will reject his people because of their rebellion, he chooses to make atonement for them rather than abandon them (Ezek 16:62). The gospel truly is the best news for the worst people.

One of the ways I think we image God best is when we run toward sinners and not away from them. For those in our faith families, there is no greater balm than when we seek to offer restoration rather than condemnation. Ahasuerus wanted nothing more to do with Vashti because she transgressed his command. I am thankful God was willing to overcome all of our rebellion in order to bring us into right relationship with him. The sweetest prize of the gospel is not that we get heaven but that we get God. He wanted us even when we did not want him. He sought us even when we were not seeking him.

What Can We Learn about Ourselves?

Without God's Grace and Intervention, We Are All like Ahasuerus

Throwing figurative rocks at Ahasuerus for his sin and condemning his actions can be easy, but if it were not for Christ, we too would continue in sinful and destructive actions. Without Christ's setting us free from slavery to the flesh, the world, and the devil, we would be "slaves to impurity, and to greater and greater lawlessness" (Rom 6:19). Ahasuerus went from one bad decision to another in our text. Even in our sanctification, sin that we do not mortify does not dissipate but escalates. We cannot feed our flesh and our faith simultaneously. Every time we choose faith over flesh, it is evidence of the Lord's grace at work in our lives.

Like Ahasuerus, we are tempted to use people for how they can benefit us without regard for their good. The king wanted to display Vashti at his feast but for his benefit rather than hers. Do we ever use people for our agendas and advancement but have no regard for their gain? Only Christ helps us see the value in others and empowers us to seek to serve them rather than just using them in our service.

When Accountability Is Absent, Rebellion Prevails over Repentance

When true voices of accountability are absent in our lives, rebellion tends to be more present than repentance. In the text Ahasuerus did not display any indicators of repentance or even regret for any of his selfish actions toward Vashti. Perhaps one reason for his lack of contrition is that those with whom he surrounded himself only pointed out how he had been wronged rather than how he was wrong. We need people in our lives who encourage us to obedience rather than disobedience. Of course, rules we make up are a lot easier to follow than the rules God has given to us. This is why we need those who will share with us not just what we may want to hear but what we need to hear from God's Word.

I have an accountability partner with whom I try to meet each week. We both seek to keep our friendship a priority because we both need a brother in Christ who exhorts us to forsake sin rather than to be comfortable with it. Every time I travel to minister somewhere, he texts me and informs me of his prayers on my behalf and exhorts me to choose Christ rather than sin. In our meetings each week, we ask each other pointed questions with regard to putting on Christ and putting off sin. We strive to help each other put away anything that pulls us away from Jesus. Were it not for the Holy Spirit using his Word in my life and his using my family's and faith family's encouragements toward holiness, I too would be guilty of more rebellion than repentance.

When Boasting, We Should Not Be Surprised if God Humbles Us

How many have heard but refuse to heed this wise counsel: "Pride comes before destruction, and an arrogant spirit before a fall" (Prov 16:18)? In seeking to declare and display his power and possessions, Ahasuerus had no clue that by the end of his feasts, his power would be diminished. He is also an illustration of the fact that those who demand honor and those who deserve honor are not always the same. The king wanted to be honored, but instead he was humbled—not just in his palace but in every province.

It may not always seem to be so, but every humbling the Lord brings to our lives is ultimately a grace. His reminders that only his kingdom will not be shaken discourage us from trying to build our own. His reminder that he has seated Christ above every title given to man, "not only in this age but also in the one to come" (Eph 1:21), frees us to live for his name rather than ours. It truly is a grace to be brought to the same conviction as Paul to "never boast about anything except the cross of our Lord Jesus Christ" (Gal 6:14). If we are overly concerned with being honored rather than giving him honor, we may miss that God "leads the humble in what is right and teaches them his way" (Ps 25:9).

What Can We Learn about Christ?

Jesus's Power Is Absolute

With Ahasuerus there was more pomp than true power, but Christ's power is absolute. At the beginning of Esther 1, we are led to think Ahasuerus is all powerful, but by the end of the chapter, we are shown that he does not even have all the power in his own house. In the Gospels, however, we see the wind and waves obey Christ's voice (Mark 4:39), we see demons and disease obey his commands (Mark 5:13,29), and even death must yield to him (Mark 5:42). We also see that those who have "authority" over Jesus, like Pilate (John 19:10-11), only have it because he allows it. In the case of Ahasuerus, absolute power is a farce. With Jesus absolute power is a fact!

Jesus's Constant Motivation Is God's Glory and Our Good

It can be scary when a leader possesses a lot of power but lacks holiness. Ahasuerus made decisions from improper motives and impaired judgment. Jobes notes, "The Persian court was not a safe place because Xerxes held great power, and he wielded it unpredictably" (*Esther*, 69). In addressing Esther 1:9-12, she goes on to say,

> When such absolute power is combined with decadence and ruthlessness, no one is safe. This scene, which shows the dangers of living under Xerxes' power in the Persian empire,

> provides a backdrop for the major conflict of the story when
> the power of the Persian empire will be turned against the
> Jewish people. (Ibid.)

Ahasuerus was fickle and untrustworthy with power; Jesus, conversely, is not. Jesus does not make decisions on a whim but according to his wisdom. All of Christ's decisions are rooted in his faithfulness and are not just for our good but for our best. His judgment is never impaired, and his motives are never improper.

Jesus Is Sacrificial

As a king Ahasuerus was selfish. As our King, Christ is sacrificial. There is no doubt Christ has all authority, yet he does not lord it over everyone like a baby having a tantrum. John records that on Jesus's final night with his disciples before his crucifixion,

> *he got up from supper, laid aside his outer clothing, took a towel, and tied it around himself. Next, he poured water into a basin and began to wash his disciples' feet and to dry them with the towel tied around him.* (John 13:4-5)

The one who had all the power in the room (and in the universe) was serving.

As a husband Ahasuerus was selfish. As the church's groom Christ is sacrificial. He does not seek to use us to our detriment and his benefit. In fact, our good actually required his detriment or, more specifically, his death. But Paul proclaims, "Christ loved the church and gave himself for her" (Eph 5:25). Likewise his sacrificial love is meant to be evident in and through us. And with regard to our homes, Duguid contends, "If Christian husbands were more like Christ and less like Ahasuerus, then perhaps we would find our wives more ready to submit to our leadership" (*Esther & Ruth*, 16).

Jesus Deserves All the Glory for Our Beauty

The gospel is not that if we do enough good things then maybe we will get Christ's attention and earn his affection. No, that is not the gospel at all, but unfortunately many believe it is. The gospel is that even when we were in our worst state, Christ set his affections on us and took action for us.

Those who are in Christ have been made beautiful, but we did not start that way. Out of concern that they would forget who they were before Christ's work in their lives, Paul reminds the Ephesians they (like all other Christians) "were dead in [their] trespasses and sins" and "were by nature children under wrath" (Eph 2:1,3). We who have repented and believed, though, have not just been informed by Christ's love but transformed by it. He has made us holy, and he has cleansed us "with the washing of water by the word. He did this to present the church to himself in splendor, without spot or wrinkle or anything like that, but holy and blameless" (Eph 5:26-27). Ahasuerus gets no credit for Vashti's beauty, but Christ deserves all glory for ours.

Jesus Deserves Honor

Much has been shared already about Ahasuerus's desire and demand to be honored, so I will not say anything further in this discussion about him. Christ, however, deserves all honor, and one day it will be declared in heaven and on earth. Consider now, as a close to this section, the sights and sounds John was allowed to see. He writes,

> Then I looked and heard the voice of many angels around the throne, and also of the living creatures and of the elders. Their number was countless thousands, plus thousands of thousands. They said with a loud voice,
>
> > Worthy is the Lamb who was slaughtered
> > to receive power and riches
> > and wisdom and strength
> > and honor and glory and blessing!
>
> I heard every creature in heaven, on earth, under the earth, on the sea, and everything in them say,
>
> > Blessing and honor and glory and power
> > be to the one seated on the throne,
> > and to the Lamb, forever and ever!
>
> The four living creatures said, "Amen," and the elders fell down and worshiped. (Rev 5:11-14)

The worship in Revelation 5 is not forced but fueled by who Jesus is and what he has done. He is worthy of eternal praise.

Reflect and Discuss

1. Why does sin tend to lead to more sin in our lives? Why is Christ our only hope of stopping this toxic decline?

2. Ahasuerus wanted to show off Vashti for his benefit rather than hers. In what ways do we use people for our good rather than theirs? How can we avoid using others to their detriment and to our benefit, and why should we?

3. Why do we need godly counselors in our lives who steadily push us to the Word? Who serves you in this way?

4. Why can we be slow to admit our sin and to seek reconciliation with those we wound?

5. Why are we sometimes slow to initiate reconciliation with those who have wounded us but are not seeking our forgiveness? How does initiating reconciliation instead of waiting for people to seek forgiveness image God?

6. We do not know that Ahasuerus ever felt regret about his decision with Vashti. If you could change one decision for the sake of the kingdom, what would it be?

7. God used Ahasuerus's wretchedness and Vashti's rebellion to open the door for Esther's future reign. What does this tell you about his sovereignty and providence?

8. Ahasuerus could not be trusted with absolute power. Why, however, can Christ be trusted with all authority? In what ways is this comforting?

9. Though our political leaders may not make every decision from pure motives or with our good in mind, we know that Christ always does. How should we respond to this truth, especially if a decision Christ makes brings difficulty and grief into our lives?

10. In what ways are you seeking to honor Christ instead of being honored?

Sin, Suffering, and Sovereignty

ESTHER 2:1-18

Main Idea: We live in a dark world, and sometimes we are part of the darkness; nevertheless, God in his grace does not discard us but delivers us, even from ourselves, and deploys us for his purposes.

I.   **In Painful Consequences, Seek Counsel That Fuels Faith Rather than Flesh (2:1-4).**
    A. Decisions made in haste and anger often lead to remorse.
    B. We need to seek counsel that fuels our faith rather than our flesh.
    C. The best proposals from the world cannot meet our deepest needs.

II. **In Painful Consequences, Live so that All Will Be Blessed Rather than Burdened (2:5-7).**
    A. Sometimes we find ourselves in situations because of the disobedience of others.
    B. At all times, even in discipline, God has preserved and is preserving his people.

III. **In Pressure to Compromise, Persevere in Commitment to the Word (2:8-11).**
    A. The Lord, in his sovereignty, can use our lack of courage and compliance with this world for his plan.
    B. Concealing convictions is not ultimately profitable.
    C. Compromise with the world in the past does not disqualify us from contending for God in the future.

IV. **In the Presence of God's Favor, Find Progress in Faith (2:9,12-15).**
    A. God's favor
    B. Esther's progress

V.   **In the Providence of God, Move into a Strategic Position without Knowing His Sovereign Plan (2:16-18).**
    A. Esther is in a position of prominence because of God's providence.
    B. God's blessings in our lives are not for selfishness but stewardship.

VI. In Pondering Christ, See That Ahasuerus and Mordecai Cannot Compare.

A. Ahasuerus exercised authority for his own gratification, but Jesus does so for our good.

B. Ahasuerus sought a beautiful and pure bride, but Jesus made us into one.

C. Ahasuerus left the women he used with shame, but Jesus has taken our shame away.

D. Mordecai could only check on Esther's situation, but Jesus can change ours.

Sometimes we experience painful consequences because of *our poor choices*. When I was a little boy, my mother used to take me shopping with her for what felt like days at a time. If she happened to be in a store with a clothing section, I would immediately look for the garments hanging on a circular rack. I would then proceed to climb into the middle of it and push the clothes out as if I were a mini-tornado.

On one particular day something caught my eye, and I shot out of such a clothes rack, hitting whatever the maximum speed is for a kid in husky jeans. My mother saw me and began to call my name. I heard her calls but replied, "No, Momma!" She kept calling, and I kept running. That is, of course, until I crashed into a glass display. Any hope I had of my mom extending tenderness and nurture to me was quickly dashed as she yanked me up and informed me what discipline she was going to administer when we got out of the store. Perhaps it was on that day that my earliest convictions about running being painful began to take shape! I made a poor choice to disobey and ignore my mother's protective calls, and for that decision I experienced painful consequences.

Sometimes we experience painful consequences because of *the poor choices of others*. I was raised in an abusive home. One of my earliest memories, in fact, is of my dad yelling and seeking to wound my mom and sister. In our town my father had a reputation for being a bit crazy. When I was in fifth grade, many of my friends were in class together. My mom wanted me to be in that class, but the teacher refused to accept me because she did not want to deal with my dad. She would not be the only one to have concerns about my father's issues. Time after time, my mother and sister and I found ourselves in painful circumstances due to the poor choices of my father.

Whether they are my choices, your choices, or the choices of another, and whether they come with blessings or burdens, every choice and consequence are always under God's sovereign care. In Esther 2:1-18 we will see that the Lord reigns over Ahasuerus's cravings and Esther's and Mordecai's compliance, and he will use all of it to accomplish his purposes. Despite Ahasuerus's fleshliness and Esther's and Mordecai's fearfulness, the Lord's favor remains present and productive.

Before we examine 2:1-18, some clarifications need to be made for those whose memories of the text are more blurry than bright. First, Mordecai is not Esther's father, brother, or uncle. He is her cousin, and he treats her like a daughter (2:15)—most likely because he raised her (2:20). Second, Mordecai does not enter Esther into a beauty pageant in hopes she will advance herself. No college scholarship was provided to the one crowned Mrs. Persia 479 BC. Third, neither Esther nor Mordecai is acting with a preconceived plan to rescue all the Jews in the empire. They will later discern Esther's position through the lens of providence but not because of their own premeditation. In other words, Esther's and Mordecai's actions are not based on any guarantee they have of prominence and certainly not because of future problems they are anticipating. Indeed, the present has enough problems of its own for them.

Even knowing that God's plan will eventually be brought to light does not completely diminish the darkness recorded in 2:1-18. Strain provides some helpful thoughts on this passage:

> Esther 2, instead of offering us an example to follow, invites us to face the reality of life in which women are often objectified and made victims, where men can be predatory, and where at least for some, fear is often more powerful than faith. ("Beauty and the Beast")

He adds,

> Esther 2 does not flinch from narrating for us this simple, ugly fact of life in ancient Persia, where people are treated as commodities. It is no fairytale story of a poor, Jewish girl falling in love with prince charming. Esther 2 is a story, the like of which when we hear it on the news we can scarcely bear to contemplate. . . . And yet it is here, amidst all the moral ambiguities and the shocking abuses that dog Esther's

steps, that we are being invited to trace the footprints of the
sovereign God who is working in and through and despite the
sin and suffering that we find here, for the good of those who
love him and who have been called according to His purpose.
(Ibid.)

Though we live in a dark world, and sometimes we are part of the darkness, God in his grace does not discard us but saves us, even from ourselves, and deploys us for his purposes. Let us now closely examine the
sin, suffering, and sovereignty recorded in Esther 2:1-18.

In Painful Consequences, Seek Counsel
That Fuels Faith Rather than Flesh
ESTHER 2:1-4

Between the closing scene in 1:22 and the opening scene in 2:1, at least
four years have passed. The events in the opening chapter occurred
during the third year of Ahasuerus's reign (1:3), but by the time a new
queen is crowned, Ahasuerus will be in his seventh year of rule (2:16).
The Bible provides no record of the king's actions in the interim, but
other historical works claim that between his third and seventh years
on the throne, Ahasuerus gathered the largest army known up to that
point and attacked Greece (Herodotus, *The Histories*, 425). His military
campaign was not successful, and he returned to Susa.

When the author raises the opening curtain of chapter 2, we find
the defeated king in a moment of reflection and remorse. He thinks
about Vashti and what happened to her. He is obviously down in the
dumps because those around him come up with a plan to cheer him.
Their idea is for all the beautiful young virgins in the 127 provinces
to be gathered in Susa, and the one who most pleases the king will
become the new queen. If chapter 1 was not enough to convince you
that Ahasuerus needed some new counselors, then perhaps chapter 2
will be sufficient. The plan reeks of something devised in a locker room
rather than in a royal court, but Ahasuerus thinks it is a great idea. (No
surprise there!) If you are a young and unmarried woman in the Persian
Empire, this is definitely a contest in which you do not want the odds in
your favor. There are a few lessons we can learn in Esther 2:1-4 about the
consequences of our own poor choices.

Decisions Made in Haste and Anger Often Lead to Remorse

One of the most regrettable decisions recorded in the Bible is in Judges 11. Jephthah has become the reluctant leader of God's people and is charged with battling the Ammonites. In his desire for victory,

> *Jephthah made this vow to the Lord: "If you in fact hand over the Ammonites to me, whoever comes out the doors of my house to greet me when I return safely from the Ammonites will belong to the Lord, and I will offer that person as a burnt offering."* (Judg 11:30-31)

The Lord had not asked or required Jephthah to make such a vow, but he did grant victory over the Ammonites. Upon Jephthah's return home, his only child, his daughter, was the first who came out of his house "to meet him with tambourines and dancing" (Judg 11:34).

As any father who had made a foolish decision to the detriment of his family would be, Jephthah was deeply grieved. "When he saw her, he tore his clothes and said, 'No! Not my daughter! You have devastated me! You have brought great misery on me'" (Judg 11:35). Just the words every little girl loves to hear when skipping out to meet her father after he's been away on a trip or at work or at war. Interestingly, in his initial phrases, Jephthah's pain is primary and his responsibility for it is minimal. While he is devastated, she will actually die. While he is expressing his misery, she will experience mortification. In his hunger for victory, he made a hasty vow. His was an unnecessary and regrettable decision indeed.

As tragic as the story of Jephthah and his daughter is, my guess is that at least on a reduced scale you can relate. Perhaps you have made a decision in anger or haste or because someone gave you bad counsel, and then later you regretted it. Perhaps you immediately regretted it. Most of my regret regarding haste and anger centers on words I have used toward or about others. One of my constant prayers is for the Lord to help me be "quick to listen, slow to speak, and slow to anger." When I fail to live James 1:19, I cannot shift the responsibility for my sin to others.

In Esther 2:1 Ahasuerus is thinking back on all the events regarding Vashti. Whether this is the first time he has done so in the four-year interval, the author does not tell us. Ahasuerus's anger is gone, but so is she. We know that he "remembered," but it seems his memory had grown a little fuzzy in the time that passed because the author says he was pondering "what was decided against her." There is an important word missing in that phrase. Do you know what it is? The word *he* is missing (no, not from the biblical record—I do believe in inerrancy and all the other I's of Scripture). But doesn't it seem that it should say, "what *he* decided against her"? We can have regret and we can have remorse, but we do not have repentance until we acknowledge our responsibility in what is wrong. Jephthah's *you* and Ahasuerus's *was* both fell short. Though his counselors may have been in agreement, Ahasuerus had no one to blame but himself. When you mess up, fess up. The beauty of the gospel is that whatever we confess, Christ has already covered with his blood. In seeking to learn from Ahasuerus's example, we can see that decisions made in anger or haste often lead to remorse.

We Need to Seek Counsel That Fuels Our Faith Rather than Our Flesh

In Esther 1 and 2 Ahasuerus is responding to the counsel of others who guide him according to his gratification rather than his good. One does not have to read far in chapter 2 to see part of Ahasuerus's error. While experiencing the painful consequences of his poor choices, the king was provided counsel by the young men who assisted him. As those of us who have been young men know, young men are not the best source from which to hear the wisdom and experience of the ages. This reality, in fact, is one of the reasons I continue to advocate for intergenerational ministry in the faith family I lead. The last thing young men and women need is to receive counsel only from their peers.

To cheer the king up, the young men proposed an idea that would be for Ahasuerus's delight but to the detriment of many families in the empire. They decided all the beautiful young virgins in the king's provinces should be brought to the palace for the emperor's pleasure. We are not told the marital status of the young advisers, but if any of them were single, this collecting of girls to do the king's bidding would also mean none of the girls could be their brides. Regardless, our concerns should lie with all the young virgins that were to be taken from their homes. Ahasuerus is not the kind of guy to whom a father would joyfully give his little girl, especially when considering his treatment of Vashti.

Up to this point in Esther, the only ideas that originate from Ahasuerus include feasts for his glory and demands for his gratification. In both instances in which decisions needed to be made, he sought and followed what others suggested. Jobes notes, "What becomes the irrevocable law of the Persians and Medes is the will of those closest to the king, who know how to skillfully manipulate his needs" (*Esther*, 100). This revelation should lead us to an important evaluation. Whom do we let influence us? On whose counsel do we place the most value? Are we surrounding ourselves with those in whom "the word of Christ [dwells] richly" (Col 3:16)? At all times in our lives, we need those whose counsel fuels our faith rather than our flesh, but especially when we are in painful circumstances due to our poor choices. Their encouragement from the Word can be used to prevent us from making further unwise decisions. Ahasuerus did not have that kind of counsel, but I hope you do and will provide that for those with whom you have influence.

The Best Proposals from the World Cannot Meet Our Deepest Needs

Ahasuerus was a king with power who ruled for his pleasure. Mathew Gilbert exhorts, "When we seek pleasure for the wrong reasons and in the wrong places, it will always evade us. When we seek pleasure in Christ, we will always find it" ("The Greatest Treasure"). In sin we are constantly seeking substitutes for God. In turning to those, we turn away from him. But only God provides what he promises. Sin never will.

The young assistants provided the king with a solution, but it (or more specifically they) will never satisfy. The best proposals from the world cannot meet our deepest needs. As Strain notes,

> Whatever pangs of remorse he had been feeling for Vashti are now forgotten as his lust ignites afresh. It's actually a classic strategy of the un-renewed human heart. Incapable of repentance, unbelieving hearts can only avoid guilt. They can ignore guilt, they can hide guilt beneath a blanket of indulgence, but they can never really remove guilt. We know, many of us don't we, there's only one thing that can do that— the blood of Jesus Christ that can cleanse our consciences from dead works that we may serve the living and true God. ("Beauty and the Beast")

If Ahasuerus were really repentant about how he treated Vashti, then he would not seek to replace her in the manner the assistants suggested. He has already wronged one woman. He will now multiply that many times over.

In Painful Consequences, Live so that All Will Be Blessed Rather than Burdened
ESTHER 2:5-7

In the next portion of the passages, the spotlight is shifted, and the author informs us for the first time that two particular Jews were living in Susa. For the original audience hearing or reading Esther, there had to be someone thinking, *Finally! Now we are getting somewhere with this pagan story.* But any joy about fellow Jews may have been short-lived when they read the names of those in the citadel. In the lineage of the Benjaminites, few are named after pagan deities. But before we rush to judgment regarding the brow-raising names Mordecai and Esther (more on that in a moment), remember that we do not know when, how, or why the two Jews living in Susa received their non-Jewish names. And just because their names were acceptable to the culture does not mean Mordecai and Esther had accepted the culture. Their Babylonian names could have been assigned or given to them.

Mordecai's name was most likely derived from the "chief god of the Babylonian pantheon," "Marduk," which admittedly is not so great for a Jew (Bush, *Ruth/Esther*, 362). If he had a Hebrew name, the author does not tell it to us. Of course, when you are living in a foreign land under the Lord's discipline and a tyrannical king, your name probably is not your biggest concern.

Even if the original readers recoiled at his name, they would at least respect Mordecai's caring for his cousin because her parents were dead. But that respect would probably vanish too when he let said cousin be taken into the king's palace, although he did at least check on her every day. In any case, I doubt the Mordecai fan club was being overwhelmed with a membership rush at this point in the narrative's first telling. Respect for him would grow (10:3), but it would not start here. His people chose not to return to Jerusalem (more on that later too), he has a pagan name, and the one he was caring for will soon be one of the king's conquests.

The female Jew in the story is named Hadassah, which means "myrtle" (ibid., 363). Several hundred years before, Isaiah said,

> *Instead of the thornbush, a cypress will come up, and instead of the brier, a myrtle will come up; this will stand as a monument for the* Lord, *an everlasting sign that will not be destroyed.* (Isa 55:13)

Isaiah meant the Lord would forgive and accept his people. *Esther* "means 'star' (a reference to the star-shaped flower of the myrtle) and is close to the name *Ishtar*, the Babylonian goddess of love" (Smith, *Ezra, Nehemiah, Esther*, 238). Bush contends, "As for the name 'Esther,' determining its etymology adds nothing to the meaning of our story, though the subject has been much written about" (*Ruth/Esther*, 363).

Our attention to the details, however, should be drawn elsewhere. Jobes asserts, "In Hebrew narrative the physical attributes described when a character is first introduced is of special relevance to his or her role in the story" (*Esther*, 96). In both her shape and appearance, Esther is lovely. The author is letting us know she will certainly be chosen to participate in the horrific upcoming season of *The Bachelor from Persia*.

Sometimes We Find Ourselves in Situations because of the Disobedience of Others

As excited as we may be to learn that Jews were in Susa, we need to ask, Why were there Jews in Susa? The first part of that question is, How did they get there? The answer is that Mordecai's and Esther's ancestors had disobeyed the Lord and were disciplined with exile. The initial verses in Daniel reveal the opening stages of that discipline and dispersal:

> *In the third year of the reign of King Jehoiakim of Judah, King Nebuchadnezzar of Babylon came to Jerusalem and laid siege to it. The Lord handed King Jehoiakim of Judah over to him, along with some of the vessels from the house of God. Nebuchadnezzar carried them to the land of Babylon, to the house of his god, and put the vessels in the treasury of his god.*
>
> *The king ordered Ashpenaz, his chief eunuch, to bring some of the Israelites from the royal family and from the nobility—young men without any physical defect, good-looking, suitable for instruction in all wisdom, knowledgeable, perceptive, and capable of serving in the king's palace. He was to teach them the Chaldean language and literature.* (Dan 1:1-4)

The second part of the question is, Why were they still there? After all, in time, opportunity arose to return home. In the book of Ezra, we are told that King Cyrus of Persia said,

> *The LORD, the God of the heavens, has given me all the kingdoms of the earth and has appointed me to build him a house at Jerusalem in*

Judah. Any of his people among you, may his God be with him, and may he go to Jerusalem in Judah and build the house of the LORD, the God of Israel, the God who is in Jerusalem. (Ezra 1:2-3)

Mordecai and Esther, then, are still in Susa because their relatives decided to stay. Any could return, but not all chose to do so. Perhaps they felt like they were heeding these words spoken through Jeremiah:

Find wives for yourselves, and have sons and daughters. Find wives for your sons and give your daughters to men in marriage so that they may bear sons and daughters. Multiply there; do not decrease. Pursue the well-being of the city I have deported you to. Pray to the LORD on its behalf, for when it thrives, you will thrive. (Jer 29:6-7)

But in doing so, they were ignoring what Jeremiah said a few verses later:

This is what the LORD says: "When seventy years for Babylon are complete, I will attend to you and will confirm my promise concerning you to restore you to this place. (Jer 29:10)

Instead of returning to and restoring Jerusalem, an unnumbered group of the Judean Diaspora chose instead to live "as expatriates in various localities in the Persian empire" (Bush, *Ruth/Esther*, 361). While the group was unnumbered, Mordecai and Esther were not unnamed. They were living in Susa—due to the disobedience of some and the decisions of other ancestors. And that disobedience and those decisions caused conflict in the lives of Mordecai and Esther.

We should strive to avoid leaving those who come after us in difficult situations. When I was single, I only had to make decisions that for the most part impacted just me. Now that I am married and have four children, I constantly think through how my decisions will affect them. One of my mother's favorite songs is "Find Us Faithful" as sung by Steve Green. These are the words of the chorus:

Oh may all who come behind us find us faithful.
May the fire of our devotion light their way.
May the footprints that we leave lead them to believe
and the lives we live inspire them to obey.
Oh may all who come behind us find us faithful. (Jon Mohr)

Indeed, may our obedience leave peace for those who follow us rather than problems.

At All Times, Even in Discipline, God Has
Preserved and Is Preserving His People

Mordecai and Esther may have found themselves in circumstances they did not choose, but that does not mean God did not care. Even in discipline God preserves his people. He told Israel,

> *I will be with you when you pass through the waters, and when you pass through the rivers, they will not overwhelm you. You will not be scorched when you walk through the fire, and the flame will not burn you. For I am the LORD your God, the Holy One of Israel, and your Savior. I have given Egypt as a ransom for you, Cush and Seba in your place.* (Isa 43:2-3)

When told there were Jews living in Susa, we should think of disobedience, we should think of discipline, and we should also think of deliverance. Moreover, the fact that there are still Jews is evidence that they have not been destroyed, and if God is not going to destroy his own people, he certainly will not let anyone else do it—even their captors. Though God disciplines us, he does not discard us. He ordains the discipline for our repentance and reconciliation and not for our ruin. The next verse in the passage from Jeremiah expresses that exact thought:

> *"For I know the plans I have for you"*—this is the LORD's declaration—*"plans for your well-being, not for disaster, to give you a future and a hope."* (Jer 29:11)

Jobes notes, "While God may be good to all his creatures in general, he is in a special relationship of protection and preservation with his covenant people" (*Esther*, 103). Strain notes this as well:

> We get the message, don't we? Mordecai and Esther are exiled. That is, though they live in Susa, they belong to the people of God, and that changes everything. They are strangers in a strange land, exiled to be sure, but they're not cut off from the covenant of promise or from the commonwealth of Israel. Whatever else happens, our author is indicating to us—"Keep your eyes on this family. God is not done with His people yet." ("Beauty and the Beast")

I'd like to make one more point here. God was using Mordecai to protect and preserve Esther's life. We are not told at what age she was taken into his care, but we will see soon that this adopted orphan would be used to save her people. Do not let anyone ever tell you, then, that adoption does not matter. As awful as it would be for Esther to be gathered into the king's harem, she was able to meet the qualifications because she had been protected and loved by Mordecai and not abandoned on the streets to settle into the arms of any passerby.

In Pressure to Compromise, Persevere in Commitment to the Word
ESTHER 2:8-11

The Lord, in His Sovereignty, Can Use Our Lack of Courage and Our Compliance with This World for His Plan

After telling us Esther was alive, she was living in Susa, and she was beautiful, the author probably surprises no one by informing his readers that Esther was taken to the palace. But the phrase *was taken* leaves one to wonder if Mordecai tried to prevent her capture or whether he was complicit. I would like to think that if a pagan king wanted my two daughters, I would fight the captors to my final breath. But if Mordecai did resist, the author does not reveal it. Surely, though, he did not think it would be good for Esther to live out her remaining days in the royal harem.

So, what was Esther thinking? Smith contends,

> Interpreters sometimes attempt to read Esther's mind, and some conclude that she remained a faithful Jew throughout this period, while others condemn her for leaving her faith and the moral requirements of the law. Although it is enticing to imagine what she might have thought and consider the things she may have done, none of this is revealed in this narrative, so it is impossible to condemn or praise her. The rest of her experiences prove that she did not totally abandon her faith, but it is impossible to know how she justified all the ethical choices she faced in the pagan world of Persia. (*Ezra, Nehemiah, Esther*, 239)

If Mordecai did not put up a fight, then did Esther? Did those who took her to the palace have bruises to prove her displeasure?

Ultimately, the author offers no commentary on the facts he or she is recording. Esther was pretty. Esther was taken. The author does not say Mordecai was wrong for letting her be taken or that Esther should have put up more of a fight. What is also missing is any evidence that Mordecai met with the Lord at a burning bush where God revealed his secret plan regarding Esther's future. Actually, the text reveals that Mordecai has no idea what is going to happen because he checks on Esther every day and tries to get any morsel of information he can. So why was Esther taken to the palace? Jobes suggests, "Esther and Mordecai may have compromised knowing that if they did not then it could cost them their lives" (*Esther*, 101). In considering my own decisions, I tend to compromise with the world even with far less personal threat. So perhaps we might be a little sympathetic with Esther's being taken captive. But then there is the issue of concealment.

Concealing Convictions Is Not Ultimately Profitable

Concealing our convictions in order to advance in this world may cause us to gain nothing of value but instead to lose what matters most. Mordecai's clashing with the captors is not revealed in the text, but his commanding Esther to conceal her ethnicity while in custody is. Again, the Mordecai fan club is not gaining traction at this point. Esther complies with his counsel and does not tell anyone about who she is or who attended her last family reunion.

Frustratingly, we are not told why Mordecai made such a command. Were Jews being targeted and threatened by Persian authorities? Not any more than usual, as far as we are aware. No indication of intentional genocide is in the text up to this point. Was Mordecai afraid Esther's ethnicity would decrease her opportunities to advance in the harem? I hope this was not true, but if that was the case, then she should have told everyone she met about her heritage. Was Mordecai right for what he commanded, or was he wrong? The author offers no answers.

There are questions we can and should answer about our own lives. For instance, are we currently concealing the fact we belong to God? Have you been shrinking back from using the Bible in your conversations at work because you are afraid it will harm your opportunity for promotion? If young and unmarried, are you not being vocal about your faith because you are interested in dating someone who is not a believer or in impressing a professor who is an avowed atheist? In short, are we seeking approval from others rather than resting in God's approval in Christ? The gospel frees us to serve because we have found security in God and are not seeking it elsewhere.

With regard to Mordecai's and Esther's actions, hopefully we can all agree that making the right decision in the right manner is not always easy. But is compromise with the world necessary? Can we blur the means as long as it justifies the end? One would be hard pressed to prove this is what Esther and Mordecai were doing since their focus was most likely on personal survival and not on building a strategy to benefit an entire ethnic group.

I had an opportunity once to go with a friend to search for one of his sons who was living hundreds of miles away. There was concern the son was involved in drugs, and some doubted that we would be able to find him. My friend had been advised that if we did find him we needed to make up a story and get him in the car and then on the plane with us at any cost. As we talked through that plan in the hotel room late one night, the Spirit brought Romans 12:21 to mind. There Paul encourages us not to "be conquered by evil, but [to] conquer evil with good." I told my friend that if we were seeking to do good toward his son then we should not have to start off our interactions with a lie. In God's good providence we did find the son, we did not lie, and soon after our visit the son chose to return home on his own.

We are called to navigate being in the world but not of it. Duguid sees Esther's actions as

> fully complying with the empire's outrageous demands with the goal of winning the "love" of an unworthy royal husband. She would perhaps have objected that she had little choice, but if someone is willing to suffer the consequences, full obedience to God's law is always an option. (*Esther & Ruth*, 29)

Jobes is not as critical as Duguid is here but offers another perspective:

> Regardless of whether they always knew what the right choice was or whether they had the best of motives, God was working through even their imperfect decisions and actions to fulfill his perfect purposes. Other than Jesus, even the godliest people of the Bible were flawed, often confused, and sometimes outright disobedient. (*Esther*, 108)

Compromise with the World in the Past Does Not Disqualify Us from Contending for God in the Future

If there is anyone who knows about denying who they are and their relationship to Jesus, it is Peter. On the night of Jesus's trials, Peter had at least three opportunities to clearly affirm his love and support for Jesus. On all three occasions he chose to conceal the truth and feign indignation about being asked if he knew Jesus. After Peter's last denial, the Lord looked straight at him, which led Peter to remember what the Lord told him and moved him to run out and weep bitterly (Luke 22:61-62).

Often, like Peter's, our level of self-reliance and self-confidence is too high, but our level of self-awareness is too low. I am certain Peter did not think he was capable of denying Jesus in the Lord's darkest hours, but he did it. J. C. Ryle offers wisdom as he cautions, "Let us settle it in our minds, that there is nothing too bad for the very best of us to do unless he watches, prays, and is held up by the grace of the Lord Jesus Christ" (*Expository Thoughts*, 370). But as we can learn from Peter, Esther, Mordecai, and a host of others in the Bible, though we may lack courage at times and choose to compromise with the world, it does not mean God is done with us.

Here are two truths for you to consider before we leave this section. First, God's people are not perfect, but his plan is. If our imperfections disqualified us from being used by God, then none of us would be used. He is not seeking a perfect servant. He sent one: Jesus. Our previous compromises with the world do not completely disqualify us from contending for God in the future. (Ask Esther and Mordecai.) Second, knowing that Peter was ultimately led to repentance and restoration, though he had repeatedly denied Jesus and even invoked a curse on himself, we can have hope that all our sins can truly be forgiven as well. Though we need almost daily reminders of this fact, God's grace is greater than all our sin.

In the Presence of God's Favor, Find Progress in Faith
ESTHER 2:9,12-15

In the middle of the gloom of custody, compromise, and concealment shines a bright spot. Esther pleased Hegai and won his favor, and he placed her on the fast track with cosmetics and food. True, she was rapidly advancing toward the king, but she was also receiving the best possible care in an awful situation. Hegai also gave her the best place in the harem. Not exactly what every girl dreams of but a blessing nonetheless.

As the story advances, we move from the search process to the special preparations. Here we learn what happens to the unfortunate contestants. They receive twelve months of treatments to prepare them for one night with the king apiece. They will be made to look and smell in a way that pleases the king, regardless of their own preferences. I wish I could say things have since improved, but many of the same pressures of appearance still exist for women today. Just consult any magazine at the checkout of your local grocery store.

After joining with the king, these girls could not return to the virgins' quarters for obvious and grievious reasons. The phrase *walk of shame* is used in our culture to describe the situation of someone who has a sexual encounter with a person to whom he or she is not married and then walks home the next morning wearing the same outfit worn the previous night. As these young girls would leave the king's bedroom and walk to a different harem where all the king's other concubines were living, it was a walk of shame indeed. But the deeper shame should fall on Ahasuerus for taking the virginity of all these women and then consigning them to a place like Hotel California, where they could check out but never leave. If the king did not call for them by name, the girls would live out the remainder of their days in the second harem having only been with the king for one night. This experience could have been Esther's as well, but for some reason it was not. Any guesses why?

God's Favor

Though she may have been faithless (unnecessarily concealing her heritage) and though she may have been fearful (who wouldn't be in that situation?), Esther still was winning favor with everyone she met. For some reason Esther is received positively by all who see her, and they help her for her good (as far as good goes in a harem). Why are the pagans so accomodating? Because "God makes even His enemies serve His ends" (Strain, "Beauty and the Beast").

We are not told that God's favor is something Esther asked for in her prayers. We are not even told she prayed. In fact, if God's blessing were based solely on bold obedience to God, Esther would be owed no favor at all. But God bestows his favor daily on those who do not deserve it and could never earn it.

Esther's Progress

Just because Esther was out of Mordecai's direct care does not mean she was out of God's. Even if we find ourselves in a pagan king's harem and not seeking God, we may find him seeking us. I am thankful for all the times God has walked with me even when I was not walking for him.

The author gives no specific reason for it, but God's kindness toward Esther is seen in how she was treated and how all received her. She was progressing instead of being punished. Her progress was because of his plan. And though it did not result in an immediate proclamation of her faith, she was certainly being advanced for the purposes of the faith.

In our lives God's kindness and favor are not any more deserved than they were in Esther's. We have acted faithlessly and fearfully as well. But when we experience the presence of God's favor (and are given eyes to see it), we are often led to progress in our faith. His grace is for our growth and for the purposes of advancing the gospel in and through us. Esther will eventually identify her ethnicity and intercede on behalf of her people, and it will all have started because God's hand is even over a harem.

In the Providence of God, Move into a Strategic Position without Knowing His Sovereign Plan
ESTHER 2:16-18

Esther Is in a Position of Prominence because of God's Providence

Choosing to skip certain details, the author gives the outcome of Esther's visit. The king decides no other virgins need be considered. He was smitten by Esther and wanted her to be his queen. In his joy he slashed taxes and gave gifts, which would have caused Esther's most ardent detractors, if she had any, to at least be slightly grateful. The girl who was adopted became the girl who was abducted who then became the girl who advanced in the harem ultimately to be adorned with a crown and announced as a queen in a feast given just for her. A provincial search process, special preparations, and the move into a strategic position all seem guided by a silent providence.

God's Blessings in Our Lives Are Not for Selfishness but Stewardship

In Esther 2 the biblical author is telling us how, despite all odds, a young Jewish woman comes into a position of power in the Persian Empire. It was not something she had sought for herself or been planning since childhood. Her being made queen certainly did not occur in a way any self-respecting woman would prefer. Being given the crown would have surprised Esther. But her rise to such a prominent position (though at this point in the story she would not have seen it as such) signaled that as sure as God had disciplined his people, he was committed to preserving them. Sometimes God moves us into position without fully revealing his plan.

Importantly, God has not placed Esther in this position just for herself. His provision for her is ultimately so he can provide for his people, and Esther will play a key role in that process. Reflecting on the chapter, Strain says,

> Their wickedness notwithstanding, the advice of the king's counselors actually leads to the positioning of Esther in the only place where she could save the people of God. The crass and abusive contest for the queen's title is utterly wicked to the core and the suffering of those subjected to it can't be minimized. And yet the painful rise of Esther to the throne of Persia meant salvation for the covenant people of God. ("Beauty and the Beast")

The king does not know she is a Jew, and the Jews do not know they will need her. God, however, knows all and always knows exactly what he is doing.

In Pondering Christ, See that Ahasuerus and Mordecai Cannot Compare

We could stop our discussion with Esther's being crowned, but it would be incomplete. Throughout our examination of the passage, I have tried to point us toward the Father and Son where applicable. Now I want to do so directly. When we consider Christ, we see that Ahasuerus and Mordecai cannot compare.

Ahasuerus Exercised Authority for His Own Gratification, but Jesus Does So for Our Good

Though in our text Ahasuerus offered tax relief and gave gifts, it was only after he had taken so many young virgins from their families. Repeatedly, Ahasuerus is seen to rule for his own good above all. Ahasuerus is not unlike many political leaders through the ages—dominated by selfishness instead of service.

My hope, however, is not in Congress's legislating for our good but in Christ living for it. As a matter of fact, "He was delivered up for our trespasses and raised for our justification" (Rom 4:25). We could examine many places in Scripture when considering Christ's leading for our good, but let me briefly mention two. In the first passage Jesus says,

> *A thief comes only to steal and kill and destroy. I have come so that*
> *they may have life and have it in abundance. I am the good shepherd.*
> *The good shepherd lays down his life for the sheep.* (John 10:10-11)

Selfish rulers think only of preserving their own lives, but Jesus presented his life as a substitute for ours. He placed our good above his own.

The second passage is in John as well. Consider these words Jesus prayed for you:

> *Father, I want those you have given me to be with me where I am, so*
> *that they will see my glory, which you have given me because you loved*
> *me before the world's foundation. . . . I made your name known . . . so*
> *that the love you have loved me with may be in them and I may be in*
> *them.* (John 17:24,26)

Jesus's desire is that we would be with him, that we would see his glory, that the Father's love would be in us, and that he himself would be in us. In his final night of prayer before the cross, Jesus prayed for us to experience the greatest blessings in the world. He would then go to the cross to secure them. Jesus does not have to use his authority for our good. We do not deserve it. But grace is never about merit.

Ahasuerus Sought a Beautiful and Pure Bride, but Jesus Made Us into One

The instructions in the king's decree were clear. There were three requirements for girls brought to the palace. Each one had to be beautiful, young, and a virgin. Their looks were to be appealing to all men, but they were to have known none of them.

The gospel, by contrast, is not a love story in which a good-looking and experienced groom meets and falls in love with a radiant and pure bride. The gospel is a love story in which a radiant and pure groom chooses to love and purify a wretched bride who has repeatedly given herself to the devouring love of the flesh, the world, and the devil. There is no beauty inherent in her, only sin and darkness. But as Duguid notes, "[Christ's] pain was the prerequisite for our beauty" (*Esther & Ruth*, 31). And the beauty treatments he puts us through are not just for his benefit but ours. Unlike Ahasuerus who took what was beautiful from others, Christ took us who were spiritually ugly and gave us his beauty. Ahasuerus sought a beautiful and pure bride, but Jesus made us into one.

Ahasuerus Left the Women He Used with Shame, but Jesus Has Taken Our Shame Away

This truth seems similar to the previous one, but here I am not addressing beauty but shame. Too often we are one-dimensional in our application of Christ's cross. We tend to think primarily of his paying the penalty for our sin. That truth certainly is important and necessary. But as sinners we also need peace and healing, which is why Isaiah says, "He was pierced because of our rebellion, crushed because of our iniquities; punishment for our peace was on him, and we are healed by his wounds" (Isa 53:5). Not only is our penalty cleared in Christ, but in him we are made whole and given peace.

Related to the context of Esther 2:1-18 is the issue of shame. I mentioned earlier the "walk of shame" some of the girls would have felt as they left Ahasuerus's chambers having had something taken away that they would never have given the king willingly. Perhaps they did not feel it immediately, but maybe shame came like a crushing blow on a girl's first night in the new harem with all of the other concubines.

Victims of sexual abuse are prone to feel shame. They feel dirty and used. This feeling comes not because of any sin they have committed personally but because they've been sinned against.

I know I have felt shame because of my own sin. I have known the good I ought to do but instead have often chosen and desired the wrong I should not. In the aftershocks of the sin that I have chosen once again failing to provide what was promised, I have felt not just guilt but shame. I have sensed the filth of my rebellion. Like Peter, I have often said to Jesus, "Go away from me, because I'm a sinful man, Lord" (Luke 5:8). Instead of running away from me, though, he runs to me.

Christ uses his Spirit and his Word to remind me that he not only provides atonement, cleansing, healing, and peace, but he also has taken my shame. Roland Muller contends,

> The overall message of the Bible is not just the story of God redeeming his people (a legal thought), but it is also the story of God raising mankind from a position of shame, to the ultimate position of joint-heir with Christ. (*Honor and Shame*, 57–58)

Muller goes on to say, "In the Gospels, Jesus continually turned to the lepers to heal them, demonstrating God's desire to reach out to those in a place of shame, and restore them" (ibid., 60).

After telling us to keep our eyes on Jesus, the author of Hebrews says, "For the joy that lay before him, he endured the cross, despising the shame, and sat down at the right hand of the throne of God" (Heb 12:2). Jesus, then, knows all about shame. On the cross Christ had not only my sin laid upon him but also my shame. The psalmist says, "My disgrace is before me all day long, and shame has covered my face" (Ps 44:15). But on the cross Jesus bore our disgrace so that one day our faces will not be covered with shame but captivated as we "see his face" (Rev 22:4). Our hope in Christ is not just wishful thinking. Our faith will not be in vain. For Paul says, "Everyone who believes on him will not be put to shame" (Rom 10:11). While Ahasuerus left the women he used with shame, Jesus has taken ours away forever!

Mordecai Could Only Check on Esther's Situation, but Jesus Can Change Ours

Though Mordecai's concern was not displayed in all the ways we may have hoped, his care for Esther was still evident. But as much as he loved Esther, Mordecai lacked the power to change her situation. He could not free her from the harem. He could not keep her from having to spend the night with Ahasuerus. There is no doubt he fully desired to help, but Mordecai lacked the ability to deliver Esther from her situation.

Jesus, however, can change ours. He has both the desire and the ability to accomplish all of his holy will. Jesus is not just full of hope for us but full of help. You can trust that "if the Son sets you free, you really will be free" (John 8:36). After calling the church at Ephesus to remember when they were "without hope and without God in the world," Paul gladly declares, "But now in Christ Jesus, you who were far away have been brought near by the blood of Christ" (Eph 2:12-13). Let us rejoice that Christ indeed can save his people, and at great cost to himself he has chosen to do so.

Reflect and Discuss

1. Why do we often go around difficult biblical texts instead of through them? What is the danger of doing so? What are some of the more difficult aspects of Esther 2?

2. Why is making a decision in anger or haste a bad idea? How can we minimize how often we do so?

3. How is remorse different from repentance? Why do we need more than just remorse?

4. Describe a time when you found yourself in a difficult situation or circumstance because of someone else's sin. How can we be faithful even in such difficult situations?

5. Describe a time when you believed the Lord disciplined you, but you also saw evidence of his sustaining you through it.

6. We do not know Esther's or Mordecai's motivations, but we do know that neither's resistance is recorded in chapter 2. Perhaps they were threatened with loss of life, and they chose to compromise with the world. Why do you and I tend to compromise for far less serious threats?

7. In what ways are you currently trying to hold on to your biblical convictions but feel tempted to compromise with the world? How can we faithfully navigate such tension?

8. Esther and Mordecai were imperfect and perhaps even disobedient, but the Lord still used them instead of discarding them. How do you feel about this? Is it any less true for us?

9. What is your response to the idea that Ahasuerus took the purity of women and left them with shame but that Jesus takes our shame and leaves us pure?

10. Ahasuerus sought a beautiful bride, but Jesus has made us into one. How should this fuel your worship and obedience?

Our God Reigns over Lots and Letters

ESTHER 2:19–3:15

Main Idea: In God's (sometimes perplexing) providence, our doing what is right may lead to our being in circumstances that feel wrong, but we can trust that God is working all things for our good and his glory.

I. **God Is Sovereign over Recognition and Rewards (2:19-23).**
   A. As we have opportunity, let us do good to all.
   B. Doing the right thing may come without immediate recognition or reward.
      1. Do not be surprised if the world does not thank you.
      2. Do not be discouraged.
II. **God Is Sovereign over Honor and Dishonor (3:1-6).**
   A. Like Haman, are we seeking our own honor?
   B. Like Mordecai, are we withholding honor where it is due?
III. **God Is Sovereign over Lots and Letters (3:7-15).**
   A. A date is set; a decree is sent; our Dad is sovereign (3:7-11).
   B. Celebrating God's deliverance and needing it again (3:12-14).
   C. No one will stop God from protecting and preserving his people (3:15).

Have you ever been punished for doing the right thing? Joseph was. Genesis 39 is a text I consider and share often. After being sold into slavery by his older jealous brothers (except Reuben, who was probably making a sandwich when the fateful event occurred), Joseph was purchased in Egypt by Potiphar, the captain of Pharaoh's guard. God blessed all of Joseph's work, and in time Potiphar placed Joseph in charge of everything he owned.

Not everyone has had to suffer in this way, but the author informs us that Joseph was "well-built and handsome" (Gen 39:6). As I noted earlier in this book, when physical features are included in a narrative, there is always a reason. At some point Potiphar's wife began to take notice of the successful slave and liked what she saw. Not hiding her intentions, she invited Joseph to be intimate with her.

What comes next in the text is one of my favorite responses in the Bible. Not only did Joseph refuse her, but he asked, "How could I do this immense evil, and how could I sin against God?" (Gen 39:9). I continue to pray that I will see sin in the same way Joseph did: as an immense evil done against God. After all, what we think determines what we do. Potiphar's wife, however, was not easily dismissed. Day after day she barraged Joseph with the same request, but he remained resilient in living according to his convictions and not her cravings.

One day, though, no one was in the house with them, and Potiphar's wife grabbed Joseph's garment and tried to entice him once more. Knowing that reason had no impact on her, Joseph opted for running, leaving his garment in her hand. (Oh, that we would all be those who run from sin rather than toward it!) Having been spurned, Potiphar's wife made up a lie that Joseph attempted to harm her sexually. And in his resulting anger, Potiphar had Joseph thrown into prison. Joseph was innocent, and his immediate reward was incarceration. After striving to be faithful to God and Potiphar, Joseph was punished instead of praised. But Joseph would also be preserved, and the Lord would bless him through all his years in prison. Potiphar would never thank Joseph for his faithfulness, but God had his own plans that would include a position of prominence allowing Joseph to help preserve God's people. In his interactions with Potiphar's wife, Joseph did what was right even though it was not immediately recognized or rewarded, and God was keeping the only record that matters.

Have you ever been confused when you have chosen obedience to the Lord, only to run into more trouble than triumph? Maybe you have asked, "God, I did what was right, so why are you going to let this bad thing happen to me?" Or maybe you are keeping a score or balance in your mind and say to him, "God, I did one good thing, and now you owe me something good as well." If we are keeping these kinds of tally sheets, then we are lousy scorekeepers. God owes us nothing but wrath. And if we were honest, we would admit that if God is basing his goodness to us on our goodness to him and others, then we definitely deserve no goodness. Yet so many of us are still holding on to (and marking) self-righteous scorecards. We do so because we are not resting in and going deeper into the gospel. We foolishly and frustratingly think we still need to earn God's affection or God's attention or at least God's good favor, and we refuse to believe that only Christ can and has accomplished it for us.

I am not sure if it is the seeming absence of praise or the presence of pain that is more surprising to some believers. Their shock is not that injustice exists in this fallen world but that they are recipients of it. For some reason they believe being a Christian means God is supposed to protect them from all pain and anxiety, especially when they have done the "right" thing.

As we turn to our study of Esther 2:19–3:15, Esther and Mordecai may have been a little confused themselves. Esther did not ask to be taken from Mordecai's home, she did not ask to be in a harem, and she did not ask to win a competition in which winning still felt in many ways like losing. But then, as if she hadn't experienced enough drama, she and Mordecai became aware of an assassination plot and shared it with the king.

The king's life was preserved, and the would-be assassins perished. Mordecai and Esther were not rewarded, but a record of the good deed was noted. Ironically, the way the king said thank you, initially, was to promote an Agagite who eventually would attempt to annihilate Mordecai and all the other Jews in the empire. Thus, though Esther and Mordecai delivered Ahasuerus from death, he practically delivered them over to death, even though he did so naively. Yep, at that moment God's providence was probably as clear to Esther and Mordecai as a windshield during lovebug season in Louisiana.

Importantly, the news of this death decree was sent out just as the Jewish people were beginning to celebrate Passover. You recall Passover, right? It's the remembrance celebration for when God delivered his people from the hands of their enemies, the Egyptians. So, on the day God's people were celebrating deliverance, they learned that their deaths had been decreed. If at this realization Esther was thinking, *God, I was trying to make lemonade out of lemons, but I am pretty sure the entire lemon tree just got dropped on us,* then few of us would blame her. In God's (sometimes perplexing) providence, our doing what is right may lead to our being in circumstances that feel wrong, but we can trust that God is working all things for our good and his glory.

God Is Sovereign over Recognition and Rewards
ESTHER 2:19-23

Do what is right, and trust that if no one recognizes you or rewards you, God is still keeping his record.

As We Have Opportunity, Let Us Do Good to All

The when of 2:19-23 is not as clear as the where and the what. After Esther was crowned queen, there was a second gathering of virgins. The author could possibly mean that the virgins who remained in the first harem were transferred to the concubines' quarters, which was overseen by Shaashgaz (2:14). The author could also mean that even after Esther was chosen, the king commissioned another gathering of women—not to give anyone a crown but to serve his cravings. Based on what we have observed of him, this possibility is not a stretch. Whatever the second gathering of women was about, we know it most likely occurred sometime between Esther's being crowned in Ahasuerus's seventh year of reign (2:16) and Haman's casting lots in the king's twelfth year (3:7). We also know that Esther's new position had not changed Mordecai's influence on her life.

Despite being crowned queen, Esther still concealed her ethnicity because of Mordecai's command. H. A. Ironside says,

> This, no doubt, would be considered good policy on
> Mordecai's part, and lovely obedience in Esther, but it was real
> unfaithfulness to God, often duplicated in our own times. . . .
> If they cover their nationality, and shame Him so that He hides
> His name too, He will make them nevertheless the instruments
> of His providence. (*Ezra, Nehemiah, and Esther,* 165–66)

A glimmer of that providence is seen in Mordecai's obtaining some critical information while going about his daily responsibilities at the King's Gate (2:19,21; 3:3). For reasons we are not told, two of the eunuchs who served at the entrance could conceal neither their anger toward nor their desire to assassinate Ahasuerus. Maybe they thought Mordecai would be sympathetic because they knew of his relationship with Esther, or maybe they just whispered so loudly that the dead could hear their plans. Either way, their secret was not safe with Mordecai.

Perhaps fearing that others in the king's court were corrupt, Mordecai passed along what he heard to Esther alone. Esther then made sure the king was made aware of the plot and of how she came to have knowledge of it. The king investigated the matter, found it to be true, and then had the two traitors either hanged from the gallows or, as some translations say, impaled on a stake. Esther and Mordecai were used to rescue the king, and all the details of their efforts were recorded in his book of chronicles. The only two Jews we know specifically in the story, then, helped save the life of a pagan, self-glorifying, woman-abusing king. If you were writing this story to win an Oscar for best picture in Jerusalem, you would be off to a rough start.

Why would Esther and Mordecai act for the king's good? I wonder if Mordecai considered not saying anything and just letting the plot unfold. Dietrich Bonhoeffer, after all, did not just know about a plan to assassinate Hitler but actively worked toward it (Eric Metaxas, *Bonhoeffer*, 380–93). Regarding both stories, some argue that by eliminating the one causing great harm thousands could be spared. Others contend, though, that we are not to kill, we are to love our neighbor as ourselves, and we are to "demonstrate the Lord's rule . . . through all meekness and patience in taking whatever suffering comes" (Piper, "Was Dietrich Bonhoeffer Wrong to Plot against Hitler's Life?"). Even though Piper expresses these hesitations, he is still slow to condemn Bonhoeffer. I know, though, that if I heard someone was thinking about killing the man who took my little girl in an ungodly manner, I would probably wrestle with the Holy Spirit's prompting to do what is right. Maybe Mordecai was afraid of what would happen to Esther in either an assassination attempt or a successful overthrow of the king. If they killed the king, what would they do to the queen? All this, of course, is speculation. The author does not tell us why Esther and Mordecai did what they did; he just tells us they saved the king.

While their reasons for doing good were not revealed, our call to it is. Paul exhorts the church at Galatia, "As we have opportunity, let us work for the good of all, especially for those who belong to the household of faith" (Gal 6:10). As we interact with our neighbors, coworkers, doctors, mechanics, plumbers, and whomever else the Lord brings into our paths, their good should be our goal. And as for those who do not work for our good? Well, I can remember reaching the end of a slide when I was in kindergarten and being met by another boy who was wearing cowboy boots and who kicked me in the shin. I remember crying and running to my aunt who was a teacher at the school and who just happened to be on duty for our recess. Thirty-seven years later I can remember all those details vividly, but I cannot recall in any form any desire in me to do that boy any good. As believers, however, we are called to forgive and work for the good of even those who wound us most. Paul tells the church at Rome to

> *bless those who persecute you; bless and do not curse. Rejoice with those who rejoice; weep with those who weep. Live in harmony with one*

another. Do not be proud; instead, associate with the humble. Do not
be wise in your own estimation. Do not repay anyone evil for evil. Give
careful thought to do what is honorable in everyone's eyes. If possible,
as far as it depends on you, live at peace with everyone. Friends, do
not avenge yourselves; instead, leave room for God's wrath, because it
is written, Vengeance belongs to me; I will repay, says the Lord. But

> *If your enemy is hungry, feed him.*
> *If he is thirsty, give him something to drink.*
> *For in so doing*
> *you will be heaping fiery coals on his head.* (Rom 12:14-20)

The gospel of Christ transforms the way we view and treat the
people who harm us most. The gospel demands that we not treat our
enemies as they deserve to be treated; rather, we treat our enemies as
Christ has treated us. What makes the gospel community special is not
just how we treat other believers but how we treat those who hate us
because of Christ. We are disciples of him who died for his enemies.
Maybe I should not marvel so much at Esther's and Mordecai's treatment of Ahasuerus and instead wonder why I am so often like the one
who asked Jesus, "And who is my neighbor?" (Luke 10:29). He was wondering whose good, in particular, he was obligated to pursue. We have
already been told whose good we should strive for: everyone's—even a
pagan king's.

Doing the Right Thing May Come without Immediate Recognition or Reward

During my senior year of college, I was up late one night, studying for
a test. I was stirred from my slumberish study by noises I heard outside
my apartment and a strange smell. I went to the back door and opened
it just in time to hear someone yell, "Fire!" Indeed, the apartment connected to mine was blazing. My first thought was that my roommate
was upstairs asleep. I ran back inside and up the stairwell to his room.
I turned on the light and began to yell for him to get up because there
was a fire. He, however, had the spiritual gift of sleeping deeply. I yelled
again to no avail and finally moved to his bed and shook him until he
woke up. The first thing he said was, "I smell smoke," to which I replied,
"You think?! GET UP!" We then did our best to gather what belongings
we could and get out. We later discovered that part of the ceiling in his
room collapsed right where he had been sleeping.

To this day my friend still refers to me as the guy who saved his life. I cannot recall anyone to whom he has introduced me in the years since who has not heard him tell about that night in some form. When someone saves your life, you tend to remember it and express your gratitude. Do you think Lazarus ever forgot walking out of his tomb or the one who called him out?

For Mordecai's and Esther's life-saving intervention, however, a simple notation was made. That was followed by no parade, no party, and no promotion. As a matter of fact, a key promotion actually went to someone other than the heroic Mordecai, but we will get there in a moment.

From birth we condition ourselves for instant gratification and reward. Watch a toddler who does something funny, gets everyone to laugh, and then repeats that action 700 times trying to elicit the same reaction. I continue to be amazed at how often my children want to be rewarded for taking care of basic hygiene like bathing and brushing their teeth. "Dad, I flossed my teeth; can I stay up late and watch a movie?" Or "Dad, I cleaned my room; can we go to Disney World?" But doing the right thing should never be about immediate reward or recognition. If we shift to that mind-set, in fact, then we may quickly move to doing what is right when it is inspected and not doing what is right just because it is expected.

As a believer who lives in a corrupt and fallen world, *do not be surprised if no one thanks you* for being a Christian. As a pastor, I constantly remind our faith family that not everyone will love them just because they love Jesus. Not everyone wants to hear about Jesus or follow him. That reality, however, does not mean we should stop trying to serve others for their good. We've got to be OK with people failing to express gratitude. And that is not always easy. I am sure Mordecai may have thought to himself once or twice, *Where was Haman when people were plotting to kill the king? I was the protector, but Haman was promoted.*

We can experience an internal struggle when we see others get positions or awards or opportunities we believe we deserved or earned. But if, like Mordecai, you find yourself having done the right thing but no one offered fanfare in response, *do not be discouraged.* God is keeping detailed records, and all will be made right. Jesus says in Revelation 22:12, "Look, I am coming soon, and my reward is with me to repay each person according to his work." God's timing is best, and he has purposes in our receiving from other people delayed or even no recognition at

all. Above all, we do not strive to do what is right toward others because
of their gratitude but because of his glory.

God Is Sovereign over Honor and Dishonor
ESTHER 3:1-6

Let us not seek our own honor or withhold it from others.

A nonbiblical proverb says, "No good deed goes unpunished." In
Mordecai's case what happens next could also be described as "kicking
a man when he is down" or "pouring salt in a wound" because of what
is said about the lineage of Haman. In the opening verses of chapter 3,
when we are expecting to read about Mordecai's reward and promotion, we are told an Agagite is elevated to being second-in-command of
the empire. For clarity, the author does not mean Haman is a graduate
of Texas A&M University! What the author could mean is that Haman
is a descendent of Agag, the king of the Amalekites whom Saul failed
to kill (1 Sam 15:8-9) but whom Samuel "hacked . . . to pieces before
the LORD at Gilgal" (1 Sam 15:33). Again, with this turn in the story, the
movie critics in Jerusalem would be throwing tomatoes at the screen
if the book of Esther were first presented as a film. Why? Because just
when it seemed that something might go well for one of God's people,
good gets shown to someone who just might be a descendant of an
enemy of God's people.

Was Haman indeed related to Agag? In 1 Chronicles 4:42-43 we are
told that five hundred descendants of Simeon combined with descendants of Ishi and "struck down the remnant of the Amalekites who
had escaped." With the death of Agag and this remnant, then, all the
Amalekites would have been gone prior to Esther's time frame. So did
the author of Esther not have knowledge of these events? If we consider
God's part in writing both 1 Chronicles and Esther, then we know lack
of knowledge is not a problem. Perhaps the author uses "Agagite" to say
that "Haman is an enemy of the Jews by birth, and the enmity between
Mordecai and Haman is tribal as well as personal" (Fox, *Character and
Ideology*, 42). Fox's proposal is one helpful way to understand what it
means to be an Agagite even if not by direct blood lineage.

Because of the one who was promoted, Mordecai had a problem.
Ahasuerus commanded all to honor Haman, but Mordecai refused to
bow to him. We are not told what fuels Mordecai's rebellion, but some
commentary writers speculate on the subject. Lewis Paton suggests

Mordecai was driven by arrogance and that his actions were "inexplicable" and "unreasonable" (*A Critical and Exegetical Commentary on the Book of Esther*, 197). Fox, however, contends Paton's portrayal "contradicts the book's image of Mordecai as wise, provident, unassuming, and never pursuing personal honor" (*Character and Ideology*, 43). Others suggest Mordecai refused to bow before Haman because God told his people, "Do not have other gods besides me" (Exod 20:3). Mordecai, however, was not being asked to worship Haman, nor Ahasuerus for that matter, but to honor him.

Whatever his reasons Mordecai refused to waver from his rebellion. On its own Mordecai's protest apparently escaped Haman's notice, which means his defiance was not loud or particularly obvious. But a couple of guys who were up to no good started making trouble in Mordecai's neighborhood. Some of the servants at the King's Gate noticed Mordecai's nonconformity and wanted to know his reason. Apparently, Mordecai was not seeking to start an empire-wide revolt because he did not try to recruit the servants to join him. Even after all their pestering, all the servants were able to ascertain was that Mordecai's being a Jew had something to do with his refusal to bow. The table of obtaining important information at the King's Gate and then passing it along to those in command was then turned on Mordecai.

When Haman found out Mordecai was disobeying the king's command and thereby "disrespecting" him, Haman was full of rage. He was certainly not full of reason, as his next steps revealed. Instead of going to Mordecai and trying to resolve the matter calmly, Haman decided his honor had been so impugned that only a total genocide of the Jewish people could satisfy the trespass. (Yeah, that sounds about right.) The two questions that keep coming into my mind when I read this scene are, "Racist much?" and "React much?" I can also hear the crowd's reaction to Zuckerman's famous pig, Wilbur, of "That's some pig" (E. B. White, *Charlotte's Web*, 210) being transferred to Haman as "That's some honor!" All that is missing is a spider spinning messages on her web in the corner of the King's Gate describing Haman's extraordinarily outsized sense of honor.

The details we really want are not supplied in the text. What was really driving Mordecai's rebellion? What caused him to reveal what he had made sure Esther so diligently concealed—their heritage and ethnicity? As much as we may want to know his specific reasons, we cannot say what they were with certainty. Let's commit right now that if we do something that threatens to get every other Christian in the world killed, we will be diligent to write down exactly what we did and why we did it!

Mordecai's passivity was a problem in 2:8, and his passion seems to at least contribute to the problem in 3:1-6. But God used both Mordecai's compliance and his complaint to put things in motion to ultimately accomplish God's plan. He used both Haman's desire to be honored and Mordecai's refusal to honor to advance his purposes. We should consider the actions of both men as we examine our lives.

Like Haman, Are We Seeking Our Own Honor?

Seeing Haman's reaction should cause us to consider how we react when people do not recognize the greatness we perceive in ourselves. To his dishonor, Haman overreacted horribly. But what do we do when people do not honor us as we feel we ought to be honored? Hopefully we do not choose the nuclear option of seeking not only to kill them but also all of those who share their ethnicity. Yet even though we may not desire to physically kill anyone, it could be that our anger burns within us like Haman's did, and we murder those who disrespect us with our thoughts. If that is the case, then we are thinking too highly of ourselves.

Here are some additional questions we should consider to aid us in determining whether we too are honor hounds like Haman: (1) Are we in any way guilty of seeking our honor over God's? (2) Are we seeking our honor to the detriment of those around us? (3) Are we more offended when our honor is impugned than when God's is? I pray we will never be like those who "loved human praise more than praise from God" (John 12:43).

But aren't there some situations in which we are supposed to be honored? For example, what if I am a parent of a teenager who seems to have never heard, "Honor your father and your mother so that you may have a long life in the land that the LORD your God is giving you" (Exod 20:12)? Don't I have a right to be angry over disrespect? Prime and Begg contend, "God's people have a unique capacity to sweeten or spoil our days, to thrill us or to cast us into the depths of depression" (*On Being a Pastor*, 281). Children are similar. When we actually deserve honor but are not receiving it, then demanding it will probably not increase any desire in the hearts of those who are withholding it. As both a parent and a pastor, I first ask myself on occasions in which I am disrespected, *Am I acting honorably? Am I setting an example for both my family and my faith family "in speech, in conduct, in love, in faith, and in purity"* (1 Tim 4:12)? If not, then I have no reason to expect honor.

But what do I do if I am not lording my authority over my children and I am striving to live honorably, but they still choose to disrespect me? I will leave the lengthy discussions of discipline and discipling to other helpful works on parenting and here just offer one thought from Paul Tripp:

> If rules and regulations had the power to change the heart
> and life of your child, rescuing your child from himself and
> giving him a heart of submission and faith, Jesus would have
> never needed to come. (*Parenting*, 49)

His point is that we cannot expect the law to do what only grace can accomplish. Ahasuerus made a command that all were to honor Haman (3:2). In Persia apparently honor had to be demanded (1:2). But that command was powerless in creating a desire in Mordecai to be conformed to it. In the same way, if your children are withholding honor from you as their parent, make sure your confidence is not in the law informing them but in God's grace transforming them. Keep praying, keep presenting the gospel in all its beauty and depth, and keep pointing them to the "presence and promises of God's grace" (ibid., 54). If all goes well, they will see the impact God's grace has in your life and will respond to it positively.

Like Mordecai, Are We Withholding Honor Where It Is Due?

When helping the church at Rome consider their responsibilities to political authorities, Paul wrote, "Pay your obligations to everyone: taxes to those you owe taxes, tolls to those you owe tolls, respect to those you owe respect, and honor to those you owe honor" (Rom 13:7). To whom, then, do we owe honor? As we just mentioned, children are to honor their parents. And as believers we are to "outdo one another in showing honor" (Rom 12:10) and to "hold people like [Epaphroditus] in honor, because he came close to death for the work of Christ" (Phil 2:29-30). The elders who work hard at preaching and teaching in your faith family are "worthy of double honor" (1 Tim 5:17).

If you are a pastor reading this book and the people God has entrusted to you have failed to follow 1 Timothy 5:17, then I am sorry, and I pray the Lord is showing himself strong regardless. You should also know that discussing financial matters with your leadership group/

elders/committee and seeking to provide for your family do not make you an unspiritual pastor.

Regarding the idea of showing honor to others, Peter provides two important passages. To husbands he says, "Live with your wives in an understanding way, as with a weaker partner, showing them honor as coheirs of the grace of life, so that your prayers will not be hindered" (1 Pet 3:7). Not acting in an honorable way toward our wives or not treating them as equal recipients of God's grace causes problems not just in our homes but in our relationship with God. As husbands our prayers can be hindered by acting dishonorably toward our spouses. Peter also says, "Honor everyone. Love the brothers and sisters. Fear God. Honor the emperor" (1 Pet 2:17). Considering this, I ask, Why, Peter? Why did you have to use honor and the two *e*'s of everyone and emperor? Oh, that's right! Because you were under the influence of the Holy Spirit.

Mordecai lived before 1 Peter 2:17 was written. In his defense God had not breathed it out yet. Regardless, honor was due to Ahasuerus (though he was not honorable), and he demanded it be given to Haman as well. I will not try to dive deeper into Mordecai's actions here, but I will ask us to assess our own. Are we withholding honor from anyone to whom it is due? If so, are we withholding it more out of convenience than conviction? Is it because we want to follow our preferences rather than the Lord's precepts? Mordecai's refusal to honor Haman would cause consequences for every Jew in the Persian Empire. The impact of our disobedience may not be as far-reaching as his, but it does not make our disobedience any less significant. Because God is sovereign over honor and dishonor, let us not seek our own honor or withhold it from those to whom it is due.

God Is Sovereign over Lots and Letters
ESTHER 3:7-15

Remember that no matter what his enemies plan, God will preserve his people.

A Date Is Set; a Decree Is Sent; Our Dad Is Sovereign (3:7-11)

When it comes to disciplining my children, there have been a few times when I ended up not doing what I said I was going to do. Sometimes I have relented because what I planned on doing was too drastic and my wife graciously helped me see that. In other instances, as time lengthened between what I declared and the moment of discipline, my desire to be as severe as I said dissipated. I take as much joy in having to discipline one of my children as I do in having to kill a snake that slithers into our yard (and I take absolutely no joy in that at all). In Haman's wrath, however, there was no evidence he thought his plan to kill all the Jews was too drastic. And if left unimpeded, his disciplinary measures spelled doom for God's people.

Phase one of Haman's plan was to set a date. Picking the right date for a party can be difficult enough when trying to align everyone's schedules and activities. But how does one pick a date for a genocide? Haman would rely on the *pur*, also known as a "lot." And in case you do not say the phrase *Pass the pur* when playing board games, let me explain: What they used to discern the date of death may have been similar to our contemporary dice (William W. Hallo, "The First Purim," 19–26). Through casting the lots, those gathered with Haman were able to determine that the twelfth month would be the most favorable day on which to slaughter the Jews. But we know something Haman and his cronies did not: "The lot is cast into the lap, but its every decision is from the LORD" (Prov 16:33). The date discerned by Haman, therefore, came not through the discretion of the gods but by the direction of God. A clear evidence of God's grace is that while Haman began scheming during the first month of the year, the massacre was scheduled for the twelfth month. As every child eager for presents knows, there is a loooooooooooong time between January and December.

Once the date was confirmed, Haman had to convince Ahasuerus to annihilate an entire ethnic group in his empire. One would hope this would be difficult if not impossible. But what should not have been a piece of cake *was* one. Haman simply gave the king a bogus scenario full of generalities. He was not interested in presenting truth, just in being manipulative, which is not dissimilar to the way we frame stories to make our way seem best. (We are never guilty of leaving out details that would be detrimental to whatever we are trying to make happen, are we?) He provided no specifics about the people he considered dangerous to the king's interests (except the lie that they were not keeping the king's laws), and the king asked for none. Never let facts get in the way of gossip or greed!

What Haman was specific about was the amount of silver he would place in the king's treasury if his plan was approved. This promise too was bogus. Gregory writes, "The bribe that Haman promises is something he will never be able to deliver, but the king apparently does not realize that" (*Inconspicuous Providence*, 63). Haman's bribe would have been between half and two-thirds of the empire's annual tax revenue, and unless Haman's uncle was Scrooge McDuck, he probably did not have access to such funds. The king, who apparently was the most easily influenced, powerful person in the history of the world, told Haman to do what he wanted and gave him his ring to validate the decrees that would be sent out. Based on what we know of Ahasuerus, his lack of regard for human life is saddening but not surprising. The king granted permission for possibly thousands of Jews to be slaughtered, regardless of gender or age, by their neighbors.

Lives were on the line, and Ahasuerus was complicit rather than confrontational. Apparently, investigation might have led the king to indigestion, so he was content making decisions without hearing what Paul Harvey called "the rest of the story." I pray you and I will never be so callous when eternal souls hang in the balance. Remember what the father in Proverbs 24 tells his son:

> *If you do nothing in a difficult time,*
> *your strength is limited.*
> *Rescue those being taken off to death,*
> *and save those stumbling toward slaughter.*
> *If you say, "But we didn't know about this,"*
> *won't he who weighs hearts consider it?*
> *Won't he who protects your life know?*
> *Won't he repay a person according to his work?* (Prov 24:10-12)

I tend to think about this text every year when churches are exhorted to consider the sanctity of life on a particular Sunday. No baby has ever driven himself or herself to an abortion clinic. No, every day in our world, babies are being taken off to death, and we are called to do something about it! When we stand before the Lord, we will not be able to pretend we did not know that something so horrific as abortion was happening every day in our country and around the globe.

It should jar us how easily a plan to eliminate an entire ethnicity of people was proposed and proclaimed. Lest we think this was just a problem for the ancients, remember the genocides in Darfur, Rwanda, Bosnia, Herzegovina, Cambodia, and Syria ("Modern Era Genocides"). And we dare not leave out the Holocaust! At the heart of each of these tragedies is one ethnic group seeking to exercise its self-perceived and self-proclaimed superiority over another. Satan is at work in all such instances, but in Haman's case there was probably a particularly hellish influence seeking to annihilate the line from which the Messiah would come.

May none of those we shepherd find the slightest bit of support for any action bent on destroying men, women, and children based on ethnicity. Whether abortion or genocide is up for discussion, each person is formed in God's image and therefore has value. Indeed, in Adam we are related to all other humans on our planet, but those of us in Christ are related more closely to a smaller group. In Adam and in Christ, our connectedness is determined by our natures. As believers, we should be pro-life in every way possible.

I do not believe those I shepherd will seek to eliminate an entire ethnicity. I am concerned, however, that some harbor thoughts of ethnic superiority in their hearts without even realizing it. In a recent sermon at Together for the Gospel, David Platt addressed the issue of racism with a particular focus on the relationships between white and African-American Christians. The merciless and slanderous reaction he received from critics on social media was overwhelming. But their tweets and posts do not make what he said any less true. As a means of working toward racial reconciliation, Platt offered these six applications: (1) Look at the reality of racism. (2) Live in true multiethnic community. (3) Listen to and learn from one another. (4) Love, and lay aside preferences for one another. (5) Leverage influence for justice in the present. (6) Long for the day when justice will be perfect ("Let Justice Roll Down like Waters: Racism and Our Need for Repentance"). For some in this world, life is cheap. But believers should know each person is created in God's image. Strive to help those you shepherd work for the good of all people. All lives should matter to us.

Celebrating God's Deliverance and Needing It Again (3:12-14)

The next phase of Haman's demonic plan was to draft one of the most heinous decrees in history. The decree was to be translated into every script and language used in the empire. Haman wanted those he was targeting to know there would be no place to hide in Ahasuerus's kingdom because even those living in its most remote areas would receive the decree. Wherever the Jews would go, all would know.

Having convinced the king, Haman no longer veils exactly what he wants done, to whom he wants it done, when he wants it done, who is to do it, or what they can gain by doing it. In the name of the king, Haman commands all people in the empire to completely anni- hilate every Jew regardless of gender or age. And after they kill the vic- tim, the murderers can then take the dolly right out of the little girl's hands, so to speak, working their way through her family's belongings. To guard against a lack of clarity, Haman uses the terms "destroy, kill, and annihilate" to convey how passionately he wants the job done. If this vindictiveness really just started with Mordecai's refusal to bow, I am not sure there has been a greater escalation of revenge known to man. Other than that it is a command from the king, no additional reasons are provided in the decree as to why everyone in the Persian Empire should turn on the Jews. Maybe they did not need any addi- tional motivation.

Of all we could consider about the edict, I want to focus on two aspects of timing. First, on the day the Jews would have been prepar- ing to celebrate God's deliverance, they found themselves in need of him once again. The edict was drafted on the thirteenth day of the first month, which would have been the day before Passover. Each year God's people remembered how he rescued their forefathers from the clutches of Pharaoh and then provided for them his law and land. Having to celebrate Passover outside the promised land was a good reminder to them of their disobedience and the Lord's discipline. Perhaps receiv- ing the edict on that particular day caused some to believe God had fully and finally abandoned his people and in eleven months they would meet their end. Certainly others would have been led to pray, "God, our death has been decreed and we are in need of you, our Deliverer, once again."

If you have not read ahead in Esther's story, I hate to spoil it for you, but God is going to deliver his people. We will leave those details for the discussions that are coming, but for now consider these two truths. (1) To do anything to the Jews, Haman did not need Ahasuerus's per- mission but God's, and he was not granting it. Duguid notes,

> The people were ultimately not [Ahasuerus's] to give into
> Haman's power. They were God's people, and He would not
> allow them to be destroyed at the whim of the empire. (*Esther
> and Ruth*, 41)

(2) Haman's promised silver bought a decree, but it could not buy the demise of God's people. Neither the silver given to Ahasuerus nor the silver coins given to Judas could thwart God's purposes. All the bribes

in the world will never be able to stop God from providing his Son with his bride, the church.

No One Will Stop God from Protecting and Preserving His People (3:15)

The second aspect of timing I want us to consider is the eleven months of waiting that God's people would experience from the time the decree went out until the date set for the purge. After the decree was placed in the mail, Haman and Ahasuerus sat down to drink together. While they were celebrating, the citadel was in confusion, the Jews were concerned, and God was still in control! What Haman and Ahasuerus and not even Esther and Mordecai knew yet was that the Jews could say, "The reports of our deaths have been greatly exaggerated."

That God's people didn't know how it would all turn out is what I want us to examine. It is one thing to hear the phrase *cancer free* after months (or years) of undergoing surgeries and treatments. But on the first day of diagnosis, even the most faithful believer may be tempted to be anxious and need to be reminded that we can cast our cares on God because God cares for us (1 Pet 5:7). In God's providence only he knows the full plan; we do not. Yes, we know how Revelation ends, and yes, we have his promises, but a lot of details for our specific lives remain mysterious. God's plan may involve our living, and it may involve our dying, but it will definitely involve our faith. The author of Hebrews reminds us that in God's providence some are spared and some suffer greatly, but in whatever circumstances we find ourselves, we are to remain faithful (Heb 11:32–12:3). So even though we do not know God's full plan or how our specific situations will turn out, we can trust God fully. Like Habakkuk, we must be able to say,

Though the fig tree does not bud
and there is no fruit on the vines,
though the olive crop fails
and the fields produce no food,
though the flocks disappear from the pen
and there are no herds in the stalls,
yet I will celebrate in the LORD;
I will rejoice in the God of my salvation!
The LORD my Lord is my strength;
he makes my feet like those of a deer
and enables me to walk on mountain heights! (Hab 3:17-19)

What can help us trust God even in our waiting? What can fuel our faithfulness? Considering his.

As a church staff we read through a chapter in Psalms to start our weekly meetings. In recent weeks we read Psalms 105 and 106, and in both the psalmist is recalling God's deliverance of his people. The psalmist reminds his readers that God "remembers his covenant forever" (105:8), "He sent Moses" (105:26), "he brought Israel out with silver and gold" (105:37), "He spread a cloud as covering" (105:39), "He opened a rock, and water gushed out" (105:41), "He brought his people out with rejoicing" (105:43), and "He saved them from the power of the adversary; he redeemed them from the power of the enemy" (106:10). Considering these works of God leads the psalmist to say, "Blessed be the LORD God of Israel, from everlasting to everlasting. Let all the people say, 'Amen!' Hallelujah!" (Ps 106:48). Even in our times of waiting, we can be empowered to trust the Lord not by considering our previous faithfulness but by recalling his. He is always working in our waiting even if it is not always evident. As Thomas Watson encourages, "God is to be trusted when his providences seem to run contrary to his promises" (*A Body of Divinity*, 112). And as is noted so clearly in Psalms 105 and 106 and eventually in Esther, no one will ever be able to stop God from protecting and preserving his people. We know no one will crush his church (Acts 12).

Conclusion

Make no mistake, in Esther 2:19–3:15 God's people found themselves in the same position we have always found ourselves in since the garden of Eden. A decree of death hangs over us from which we cannot deliver ourselves. Far worse than Mordecai's refusal to honor Haman is our refusal to honor the Lord. We have not desired to give him the glory and honor he is due but instead have chosen to live for our own glory. We thus stand in need of rescue from our rebellion. God alone can save his people, and he has chosen to do so at great cost. Though Haman used his money to purchase death, God uses Christ's death to purchase life. No greater price has been paid for liberation, and that price has been paid in full.

Reflect and Discuss

1. Why is doing what is right for people who have done us wrong so difficult? How can the gospel fuel our obedience here?

2. Why do we so easily seek earthly rewards and forget about kingdom rewards? How can we give more consideration to the eternal rather than the temporal?

3. Why do you think we're surprised when, after walking in obedience, we seem to be rewarded with struggle?

4. In what ways do we treat God as if he owes us? How can the gospel free us from thinking we are owed something after doing what we should be doing all along?

5. How can we minimize our personal desires to be honored and maximize our interest in God's honor?

6. How can we demonstrate compassion even to those who conspire against us?

7. How can recalling God's faithfulness in the past fuel our trust and faithfulness in the present?

8. In what practical ways can we join Paul in saying, "My eager expectation and hope is that I will not be ashamed about anything, but that now as always, with all courage, Christ will be highly honored in my body, whether by life or by death" (Phil 1:20)?

9. The Jews would have certainly been tempted to be fearful and anxious because of the decree. What, if anything, are we as Christians currently fearful or anxious about? How can we cast our cares on him?

10. In what ways are you demonstrating that you are pro-life?

Rejecting Passivity and Risking Perishing

ESTHER 4

Main Idea: As God entrusts us with positions of opportunity and empowers us for obedience, may the stewardship of faith lead to our participation in his plan and away from the selfishness of passivity.

I. Mordecai's Reaction (4:1-8)
II. Mordecai's Request (4:9-11)
III. Mordecai's Realization and Reminder (4:12-14)
    A. Mordecai's exhortation
    B. Mordecai's expectation
    C. Mordecai's evaluation
IV. Esther's and Mordecai's Resolve (4:15-17)
V. Christ's Role

When God rewards his people in heaven for faithful service, some of us will miss out on rewards because we were fearful rather than faithful. Will someone else be rewarded because they participated in God's plan where perhaps you were passive? Understand that our fearfulness, passivity, and selfishness will not thwart God's ultimate plans, but they will diminish our eternal rewards. And if you say we should not obey just for the rewards, I would heartily agree with you because I hope the gospel is fueling our obedience above all. But in his preaching Jesus himself kept pointing to eternal treasure and rewards because he knew we are far too occupied with perishing trinkets and trash. So think about it: When God rewards us in heaven for faithful service, will you miss out on rewards because you were fearful rather than faithful? How can we be moved to serve boldly and faithfully?

On a Tuesday evening in 1925, Gladys Aylward had her soul stirred for the sake of missions by a young man she heard preach in England (Carol Purves, *Chinese Whispers*, 8–9). She became burdened for China and knew "somebody" needed to go there and declare the gospel of Christ. Gladys decided to contact every important person she knew and ask them to consider going to China on mission. Purves writes, "She approached doctors, clergymen, bank managers, and solicitors. She wrote to the wealthy and influential people who she knew slightly or whom she had met in the course of her work" (ibid., 12). When they turned her down, Gladys next approached her brother Laurence. He was not particularly burdened to see the lost come to Christ, but God would use him in Gladys's life. Laurence said to her, "If you're so keen why don't you go yourself?" (ibid.).

After trying to convince every man she knew of the great need for missionaries in China but seeing none of them respond to the call, Gladys finally realized the "somebody" God wanted to use was her. She prayed, "O God, here is my Bible, here is my money, here am I. Please use us, God, please use us" (ibid., 15). After that, she made two resolutions. Her first resolution was that "never again would she ask someone else to do a job God was asking her to do. Secondly, if God would show her the way, she would go to China even if it meant being unsponsored" (ibid., 16). Gladys kept both resolutions, and God used her in amazing ways for the advancement of the gospel. If you have not read her full story, please do so. In order not to reduce Christianity to what is safe, easy, and comfortable for me, I constantly consider the cross and read biographies of missionaries.

One last thought on Gladys: She once shared that she had prayed for God to send a husband to join her on mission to China. However, none appeared. She believed God called a man not just to marriage but to mission, and he never chose to obey.

When considering Esther 2:19–3:15, I referenced Proverbs 24:10-12, in which a father tells his son that if he sees people being carried away to death or others stumbling toward it themselves, then the son should not look around and hope somebody else does something but should intervene. Too often we find ourselves in situations in which everybody knows that somebody needs to do something about an issue, but nobody does. I, in fact, have had multiple moments in my life where I felt "somebody" should do something but then failed to act on what I could do. There is one moment that always stands out in my mind.

I had been teaching in Uganda but made a trip with a friend to Rwanda. He was there on behalf of an organization that was seeking to minister to some of the widows of the genocide who made handicrafts to try to provide for their families. A local church was trying to support these women by helping them develop skills, organize their efforts, and promote their products.

On our first night in Rwanda, we attended a service at the church I just mentioned. Their pastor was not in town, but he had a guest pastor from the Congo preaching in his stead. The guest was speaking in one language; someone on the stage was interpreting what he was preaching to those in the congregation; and the church provided someone to sit next to me to interpret it in English.

As the "preacher" was sharing, I began to get nauseated. Not because of the travel but because of his teaching. He started telling the congregation that if they wanted their enemies dead, then they just needed to pray for that. If the congregation wanted their enemies to have a disease, then they just had to ask God to move in that way. Providentially I had preached on Matthew 5:43-48 the Sunday before I left the United States. I knew that what he was saying was not just wrong but demonic. People in the crowd, however, began to run up to the stage and throw money onto it as a sign of their approval and appreciation for his teaching.

I knew "somebody" needed to stand up and say something. I looked around to see if anybody would. But everywhere I looked, I saw affirmation rather than anxiety. I then began to rationalize my delaying by saying that I was only in Rwanda to support my friend, and I did not want to mess up the ministry he was working toward. And I regret to inform you that I did nothing. By the time we left the building, I had a migraine because I was sick from his "sermon" and sick at myself for shrinking back in fear.

I confessed my disobedience to the Lord and asked his forgiveness. I resolved should I ever find myself in a similar situation in which I know "somebody" needs to do something and believe God is calling me to be that "somebody," I will trust his empowerment and intervene however he is directing me.

In Esther 4:1-17 Mordecai will challenge Esther to be the "somebody" to help meet the needs of her people, the Jews. By chapter 4, he is starting to see that her position as queen has perhaps been God's providential plan all along. If she rejects his request, her passivity will not mean the destruction of all her people; it will mean her own, and God will find another means of delivering them.

Before we dive into the text, let me ask another initial question: Is there something you are hoping "somebody" will do in your faith family or in your city? With regard to your church or town, do you ever think to yourself, *Somebody ought to . . .* , or *I wish somebody would . . .* ? Maybe you should step up.

As God entrusts us with positions of opportunity and empowers us for obedience, may the stewardship of faith lead to our participation in his plan and away from the selfishness of passivity. Maybe the Lord is saying to you, "I have put you in this position; now, be faithful with what I have entrusted to you." If so, I hope stewardship outranks selfishness in your list of concerns. God would preserve his people through Esther's and Mordecai's obedience.

Our obedience is God's ordinary means for accomplishing his extraordinary plans. I need to be clear, though. The message of Esther 4:1-17 is not "Be a hero like Esther." Nor is the message "Do not be a problem causer like Mordecai, but be a problem solver like Esther." Instead, the message is that God is choosing to save his people through the ordinary means of two Jews who transition from compromise and concealment to conviction. Jobes challenges us:

> Perhaps, like Esther, you have been brought to this moment in your life by circumstances over which you had no control, combined with flawed decisions you made along the way. Perhaps instead of living for God, you have so concealed your Christian faith that no one would even identify you as a Christian. Then suddenly you find yourself facing calamity. . . . Regardless of the straits you find yourself in, turn to the Lord your God. His purposes are greater than yours. (*Esther*, 142)

Mordecai's Reaction
ESTHER 4:1-8

In times of crisis, let us be more concerned with confessing our fear and feelings than with concealing our faith.

When I was in my early teens, there was a television character on a certain sitcom who, every time he made a mess, would ask, "Did I do that?" And the answer every time was clearly, "Yes! You did that!" Mordecai finds out about Haman's plan and knows his defiance ushered in consequences for so many more than just himself. A phrase I repeatedly emphasize to the faith family I shepherd is this: "My sin but our consequences." The point is that our sin never just affects us as individuals; there tend to be consequences for our families and faith families. Breneman contends, though,

> There is no indication that Mordecai was sorry for his actions
> in refusing to bow down to Haman. This would support the
> idea that his action was based on religious convictions. Rather,
> he grieved over the signed fate that his people would perish.
> (*Ezra, Nehemiah, and Esther,* 334)

In his reaction to the edict, Mordecai chose certain actions while avoiding others. Though the letter was in the king's name and signed with his ring, Mordecai did not attempt to seek an audience with the ruler himself. Serving at the King's Gate meant that Mordecai was a public official, but probably not one with a lot of royal privileges. And as Esther will note, anyone who approached Ahasuerus uninvited risked death (4:11). Another thing Mordecai avoided was trying to make things right with Haman. Even after the edict Mordecai still refused to honor him (5:9). Apparently, in Mordecai's mind, apologizing to Haman was not an option.

When we are wrong (and the author never tells us that Mordecai was), I hope we will be quick to seek reconciliation with any we have wounded. And when we are wronged, I also hope we will be quick to seek reconciliation. One of the clearest ways we image God is by initiating reconciliation and offering forgiveness to those who have sinned against us.

So, what did Mordecai do? He responded as God's people had in previous generations: he put on sackcloth, which was used to express grief, guilt, deep distress, or despair. This public lament over the edict at the entrance of the King's Gate suggests he was no longer worried about concealing anything. And as Breneman suggests, "One should not hide one's concern in crisis situations" (*Ezra, Nehemiah, and Esther,* 333). Considering the death decree that had been issued, Mordecai did not have time for religious pretense. He was genuinely moved with grief and expressed it in the clearest way he knew.

In our Western, individualized world we often have little grasp on how both our obedience and disobedience will impact others. We tend to think only of I, me, my and not about we, us, and our. Like Mordecai, we may make bigger messes than we intended, and we cannot fix them on our own. Remember: "My sin but our consequences." And know that its sister principle is also true: "My obedience but our blessings."

Blessings seemed in short supply for God's people living under Ahasuerus's reign. Mordecai's reaction was multiplied many times over by all the Jews in each province. They too donned sackcloth and ashes and expressed laments. We are not told about their specific expressions or cries, but Lamentations 3:40-66 offers a possible example. Because of space considerations, I will not include that passage here, but I hope you will take time to turn to and read it now. I also hope, at some point, you will consider shepherding your people through the book of Lamentations. As Kaiser notes,

> God has placed personal and national laments in Scripture, it would appear, as a corrective against euphoric, celebratory notions of faith, which romantically portray life as consisting only of sweetness and light. . . . God has given us in the laments of Scripture a solace where the full spectrum of our earthly journey can be represented. (*Preaching and Teaching from the Old Testament*, Part 2, Section 8, CBD Reader Edition)

Through Lamentations we are encouraged to deal with suffering by directing our despair not away from God but toward him.

When Esther heard about the scene Mordecai was making near the King's Gate, she expressed her concern by sending clothes for him to put on. In our concern, however, let us not try to cover grief without first determining the cause of it. Esther was trying to provide answers when she needed to be asking questions, which she eventually did. Esther apparently had no knowledge of the edict, so Mordecai sent her a copy and a command of his own. Through her servants he told her not to worry about clothing or consoling him but to focus on communicating with the king. (If only God had known this was coming, then maybe he could have had someone in place to help . . . oh wait!)

While Esther and Mordecai may have been surprised and worried about Ahasuerus's and Haman's edict, God was not. God never paces in heaven, hoping things work out. Like all things the edict was foreknown by the Lord, and in his foreknowledge he had made provision. The events in Persia, after all, were not his first rodeo. Remember when God told Abraham what would happen to his descendants even before Abraham had a child (Gen 15)? Or remember when God used massive events in Joseph's life to get him to be second-in-command of Egypt so that Joseph's father Jacob and Joseph's eleven brothers would have provision during a famine? Remember when God said, "I declare the end from the beginning, and from long ago what is not yet done, saying: my plan will take place, and I will do all my will" (Isa 46:10), so we would have no doubt of his awesomeness and control? Yeah, if only God had known that Haman would try to wipe out all of his people.

The human heroes of this story could not yet see that God already had a plan of salvation in place for them. Nevertheless, even here in chapter 4, Esther and Mordecai were starting to understand providence a little more clearly. It may have initially felt like the situation of the blind one Jesus was healing who saw people who looked like trees walking (Mark 8:24). But as sure as he saw clearly before the Son of God was done with him, they too would eventually gain clarity.

Before moving on to the rest of our discussion, I want us to consider two questions. First, how do we react when we get bad news? Do we panic, or do we pray? In Acts 12 the church learned that James had been executed and that Peter was in prison, but Luke says, "The church was praying fervently" for Peter (Acts 12:5). I love that though they were grieved because of James's death, they were not dissuaded from interceding for Peter. I also love that the reason they are praying in Acts 12 is because they had devoted themselves to it in Acts 2. Prayer, then, was not just about crisis but commitment. Neither Mordecai's nor the Jews' reactions were wrong. When they learned of doom, they did what they had been discipled to do in hopes the Deliverer would hear and help.

Second, why does it often take God's using drastic matters to get us to the point of repentance, remorse, dependence, or even wanting to communicate with him? Receiving an empire-wide decree giving those who live in our village permission to slaughter each member of my family would certainly get my attention. The Lord, I think, would not have to use "drastic" means if we were committed to "daily" means. The greatest gift of the gospel is that God gives us himself. He reconciles us for the purpose of relationship. Losing sight of this great grace is always to our detriment.

Mordecai's Request
ESTHER 4:9-11

Like Mordecai we should encourage others to leverage their positions of influence for the sake of the kingdom.

Mordecai wanted Esther to intercede on behalf of all the Jews. The time for secrets was over. Through Hathach, Mordecai encouraged Esther to leverage her influence with Ahasuerus. Passivity was not an option. Esther, however, wavered at her cousin's prompting, and you can hear "Houston, we have a problem" in her response. In case Mordecai

had completely lost his mind, she educated him on basic royal protocol that everyone in the empire apparently knew. Even though she was
the queen, her access to the king was restricted. The penalty for breaking protocol was death. She then revealed that it had been a month
since she was last summoned before Ahasuerus, which in any other circumstance would probably have been a blessing. Esther's people were
in trouble, but instead of immediately jumping at the chance to help
them, she hesitated. Her first thought was not their deaths but her own.
She was not certain she wanted to take such a risk.

I would be the last to throw a stone at Esther. After all, like her,
you and I may be hesitant to seize opportunities the Lord entrusts to
us for his sake. You may even be deliberating right now about a specific situation in your life. But why was Esther hesitant? It could be that
she thought she could ignore the announcement and remain safe in
the citadel. Maybe she thought it was not her problem. That possibility
brings to mind a member of the church I pastored in Baton Rouge, who
shared with me once that her eighty-year-old father had taken a thirty-
year mortgage out on a mobile home. When she asked him about the
possibility of his dying and leaving that financial responsibility unmet,
he responded, "Not my problem!"

Esther was obviously concerned the king would not grant her permission to be in his presence. After all, Vashti had refused to go before
the king when summoned, and everyone knew how that turned out.
Suddenly asked to approach the king unsummoned, Esther knew there
was no room for playfulness in the protocol. Entering the throne room
and asking, "Ahasuerus, did you call me, Sweetie?" would bring a swift
response: "No. Kill her."

What is encouraging to many is that her obedience was not immediate and courageous. Like us, Esther may have had a "natural proneness
for seeing the difficulties rather than anticipating what God could, and
would, do" (Prime, *Unspoken Lessons*, 76). My wife always says that if I
were not in ministry I would be in insurance because I can assess all the
ways something can go wrong in about five seconds.

Perhaps since Esther had not been in the king's presence for thirty
days, she reasoned that she was not the right mediator. Maybe you
have been there before too. Maybe you are there now and are listing
all the reasons that you are not the right person for whatever opportunity God seems to be granting. We tend to set our gaze on our defi-
ciencies or disqualifications rather than the Lord's sufficient grace and

empowerment. Know that if you are delaying obedience out of fear, that is actually disobedience.

Mordecai's Realization and Reminder
ESTHER 4:12-14

Like Esther we often need others in our lives to encourage our obedience and faithful stewardship of what God entrusts to us.

Mordecai's Exhortation

When Mordecai was informed of Esther's deliberations, he told Hathach to make sure she understood she would not escape the edict. Even in the palace, there would be no exemptions. Mordecai was certain God's people would be preserved; but if Esther faltered, she and her lineage would perish. In assessing Mordecai's boldness, Prime contends,

> We sometimes need to be extremely forthright in exhorting
> one another to do the right thing, just as Mordecai did with
> Esther. Our best friends are those who love us enough to be
> genuinely honest with us. . . . When relationships are good,
> reprimands can be given, even welcomed, and accepted in the
> spirit in which they are given. (*Unspoken Lessons*, 79)

Let's consider Prime's statement for a moment in light of our lives. Within your family and faith family, are there good relationships, are reproofs voiced in appropriate and loving ways, and are reprimands welcomed? The author of Proverbs tells us, "The wounds of a friend are trustworthy" (Prov 27:6).

One of the most transparent examples I have ever read of one Christian brother exhorting another to do the right thing and finding that exhortation received is in a blog post by Garrett Kell. In the piece Kell admits he was at one time a pastor enslaved to the sin of pornography. In preparing to launch a new church plant with one of his friends, Kell decided to reveal his sin and lengthy struggle through a letter to his planting partner. Kell records what happened next:

> That trip to Jersey began an intervention that I believe saved
> my soul, my marriage, and my ministry. Carrie and I met
> Reid at a coffee shop and through tears he said, "I love you,
> brother, but after reading your letter, I don't feel like we can
> move forward as partners. And to be honest, I don't think you

should be a pastor right now." No one had ever gotten in my face like that—or at least I had never listened. Most people were willing to overlook my struggles because of my perceived giftedness or personality. But Reid didn't care about any of that. He loved God, and he loved me. ("I Was a Pastor Hooked on Porn")

To remain silent when those we care for are chained to sin is never loving. Kell would return home, confess his sin to the elders of his church, and then confess to the entire congregation, even repeating it for those who were not in attendance.

Kell did not run from his church, and they did not run him off. He notes that almost a year later, "many [members] began confessing their own hidden sins. Self-righteousness was expelled, and supernatural healing came for me and for the church family that remained" (ibid.). At the end of his blog post, Kell exhorts his readers,

You need someone in your life who knows you—who *really* knows you. Not who generally understands how you struggle, but who has a pulse on the state of your affections and sin struggles today. We all need someone along with whom we're constantly confessing and repenting and trusting in Jesus. (Ibid.; emphasis in original)

In his grace God used the exhortation from a loving friend to move Kell not to do what was easy but to do what was holy and right. Esther had a similar relationship with Mordecai. You and I need that as well. Who needs your encouragement to obey the Lord, and who is encouraging you? I hope you are modeling how to give and to receive loving reproofs.

Mordecai's Expectation

After hurricane Katrina, I had the opportunity to serve at a staging area at the New Orleans airport, helping families transition from rescue helicopters to inside the terminals. According to some of the evacuees' stories, not all of them had been convinced help was going to arrive on time; for some caught in the floods, it did not. My wife and I asked one of the evacuees, who was seven months pregnant and had a two-year-old son, to stay with us until we could reconnect her with her family. She told us they had to cut their way through their roof to escape the rising waters. When she and her son were rescued, they left her daughter and mother standing on the roof. Though the pilots promised to return immediately to her roof, help had to be found elsewhere.

Regardless of Esther's actions, Mordecai was certain God's people would be preserved. If she faltered, it would be to her detriment, but the Jews would be delivered. From where and from whom would other help arise? Bush contends,

> Given the facts of the story that the narrator has emphasized, such as the character of the king, the power of Haman's position, the diabolical nature of his edict, and the irrevocability of Persian law, a plausible source for another human agency that could deliver the Jews is hard to imagine. (*Ruth/Esther*, 396)

Bush also rejects notions of "Jewish officials, a Jewish armed revolt, or the goodwill of the inhabitants of the empire" because they were "lamentably implausible" (ibid.).

So, does Mordecai mean "God" when he says the Jews will receive help from "another place" (4:14)? For those who believe Mordecai's confidence is related to his conviction of divine providence, Bush contends, "There is simply nothing in the story even suggesting that the narrator characterizes Mordecai as a man of such firm faith and piety" (ibid.). While I agree with Bush that up to this point in the story there is little evidence to support a claim that Mordecai possesses unwavering faith, I do believe the author of Esther will provide glimmers of that hope in the passages to come and even in the final question of 4:14. Once again, though, we find ourselves wishing for specificity and clarity where none is provided. What is clear is that even if Esther does nothing, something will ultimately be done for the good of God's people.

Either way, Esther herself is facing loss. In one scenario she risks losing her life. In another scenario she risks losing the blessings that come from doing the good she ought to do. I am always grieved when the Lord has to work around me instead of through me. Mordecai did not want this to be the case for Esther.

Mordecai's Evaluation

One of the most remembered and recognized phrases in the entire book of Esther is found at the end of verse 14. After evaluating the Jews' problem and Esther's placement, the lights of providence are possibly just beginning to gleam for Mordecai as he asserts that perhaps Esther's being taken and then her becoming queen are not a random tragedy after all. Maybe the reason she has such a position is for a higher purpose. These musings reveal what we noted earlier in this book: Esther and Mordecai were not part of a well-organized coup to take power and remove Ahasuerus. No, in Mordecai's ponderings of Esther's position, there is much more the sound of Gomer Pyle's "Gawl-lee" than of Sherlock Holmes's snarky "Elementary, my dear Watson!" Mordecai may not have fully reached the answer of "4," but he is at least beginning to frame the equation of "2 + 2" with this statement.

Mordecai's point is clear enough. Obtaining a royal position is a matter requiring stewardship. Esther was entrusted with an opportunity and the responsibilities that came along with it.

Prime asserts, "We should all be asking, 'What work has God especially for me to do because he has allowed me to be alive at this particular time?'" (*Unspoken Lessons*, 81). The Lord determines both when and where we live. As Paul says of God, "From one man he has made every nationality to live over the whole earth and has determined their appointed times and the boundaries of where they live" (Acts 17:26). There is not another time period in which you should have lived. The places where we are, the positions we hold, and the people by whom we are surrounded have been entrusted to us for the purpose of gospel advancement. God is no less intentional with our lives than he was with Esther's and Mordecai's. And just in case you need to be reminded, this "time" is our only time to make disciples, and the time decreases each day. May our lives be gripped with gospel urgency.

Esther's and Mordecai's Resolve
ESTHER 4:15-17

Like Mordecai and Esther, let us seek God's power through prayer so that we will be resolved and faithful rather than resistant and fearful.

Where there initially had been reluctance, now in Esther there is resolve. The one who was given a command (4:8) would end up giving one of her own (4:16-17).

Several years ago I led a large group of teenagers on a mission trip to Germany. One of the requests of the missionaries with whom we were partnering was that our group spend time prayer walking through universities, apartment complexes, and city blocks. The students (and regrettably some of the other adults) were not really excited about this.

In various forms they kept saying, "We came all this way to do something. We did not make the trip just to pray." To their complaints, the missionary responded, "Prayer *is* doing something. No one else comes and prays in these places, and before we do anything else, we need to pray." Pausing for prayer is not the same as pausing obedience for procrastination or passivity. As a matter of fact, prayer is never a bad first step.

But the text does not say anything about prayer. Frustrating, isn't it? If there was ever a good place in Esther (and indeed we have seen several possibilities already) to make a few extra swipes with the pen to specifically tie actions with reliance on God, then this would be a great candidate. The author, however, refrained from doing so. Nevertheless, Prime contends that Esther's statement "tells us what she did not trust in: she did not place her confidence in her own beauty, position, or eloquence. The mentioning of fasting indicates where Esther placed her trust" (*Unspoken Lessons*, 82). We would affirm that fasting reflects dependence on God. But could not her fasting have been an attempt to earn favor through asceticism? Sure, but from whom or what would she be earning that favor? Certainly not Ahasuerus, since he liked his women to have their cosmetics and food! In connecting prayer and fasting, Prime says,

> Prayer is the principal purpose of fasting, in that fasting
> concentrates the mind and helps to detach it from current
> preoccupations. Fasting, therefore, is a way of abstaining
> from what may interfere with prayer. It is an expression of
> earnestness, and recognition of the seriousness of a situation,
> expressing either sorrow or repentance. (Ibid., 83)

Prime believes Esther, Mordecai, and all the Jews they could gather in Susa prayed along with their fasts, and I do as well.

When is the last time you fasted and prayed because you were seeking the Lord's direction? When I was trying to discern whether I should pursue marriage with Tara, I fasted four days and prayed through Proverbs 3:5-6, taking one phrase per day as a focus for my prayers. David Mathis says, "Fasting has fallen on hard times—at least, it seems, among our overstuffed bellies in the American church." He then admits, "I speak as one of the well-fed" (*Habits of Grace*, 117). Nevertheless, he contends that how we view fasting is important:

> If we are awakened to see fasting for the joy it can bring, as
> a means of God's grace to strengthen and sharpen godward

affections, then we might find ourselves holding a powerful new tool for enriching our enjoyment of Jesus. (Ibid.)

In his book *Spiritual Disciplines for the Christian Life,* Don Whitney says many purposes for fasting can be found in Scripture. One of the purposes he lists is to strengthen prayer. He notes that Nehemiah (Neh 1:4), Daniel (Dan 9:3), Joel (Joel 2:12), and the church at Antioch (Acts 13:3) all fasted and prayed. He does offer two important cautions. First, he says,

> The Bible does not teach that fasting is a kind of spiritual hunger strike that compels God to do our bidding. If we ask for something outside of God's will, fasting does not cause him to reconsider. Fasting does not change God's hearing so much as it changes our praying. (*Spiritual Disciplines,* 166)

Whitney's second caution is that

> we cannot use fasting as a way to impress God and earn His acceptance. We are made acceptable to God through the work of Christ Jesus, not our work. Fasting has no eternal benefit for us until we have come to God through repentance and faith. (Ibid., 165)

The fasting in this chapter of Esther certainly is a stark contrast to all of the feasts that are recorded. I hope fasting, however, is not unfamiliar to you but is a discipline you use often as you continue to grow in and pursue Christ. I have always appreciated the idea that

> the root of Christian fasting is the hunger of homesickness for God, [which means] we will do anything and go without anything if, by any means, we might protect ourselves from the deadening effects of innocent delights and preserve the sweet longings of our homesickness for God. (Piper, *A Hunger for God,* 15)

Like Esther we should fast to express that our confidence and trust are not in ourselves but in God. Sure, the possibility exists that Esther and the others only fasted and did not pray. But I would say what is possible in this case is not probable. In fasting we are able to say to God, "We hunger for you more than anything else. We can do without some things but not without you. As I fast, I express to you that I do not live by bread alone but desire to live on your words. And I need you to show me in your Word the way you would have me go."

Through Mordecai's exhortation, expectation, and evaluation, we have seen Esther shift away from self-preservation to be willing to sacrifice her life if necessary. With each opportunity the Lord gives us, our responsibility is obedience, not results. Neither Esther nor Mordecai knew how things would turn out. They both knew that Esther should intercede for her people and that it could cost her life. Abraham did not know how things would turn out with Isaac; he just knew what God was asking him to do (Gen 22). Paul did not know how everything would turn out; he just knew he was being compelled to go to Jerusalem (Acts 20:22-23). What is needed is not our full knowledge but our faithful obedience.

Christ's Role

Since Christ is our great high priest, let us draw near to God in full confidence.

If left to our own resources with regard to holiness, we, like Mordecai, should don garments of mourning and never take them off. But as Isaiah says,

> *I rejoice greatly in the* LORD*, I exult in my God; for he has clothed me with the garments of salvation and wrapped me in a robe of righteousness, as a groom wears a turban and as a bride adorns herself with her jewels.* (Isa 61:10)

Esther tried to cover Mordecai, but God has succeeded in clothing us. He was able to do this by making "the one who did not know sin to be sin for us, so that in him we might become the righteousness of God" (2 Cor 5:21).

That same one is the "one mediator between God and humanity, the man Christ Jesus" (1 Tim 2:5). Esther interceded on behalf of her people, but there is no greater mediator than Jesus, our great high priest (Heb 7:22-28). Becoming our mediator did not merely require the possibility of his death but the certainty of it. Keller notes, "Esther saved her people in two ways: identification and mediation. Does that remind you of anyone? Jesus didn't say 'If I perish, I perish,' He said, 'When I perish'" ("If I Perish, I Perish").

Other than in Christ, there is nowhere we can hide from God's wrath. Esther would not be safe in the citadel, and we are never safe in our sin. Christ is our only refuge. Once we are in Christ, we can draw near to God in full confidence that he welcomes us and desires our presence (Heb 10:19-22). Let us then never neglect an opportunity to draw near, for in his presence is "abundant joy" and at his right hand "are eternal pleasures" (Ps 16:11).

Conclusion

There has only been one perfect person God used in accomplishing his purposes. For the rest of his agenda, God uses imperfect people. He uses our daily and ordinary obedience to accomplish his extraordinary plan. Perhaps you feel you have concealed your faith too long or compromised with the world too much. Here is where Esther and Mordecai provide us a lot of hope. It is not just that we should see what they did right and do that, but we should also see all they did wrong and know it did not disqualify them from being used by God. The same is true for us.

Reflect and Discuss

1. Describe a time the Lord called you to do something but you were full of fear rather than faith and did not obey. Why is Esther 4 a good chapter for many of us who have been in this position?
2. In what ways, if any, are you currently hesitating to obey the Lord? How can the gospel fuel obedience?
3. In the time of crisis, how far do you have to make it down your reaction list before you get to prayer? Why is prayer always the best reaction to difficult circumstances?
4. Why do we tend to conceal our grief or struggles rather than sharing them openly?
5. Who is someone God has used to encourage you to be obedient to something God was calling you to do? Why do we need others who will help spur our obedience? How can we encourage one another to be obedient?
6. What, if anything, are you hoping "somebody" will do in your faith family or in your city? Why do you think you are not the "somebody" to do it?
7. How might the gospel bring us to the point where we are willing to say, "If I perish, I perish, but I am going to obey at all costs"?
8. How often do you consider and take advantage of the fact that through Christ we have full access to meet with God the Father?
9. To what degree are you amazed that the Father wants us to be in his presence? Explain.
10. How often do you express gratitude for Christ's identification with and mediation for us? Why is Christ called our great high priest?

A Tale of Two Plans

ESTHER 5

Main Idea: As we act on plans we discern from God's Word rather than plans we devise from our wills, the Lord will use us for the development of his kingdom and not its detriment.

I.   **How to Be Used for the Development of the Kingdom**
   A. Put feet to faith (5:1).
   B. Experience God's favor (5:2).
   C. Be selfless (5:3).
   D. Be strategic (5:4-8).
   E. Be obedient to the "whats" of God's plans without fully knowing the "whys."

II. **How to Be Used for the Detriment of the Kingdom**
   A. Fuel idolatry rather than forsake it (5:9).
   B. Be convinced of your own significance (5:10-13).
   C. Surround yourself with voices of compliance rather than conviction (5:14).
   D. Devalue the lives of others and eliminate anyone in the way (5:14).

Of all the subjects I miss from elementary school, recess ranks at the top (nap time is a very close second, especially since I spent two years in kindergarten). I miss the slides and swings to some extent, but I miss the playground sports the most.

At one recess period in third grade when we were playing football, I got as close to the line of scrimmage as possible. The quarterback was in the shotgun, and I was studying his cadence. I timed it so that just as the center snapped the ball, I darted across and caught it before the football reached the quarterback. Technically, I might have been a little offsides when I started, but there is not a lot that's technical about playground sports.

Once I had the ball, I sprinted with all of my might, which is saying a lot since I was a chunky kid. Somehow, I literally outran everybody and spiked the ball in the endzone for a touchdown. It was only then that I figured out I had just scored a touchdown for the opposing team. Instead of turning toward my opponent's goal line behind them, I had turned toward the goal line we were defending and then blazed a trail for a touchdown. I had unwittingly been an accomplice to the other team's victory because at that moment the bell rang for us to return to our classes (probably to read *Where the Red Fern Grows*).

As I have gotten older, I have come to realize this happens in other places besides the playground. In our daily lives, spiritual warfare rages. The flesh, the world, and the devil do not take holidays. I am afraid most of us tend to be oblivious despite Jesus's, Paul's, Peter's, John's, and James's warnings recorded throughout the New Testament exhorting us to be alert. Perhaps without our realizing it, the enemy can use our actions, our conversations, or even our ambitions for the detriment of God's kingdom rather than its development.

God certainly is not the only one who makes plans, but his plans are the only ones that will ultimately prevail. Esther 5 is a tale of two plans. Esther had a plan, and Haman had a plan. These two plans originated from two different sources, one was birthed from prayer and one was created from rage and hatred. The plans in Esther 5 had two different purposes as well. One plan was drafted as an attempt to save lives, and the other plan was created to take a life. The plans differed in perspective also. One plan was from selflessness, and one was full of selfishness. Ultimately, the plans had two different outcomes (as we will soon see). The outcome of Esther's plan will be one of incredible deliverance while the outcome of Haman's will be one of inevitable destruction.

Whose plans are we carrying out? Are the plans we act on for the purpose of making our names or God's name great? Are they about our kingdoms or his? Are they marked by selfishness or selflessness? Do the plans we carry out involve our living by faith at all? Do they involve our experiencing God's power as we walk in obedience? Do they result in the advancement of the gospel? In Esther 5 God's people are beginning to see God's providence, and they move from asking for to acting on God's plan to preserve his people. As we act on plans we discern from God's Word rather than plans we devise from our wills, the Lord will use us for the development of his kingdom and not its detriment.

How to Be Used for the Development of the Kingdom

Put Feet to Faith (5:1)

Having either attended or led youth camps for twenty-eight years, I am well aware that when we say we are going to do something for the Lord, we sometimes do not even make it to the parking lot before breaking our commitments. My youth minister once played Al Denson's song, "Be the One," on repeat as we traveled back from camp at Glorieta, New Mexico, because some who had kept their commitment on the ride through the parking lot were in danger of breaking it on the bus! Student ministry is not for the faint hearted. Even for those students who actually make it home with their commitment to the Lord still intact, some begin to waver when the camp "warm fuzzies" and the camp t-shirt both begin to fade. Now before we all move into Debbie Downer's neighborhood, remember there are countless examples of God, through his Spirit and Word, calling students (and adults) to action, and in his power they have followed through.

After the period of fasting, there was no failure to launch with regard to Esther. What she said she would do, she did. She put on her robes, she squared her shoulders, and she made her way to the throne room. Smith asserts,

> People who hope to be used by God must boldly put
> themselves in a position where God can work through them,
> rather than sitting back, doing nothing, passively hoping or
> waiting for God to do something. (*Ezra, Nehemiah, Esther,* 260)

We are to make the most of every stewardship the Lord entrusts to us.

How often do we decide to pray about something not because we are still trying to discern the good we should do but because we are delaying? Perhaps we say, "Let me pray about that," but then we keep praying and keep praying and never arrive at a decision or take action. Or perhaps we know the Lord has said, "Go," and we say, "No!" Instead of choosing faith in the Lord and walking in obedience, we choose fear and walk in disobedience. Some of us may even be paralyzed by procrastination, but behind procrastination is the dangerous presumption: "I will have more time and opportunity to do this in the future." James exhorts us,

> *Come now, you who say, "Today or tomorrow we will travel to such*
> *and such a city and spend a year there and do business and make a*

profit." Yet you do not know what tomorrow will bring—what your
life will be! For you are like vapor that appears for a little while, then
vanishes. (Jas 4:13-14)

Esther did not postpone following through with her commitment. In
her, there was no more reluctance or rationalizing, just resolve.

Esther's determination is similar to what Christ displayed as he fulfilled the Father's plans. Luke writes, "When the days were coming to a
close for him to be taken up, he determined to journey to Jerusalem"
(Luke 9:51). Jesus was not walking away from the cross but toward it.
Mark provides another picture of Christ's resolve when he records Jesus
saying to his sleepy disciples in Gethsemane, "Get up; let's go. See, my
betrayer is near" (Mark 14:42). The time for praying in the garden was
finished; the time for propitiation at Golgotha had arrived. In Christ
there was no reluctance or rationalizing, just resolve. Esther was uncertain she would live; Christ was certain he would die.

For Esther, asking in prayer led to action in the palace. Her fasting
led to faithfulness. God never puts us in positions of opportunity just
so we can *consider* doing something or *almost* do something or *maybe* do
something. He puts us in positions of opportunity to be obedient and
"be strengthened by the Lord and by his vast strength" (Eph 6:10). In
Joshua 1, the Lord commanded Joshua three times to "be strong and
courageous" (1:6,7,9). God was calling Joshua to lead his people into
the promised land, but he did not expect Joshua to be faithful based on
self-motivated fervor but on some very important facts. God reminded
Joshua of his presence and promises. Joshua could choose to be fearful and disbelieve God and ultimately disobey, but that would not stop
God's plan. And Joshua would not be rejecting just an opportunity but
a direct command from the Lord.

We have been given a command as well. The one with all authority
told us,

> *Go, therefore, and make disciples of all nations, baptizing them in the*
> *name of the Father and of the Son and of the Holy Spirit, teaching*
> *them to observe everything I have commanded you. And remember, I*
> *am with you always, to the end of the age.* (Matt 28:19-20)

Are we delaying obedience to this command in any way? The date of
death was set for the Jews. There was no time for Esther to delay. In
our world people perish every day, and some have never heard the gospel a single time. There is, then, no time for our delaying either. Are

the people we shepherd paralyzed by fear at either making disciples or going to the nations? How many times have they committed to living these verses but failed to launch? As we consider Christ's plan, presence, and promises, he will provide all the courage and strength we need to obey his commands.

Every opportunity God puts before us is a call to faith in the promised strength of God (Piper, "Be Strong and Courageous in Jesus"). For Esther, there would have been ample fuel for fear. In particular, she had not been summoned by the king and was about to reveal her ethnicity to him after his ring and name had been used to sign a death decree for all of her people. Each gospel opportunity we are given is a choice between fear and faith. We can do what we committed to do, not because we are strong but because Jesus is. When we do follow through, choosing faith and not fear, something very important occurs. Peter writes, "If anyone serves, let it be from the strength God provides, so that God may be glorified through Jesus Christ in everything. To him be the glory and the power forever and ever. Amen" (1 Pet 4:11). When we serve in his strength, it will not just be for our good and the good of those around us, but for his glory. We need to be faithful with each opportunity he entrusts to us. Is there anything you have been saying for a while now that you were going to do for the kingdom but still have not gotten around to doing? By his grace and for his glory, hop to it.

Experience God's Favor (5:2)

The moment of truth arrived. Would Esther be received or rejected? Would she live or die? Gregory writes,

> Of course, she does not know—cannot know—what the outcome will be when the king sees her. She does not know whether the king will be in a generous mood or an irritable mood. She does not know whether she will make a good impression on him or not. She does not know whether she will find favor with him or not. Nevertheless, with courage, conviction, and perhaps some faith, she goes. (*Inconspicuous Providence*, 95)

Esther did everything she could do. She fasted, she put on her royal robes, but whether she lived depended on his look.

Have you ever been there before? You knew you were acting in faith but still you were uncertain of how it would all turn out? I certainly have.

One Sunday morning as I was getting ready to lead our congregation, the Holy Spirit brought Abraham and Isaac to my mind (Gen 22). I had been praying through two weighty issues, and I desperately needed the Lord's direction. When the Spirit brought Abraham to my memory, I realized that Abraham did not know how the Lord would ultimately resolve everything; he was just called to step out in faith. For my two areas of concern, I knew this meant I could not control any outcomes, but I was responsible for my obedience. I chose to trust the Lord and obey, and in both situations the Lord's grace was apparent. When we put feet to faith we should not be surprised to find God's favor.

The same was true for Esther. And as soon as the king saw her, he granted her life because in his eyes she "gained favor." This is now the fourth time the author described the reaction of those around Esther in this way (2:9,15,17). Bush notes, "Again the narrator uses the active expression 'she won his favor' rather than the more passive expression 'found favor'" (*Ruth/Esther*, 404). Certainly, Esther's strategy and subtlety, which we will discuss in a moment, were helpful aids in acquiring favor, and they continued to be utilized with her next steps. The king extended the scepter, and she at the very least touched it but may have even kissed it. She may have broken protocol by appearing in the court, but she did not want to break it once she was received favorably. Any misstep could jeopardize her audience with the king and his approval of her. As we know, her goal was not just to enter the court, but to end the edict. Objective 1 of gaining access was achieved. Objective 2 of addressing the king was the next phase of her plan.

Be Selfless (5:3)

Now that Esther's life was spared, would she make an appeal for just herself with regard to the death decree, or would she advocate for others as well? An opportunity was afforded her when Ahasuerus asked for her request and offered up to half of his kingdom if necessary for the answer. This moment is one of the few in the book when the king actually seems perceptive. In most other situations he comes off either drunk, dense, or depraved. In this exchange, however, he sensed something was important enough for Esther to take the actions she had, so he inquired as to what might be the cause.

Was he really willing to give her up to half of his kingdom? Since he ruled almost all the known world at that time (except Greece, which he had failed to conquer), he does not come across as someone willing to divide his power or property easily. Nevertheless, he will repeat the phrase two more times (5:6; 7:2), so it was not just a slip of his tongue. Technically, the offer was a formality indicating his willingness to be generous and not an absolute blank check. Herod once made the same promise to Herodias's daughter, who dazzled him with her dancing, and she requested the head of John the Baptist on a platter. Herod regretted his offer and her request, but he did not refuse her (Mark 6:21-29). According to Herodotus, Ahasuerus himself had a bad experience in extending the same offer to one of his daughters-in-law, who was also his lover and his niece. (And you thought your family was messed up.) The result of her request would ultimately lead to the murders of the king's brother, sister-in-law (whom he also desired at one time), and nephews (*The Histories*, 598–600). What a mess.

In Esther's case, a window was open for her to say she desired not his possessions but her people, but as wisdom was needed in determining what he would see (5:1), it was still needed for determining what she should say. We know she did not enter the throne room just for herself but for all those who had no opportunity or ability to go into the king's presence. Selflessness is always a mark of those God is using to build his kingdom (Phil 2:3-4). Paul told the Corinthians he would "most gladly spend and be spent" for them (2 Cor 12:15). He told the church at Colossae that he was commissioned as a servant of God's church and rejoiced in any sufferings required for their sake (Col 1:24-25). Selflessness should be evident in our homes also, as husbands sacrificially love their wives (Eph 5:25). For Esther, though, presenting her request would require not just selflessness but also sanctified shrewdness.

Be Strategic (5:4-8)

After all the anticipation, the moment for petition finally arrived. Esther was alive, she had the king's attention, and she could plead her case on behalf of her people. But just as we think she will ask for freedom from the edict, she . . . invites him to a feast . . . with Haman! I know. Her people are in peril and she is throwing a party? Well, in her defense, it has often been said the way to a man's heart is through his stomach, so it does not seem to be the worst idea ever. But is she just delaying? Stalling? Panicking? No, she had a plan.

The fact the meal was already prepared reveals two things: Esther was really hopeful she would live, and Esther had a plan. Her decision not to admit her true request was not just nervous delay but deliberate strategy. Smith notes the clear evidence of Esther's intentionality:

> Esther dressed appropriately by wearing her royal garments, behaved properly when the golden scepter was stretched out to her, and responded to his generous offer by modestly offering to serve the king. She did not act like an emotional basket case who was about to fall apart, like an angry spouse who was jealous because she was ignored, or like someone who was trying to push her agenda on the king. Since her primary goal was to "find favor in the eyes" of the king, she did what she was supposed to do. (*Ezra, Nehemiah, Esther*, 260)

I admit that when I asked Tara's father, who was a major general at the time, for his permission to marry her, I did not do it at the restaurant while we were eating; I did not do it when we initially returned to their house; I finally did it after Tara's mom left the kitchen where we were visiting, and only after it had been hours since we started talking. Unlike Esther's, my delay was all panic and zero planning. Fortunately, Tara's parents were very patient!

Why would Esther need to be strategic? If Ahasuerus already offered her up to half his kingdom, then why not just go for the win? Duguid offers several reasons for Esther's shrewdness: (1) She was asking for the reversal of an irreversible law, which had been sponsored by the most powerful advisor in the empire and signed with the king's own signet ring. (2) Granting her request would cost the king ten thousand talents—as much as half the annual tax revenue of his empire, and no small sum. (3) Perhaps even worse, though, it would be hard for the king to accede to her request without losing face, since the edict had been officially authorized by his own royal person. (4) Finally, in order to make her request, she would have to reveal her hidden Jewish identity, risking a potential backlash from the husband she had been deceiving for the past five years (*Esther & Ruth* 62). The feast would provide an opportunity for some of the formality to be diminished and would eliminate the risk of Esther embarrassing the king while on his throne and in his court. Any of the reasons listed would be sufficient cause for some measure of strategy. When they are considered all together, the feast does not sound foolish after all.

Now the moment we have been waiting for (again). The king is full, the wine has flowed, and he's ready to fulfill his wife's request. We are ready for Esther to spring her trap—and possibly admit she's poisoned Haman's food, though few of us would blame her if a little spilled in Ahasuerus's bowl as well. There is no admission of poisoning, however, just an invitation to another party.

Esther! What are you doing? You had the moment and you missed it! But did she? As the great Lee Corso says so often, "Not so fast, my friend!" Look carefully at her wording. She did not just invite the king to another feast; she connected his attendance with his answer to her as-yet-unnamed request. If he really would grant her plea, then his presence the next day would be her assurance. Both the king's curiosity and his commitment level would be piqued.

Not only would the king be present, but so would Haman. She would be dining with the devil, again. We should give special credit to Esther for having Haman attend these feasts. Few enjoy confrontation. Even fewer handle it in a biblical manner. Talking about people is a lot easier (but not holier) if they are not in the room. What Esther has to say about Haman she will say in his presence. It would have been easy to just invite Ahasuerus and then have him handle Haman. But Esther will confront her enemy (7:6).

For carrying out the plan she discerned through fasting, Esther gets a lot of grief from people sitting somewhere drinking coffee (or better yet, Mountain Dew) and writing books about her. Some believe she should have gone in, guns blazing, and been bold like Vashti. Esther's use of a plan, though, required no less boldness than Vashti's refusal. While Vashti faced deposal, Esther risked death.

Others suggest Esther resorted to worldly methods of scheming to get what she wanted. Assuredly, we are called to be in the world but not of it. Subtlety and strategy, however, are not necessarily anti-gospel. Jesus told his disciples, "Look, I'm sending you out like sheep among wolves. Therefore be as shrewd as serpents and as innocent as doves" (Matt 10:16). When we consider participating in missions in places where governments are not just opposed but hostile toward the gospel, strategy is not evil or worldly. For example, we could get on a plane bound for North Korea and announce to everyone mid-flight that we are boldly taking the gospel to that communist nation. Upon landing, however, if we were even allowed to deplane, it would only be for one of two destinations: detainment or deportation. I am not advocating lying. I am just saying that since the Lord called us to shrewdness, utilizing strategy does not make us children of the devil or the world.

Knowing when to say what is also important for gospel purposes, but it should not lead to unending silence. Each of Esther's words that are recorded for us are measured, but she would eventually give Ahasuerus the details of her request. When seeking to see those around us come to Christ, we may be strategic with what, where, and when we share with them the gospel, but we cannot be silent forever. There comes a time when the content of the gospel has to be shared. We cannot hope people will make it to heaven just by observing our lives anymore than Ahasuerus could discern what Esther wanted just by attending her feasts.

Be Obedient to the "Whats" of God's Plans without Fully Knowing the "Whys"

As we seek to be used by God for the building of his kingdom, we need to follow the Lord's plan and his timing even if we do not fully understand either of them. Esther did not know how God would use the night between the feasts. She just knew she discerned a two-feast strategy. When an angel of the Lord told Philip, "Get up and go south to the road that goes down from Jerusalem to Gaza," he did not tell him why (Acts 8:26). Unlike many of us who refuse the "what" until given a "why," Philip obeyed and would eventually be used to share the gospel with an Ethiopian man (Acts 8:35). Just because we may not understand the Lord's plan fully does not mean we lack the information we need to act faithfully.

Perhaps God does not give us all the details because he wants us to trust in his presence, his provision, and his promises. As noted previously, our dependence is not just for our good, but for his glory. When the outcome arrives, we can be quick to say, "Look at what God did" instead of "Look at what I did." Gregory notes the eventual outcome of these feasts was

> not just a product of Esther's shrewdness. Even with all her shrewdness, the king did not have to extend the scepter, but he did. The king did not have to invite a request, but he did. The king did not have to come to the banquet, but he did. (*Inconspicuous Providence*, 100)

While Esther's planning was important, Someone else was integral in the king's participation. The author of Proverbs says, "A king's heart is like channeled water in the Lord's hand: He directs it wherever he chooses" (Prov 21:1). As Gregory points out, "Persian kings are not exempt" (ibid., 101).

How to Be Used for the Detriment of the Kingdom

The Lord is not the only one who makes plans, but he is the only one whose plans will be fully accomplished. Satan makes plans all the time for the destruction of God's people and then uses others to carry them out. Haman probably had no clue that Satan was at work in his life to attempt to wipe out the messianic line. He was most likely operating from the desires and evil that were already in his heart. Regardless, we should examine our lives to be sure we are not even unwittingly carrying out Satan's plans rather than our Savior's. We tend to be used for the detriment of the kingdom when we fuel idolatry in our lives rather than forsaking it (5:9), are convinced of our own significance (5:10-13), surround ourselves with voices of compliance rather than conviction (5:14), or devalue the lives of others and eliminate anyone standing in our way (5:14).

Fuel Idolatry Rather Than Forsake It (5:9)

What is the fastest you have gone from full joy to explosive rage? If you have never had such a transition, then what is a memory you have of shifting from being joyful to whatever emotion came next? Unfortunately, a lot of my swings from joy to mourning are linked to sports. You think your team is going to win the game only to have victory ripped out of your hands and heart in the last moment.

After being invited to a private feast with the king and queen and then receiving an invitation to do it all again the next day, Haman felt like he was on top of the world . . . until he saw Mordecai. Once again, Mordecai was neither apologetic nor anxious about refusing to show honor, and Haman refused to accept such disrespect.

We need to ask ourselves two important questions: In what or whom do we take joy? What or who kills joy in our lives? In his last lengthy conversation with his disciples on the night before his death, Jesus told them, "You also have sorrow now. But I will see you again. Your hearts will rejoice, and *no one will take away your joy from you*" (John 16:22; emphasis added). Some will argue about whether Jesus meant his resurrection or his second coming (I believe it is the former), but at some point in the future Jesus's disciples would be reunited with him and have irrevocable joy.

Piper calls the incarnation "the dawning of indestructible joy because the joy Jesus was bringing into the world was like no other kind in history. Once we have it, it cannot be destroyed" (*The Dawning of Indestructible Joy*, 8). He adds,

> The joy that Jesus came to bring is from outside the world. It is the very joy that Jesus himself has in God the Father—which he has had from all eternity and will have forever. There is no greater joy than the joy that God has in God, because God is the greatest object of joy, and God has the greatest powers to enjoy. (Ibid., 8)

On that last night with his disciples, Jesus talked a lot about joy. He said, "I have told you these things so that my joy may be in you and your joy may be complete" (John 15:11). Do you have complete and irrevocable joy? The only place you'll find it is in Christ. Haman's joy rapidly evaporated because the object of his joy was his experience at the feast and his expectation of another rather than in the Eternal One. Earthly pleasures and possessions lack the weightiness and worthiness to sustain our joy forever. Often, the best the world has to offer cannot fuel our joy minutes after the joy began.

While those who are in Christ can have indestructible joy, the full experience of it will not be realized until heaven. In the intermediary period, our joy will never be fully removed, but it can be diminished. And each time our joy is diminished, the reason is because we have pursued "fool's joy" (I am playing off the term "fool's gold" because, like those worthless rocks, earthly joys never provide what they promise). Wilson contends, "All sin is idolatry because every sin is an exercise in trust of something or someone other than the one true God to satisfy, fulfill, or bless" ("The Church and Idolatry"). Nothing, in fact, diminishes our joy faster than our pursuit of sin. Haman's joy was quickly overcome when he embraced anger fueled by pride and coveting. He was mad because he was not getting what he desired and felt worthy of receiving. Haman could blame Mordecai all he wanted for stealing his joy, but the blame lay solely with Haman. All sin is a choice, and all sin comes with a cost. Because the object of Haman's joy was too small, it could not sustain the attack cast upon it by the trifecta sins of anger, pride, and coveting.

The battle for our joy is no less vicious, and it rages daily. In whom or what are you taking joy? What or who is currently killing joy in your life? Segal contends,

We can be infinitely and enduringly more happy with Jesus
than with anything or even everything in a world without
him—even when that world is filled and overflowing with
promotions and bonuses at work, on-demand television, all-
you-can-eat sushi, grossly accessible pornography, always new
and better technology, and countless other goods become
gods. (*Killjoys*, x)

The one thing Haman wanted more than anything else was honor
from Mordecai (5:13). (Why do we so often crave what we lack?) We
have to guard against making an idol out of what we do not have.
Perhaps you think to yourself, *If I just had that promotion or new vehicle or a
spouse or children or if people recognized how awesome I am,* but none of those
things can bring lasting satisfaction. Duguid warns,

When we seek to feed our idolatries rather than starving them,
we end up emptier than ever, in even greater bondage than
before, and it is only a matter of time before something else
reignites our negative emotions. (*Esther and Ruth*, 67)

He goes on to note that the identities of our idols are . . .

most easily exposed by analyzing our strongest emotions, both
good, and bad. What is it that causes us to be angry out of all
proportion to the offense? There is a clue that one of our idols
is being threatened. What is it that makes us feel an unusually
strong sense of achievement? It may be one of our idols being
stroked. Our strong emotions are clues enabling us to read
our own hearts better. (Ibid., 67)

Ask God to use his Spirit and his Word to help you identify any idols you
may have. Then ask for his grace to help you forsake them immediately
rather than continuing to feed them.

Be Convinced of Your Own Significance (5:10-13)

In his book to pastors, H. B. Charles writes about the time one of his pulpit heroes preached at his church. During a conversation following the
service, his hero took him to task. Charles says his pride was confronted
when the guest pastor said, "I think you want to be somebody. I don't
want to be somebody. I just want to preach. But I think you want to be
somebody" (*On Pastoring*, 46). Charles admits God used that conversation to change his life and the trajectory of his ministry. He notes,

As pastors who preach the gospel to others, we need to
constantly preach the gospel to ourselves, as well. We must
not forget that our identity rests in the finished work of
Christ, not in church size, speaking schedule, or ministry
accomplishments. . . . When we are tempted to be somebody,
we must refuse to boast in who we are or what we have or what
we accomplish. Our boasting should be in Christ alone. (Ibid.,
46–47)

Too bad Charles's hero couldn't have a conversation with Haman as well.

Haman did not just want to be a somebody: he was convinced he was
somebody. Duguid believes what "Haman craved above all things was
not simply significance, but rather being seen to be significant" (*Esther
and Ruth*, 64). After failing to receive honor from Mordecai, Haman
took a play out of Ahasuerus's playbook and decided to invite people
over so he could recount his glory and greatness to them. If he had a
phone, he would have texted them to "Come to my party so I can let you
know how awesome I am." His significance and security were found in
accolades, assets, and achievements. He lists what many would consider
blessing upon blessing, but he expresses no gratitude to the Lord, just
contempt for Mordecai. Prime warns,

Pride is one of the greatest sins because it makes us treat
God's gifts as if they rightfully belonged to us, and were
created by us. Our pride robs God of his right to be
acknowledged as the source of all the good we know and
enjoy. (*Unspoken Lessons*, 94)

Haman was not interested in acknowledging the Lord as the source of
his good because he was too consumed with having his own glory recognized. Prime continues his warning by writing, "Our pride is a form
of dishonesty since it gives us false views of our own importance. It is
frequently the substitution and exaltation of ourselves in the place of
God" (ibid., 95).

If we are substituting and exalting ourselves in the place of God,
we will not be doing it for very long. The author of Proverbs says,
"Pride comes before destruction, and an arrogant spirit before a fall"
(Prov 16:18). Pharaoh, for instance, thought he was somebody; he found
out he was not (Exod 7–15). King Sihon thought he was somebody; he
found out he was not (Num 21:21-30). King Og thought he was somebody; he found out he was not (Num 21:31-35). Balak thought he could

pay somebody and overcome God's people; he found out that the some-body he paid was a nobody in comparison to God (Num 22–24). King Herod thought he was somebody; he found out he was not (Acts 12). Haman thought he was somebody, and he soon found out he was wrong (Esth 7:10).

While Haman wants all eyes on himself, an important question remains: On whom does the Lord cast his gaze? In Isaiah 66:2 the Lord says, "I will look favorably on this kind of person: one who is humble, submissive in spirit, and trembles at my word." In James 4:6 we learn that God does not just look favorably on the humble, but he also helps them: "He gives greater grace. Therefore he says: God resists the proud, but gives grace to the humble." If you are more convinced of God's greatness than your own, then you are on solid ground. If you do not just acknowledge you need God's help but ask for it, then humility will flourish and pride diminish. If you think back through each day and carefully give God glory for each evidence of his grace, then your culti-vation of gratitude will help you avoid fueling the foolishness of pride.

One last thought here. How do you think Haman's sons felt when he included them in the list of things that failed to satisfy him or that were worth nothing to him in comparison to wanting honor from Mordecai? How oblivious we can be to how deeply we wound others around us when we are blinded by pride and driven by idolatry. Father, give us eyes to see you rightly so we will see ourselves rightly and serve others joyfully.

Surround Yourself with Voices of Compliance Rather Than Conviction (5:14)

Instead of encouraging him to mortify his sin, the group gathered in Haman's home encouraged him to kill Mordecai. Prime declares, "They would have been better friends to him if they had warned him of the danger of his wounded pride and where it would lead him" (ibid.). They contributed to his sin rather than confronting him about it. We do not need nor is it loving to be these kinds of friends. As a faith family, we are called to speak truthfully to one another in love (Eph 4:15). I have asked my congregation, my accountability partner, and my wife not to aid my sin but to address it and help me forsake it.

Tripp says, "My self-perception is as accurate as a carnival mirror" (*Instruments in the Redeemer's Hands*, 54). He contends we need to hold the Word in front of each other so we can see ourselves clearly. I have a mark on my face where in sixth grade I sneezed and accidentally jabbed my pencil into my cheek. The only time I remember it is there is when someone points it out or, worse, licks their thumb and tries to wipe it off my face. Because I cannot see it, I am not bothered by it. We need others who can see and are bothered by our sins to lovingly and graciously speak God's Word into our lives. Mahaney admits, "Without others' help to see myself clearly, I'll listen to my own arguments, believe my own lies, and buy into my own delusions" (*Humility*, 128).

Far different from Esther's plan discerned through prayer, Haman's plan was devised by people in a moment of reaction. Their plan would benefit only one person—Haman. He was willing to kill someone just so his ego would no longer be bruised! Sombody needed to tell this brother to get over himself.

Devalue the Lives of Others and Eliminate Anyone in the Way (5:14)

In Proverbs 12:15 we are told, "A fool's way is right in his own eyes, but whoever listens to counsel is wise." Unless, of course, that group of counselors is comprised of a bunch of fools. In that case, you are no better off than if you had only taken counsel from yourself. Both Ahasuerus and Haman needed new counselors because they were both too easily pleased by the horrific recommendations of the yahoos that surrounded them.

One would be hard pressed to find a more stunning example of the devaluing of human life than the advice from Haman's friends to have Mordecai killed and then to go enjoy himself at the feast. This is worldly thinking at its prime. Haman's happiness is more important than Mordecai's life? Eliminate *anything* standing in the way of his getting what he wants? Importantly, killing Mordecai would not kill the root of Haman's issues. Eventually there would be someone else who would not give him the honor he wanted, so would he then have to have that person killed too?

I guess his home owners' association did not have restrictions against building gallows, which was unfortunate for Haman. As he ordered the gallows to be constructed, he was oblivious to the fact he was building a device for his own doom. Haman's refusal to see value in Mordecai's life would lead to the loss of his own.

Is there any way that you are currently elevating your interests above the needs or interests of those around you? Are the people around you only valuable to you when they contribute to your agenda; and should they fail to do so, do you dispose of those relationships? Paul exhorted the church at Philippi,

> *Do nothing out of selfish ambition or conceit, but in humility consider others as more important than yourselves. Everyone should look out not only for his own interests, but also for the interests of others.*
> (Phil 2:3-4)

Selfish ambition and conceit drove Haman, and there is no evidence in the text that he ever considered the interests of others. Do not be Haman. Do not devalue the lives and worth of those around you just because they do not cater to your conceit. I hope that when I give an account to the Lord one day that there will be more evidence of my serving others for their good than of my using them for mine.

Conclusion

What a cliffhanger we have as we come to the end of Esther 5! Esther and Haman both have plans, but neither is fully aware of the other's. Will Haman's plan be carried out first? Will he murder Mordecai and then munch on muffins? Reading the text is like watching a baseball player running home and an outfielder throwing the ball to the catcher. The fans wait to see which will arrive to the plate first. Will the runner beat the ball, or will the ball arrive before the runner? Because lives are on the line in Esther 5, the stakes are even higher. Whichever plan gets enacted first will determine who lives and who dies. What neither Haman nor Esther anticipated, though, was that while they slept Ahasuerus would not, and his providential insomnia would have an impact on all their plans.

In light of all we have discussed in Esther 5, let me close by offering one more reminder. The gospel answers the need for true significance. Nothing speaks more to your significance than God the Father caring enough to be involved in your situation and sending God the Son to lay down his life in your place and then to empower you with his Spirit for the purposes of the kingdom. These truths are of utmost and eternal significance. We just fail at times to apply the gospel to our lives. We search for fleeting significance rather than resting in an eternal one. You have been approved by God in Christ. You cannot be more significant, and you cannot be more set free to serve in obscurity because it is about his name and not ours. I hope wherever you are today, the joy in the gospel is fueling your obedience. May you be used for the development of God's kingdom and not its detriment.

Reflect and Discuss

1. Describe a time when you were used to the detriment of God's kingdom. How and when did you experience conviction over it? What did you learn from the experience?
2. How can we know we are being used for the development of God's kingdom rather than its detriment?
3. Describe a time when you followed a plan that was determined by your will rather than God's Word. How did this turn out for you (and others)?
4. How can we be certain we're discerning God's plan for our lives from his Word rather than devising plans from our wills?
5. Have you ever used prayer for delaying rather than obeying? If so, why? How can we minimize this tendency in our lives?
6. Describe a time you walked obediently in faith and experienced the Lord's favor, provision, and blessing. How do we know he will provide all we need if we obey?
7. In what ways can we feed idolatry in our lives rather than forsaking it?
8. How does the gospel answer our need for true significance?
9. What can we do to surround ourselves with voices of conviction rather than just voices of compliance?
10. In what ways are you hoping the Lord will use you in the development of his kingdom this year?

Providential Peripety[1]

ESTHER 6

Main Idea: Through the ordinary means of insomnia in Ahasuerus and an insatiable desire for honor in Haman, God will turn the tables on the enemy of his people, initiating Haman's downfall and his people's deliverance.

I. Consider the Providential Insomnia (6:1-2).
II. Consider the Providential Investigation (6:3).
III. Consider the Providential Interruption (6:4-5).
IV. Consider the Providential Irony (6:6-11).
V. Consider the Providential Insult (6:12-13).
VI. Consider the Providential Invitation (6:14).
VII. Conclude that There Is Nothing like God's Providence and God's Peripety; None Is Worthier of Glorious and Glad Praise.
  A. God's providence
  B. God's peripety
  C. God's praise

February 26, 2017, will be remembered in Hollywood for a long time. On that night at the Oscars, Warren Beatty and Faye Dunaway had the privilege of presenting the Academy Award for Best Picture. After introducing the nominees and then some brief banter, it was time to announce the big winner. Beatty opened the envelope, seemed a little confused, and then handed it to Dunaway. She then announced *La La Land*, and "the musical's cast, director, producers and crew then took the stage to accept the night's top prize and began their thank you speeches" (Nicholas Hautman, "Oscars 2017 Best Picture Mix-Up: Everything We Know So Far, Plus What Went Wrong"). The only problem? *La La Land* was not the true winner.

Hautman writes,

---

[1] I am thankful to Karen H. Jobes for introducing me to the term *peripety*. It "refers to a sudden turn of events in a story that reverses the intended and expected action" (Jobes, *Esther*, 155).

> In one of the most surprising reversals in the history of live television, headset-clad members of the Oscars crew scurried on stage to alert the *La La Land* team that something was wrong. The film's producer, Jordan Horowitz, quickly grabbed the microphone and announced, "There's been a mistake. *Moonlight*, you won best picture. This is not a joke." (Ibid.)

So, what happened? How could such a mistake happen on such a large stage? It turns out there was no malice and really no mystery. Prior to walking on stage, Beatty was simply handed the wrong envelope. He was given the announcement for Best Actress in a Leading Role, which happened to be Emma Stone, who happened to star in *La La Land*. When Beatty opened the envelope, he knew something was not right. When he handed the envelope to Dunaway, she thought he was simply drawing the moment out. She only saw the *La La Land* portion of the announcement, and that is what she shared. After the chaos calmed, the cast and crew from *Moonlight* walked on stage and accepted the honor that rightly belonged to them. It was quite a reversal.

In Esther 6 a reversal of epic proportions is recorded as well. Haman wanted to be honored by all, especially by Mordecai, but (spoiler alert) Mordecai would be honored by all, with Haman leading the call to honor. You may have seen it coming because you are familiar with the story, but Haman never did. He experienced a bit of "that's not what I envisioned." He never in his wildest nightmares imagined he would be used to bring honor to the one who refused to honor him.

In Esther 6 we are also going to see that God's timing is always perfect. God is going to save Mordecai from Haman's foolishness. Indeed, Mordecai's words to Esther in 4:14 prove prophetic in his own life, since help for him comes "from another place" besides Esther (unless you count her cooking, which may have contributed to the king's insomnia). As a part of God's preserving Mordecai, we will also see why he did not allow Mordecai to be rewarded earlier by the king when he divulged the assassination plot. As always, God's plans and timing are for our best and are beyond what we could imagine.

Consider the Providential Insomnia
ESTHER 6:1-2

When we last visited our text, the king and Haman had attended a feast that Esther prepared. We thought she was going to intercede for her people, but instead she invited the king and Haman to another feast to be observed on the following day. Unbeknown to her, Haman left her feast and had another run-in with Mordecai. Then, after receiving counsel from his family and friends, Haman decided to have gallows constructed and to have Mordecai hanged on them before attending the second feast with Esther and Ahasuerus.

Since Esther did not know about Haman's plan, she could not throw her royal robes back on, run to the king, and attempt to intervene for her cousin. Since Mordecai did not know about the plan, he was not packing his bags in the middle of the night and trying to catch the next camel caravan headed out of town. Neither of the two protagonists in our story had any clue about the peril Mordecai was in. And unlike when Mordecai was made aware of the plot to kill Ahasuerus, none of those in Haman's camp would prove willing to break ranks and send a message to Mordecai, Esther, or the king. They were in solidarity, and Esther and Mordecai were asleep. They did not know about the danger awaiting them, much like the way I did not when I picked up a cooler by our back door late one night that a snake hid beneath.

The tension in the story of Esther reminds me of scenes from a movie in which someone is held captive and some instrument of death moves closer and closer with each passing second. If the hero does not show up, doom awaits. As the one who draws nigh to death is well aware. Mordecai, by contrast, is clueless. But you know who did know about it? God. Isn't it interesting that while Esther and Mordecai were sleeping God was not, and he made sure he was not the only one awake.

Initially, the revelation that the king could not catch any Zs seems like an insignificant detail. After all, you may be like my wife, who says, "Sleep escapes me every night—because my spouse snores!" Maybe Ahasuerus needed a CPAP machine (I do). Maybe he had indigestion from the feast that robbed him of winks. But what seems like a run-of-the-mill detail could not be further from ordinary. The human authors of the Bible, who were under the inspiration of the Holy Spirit, did not have word counts they were trying to reach for their publishers. There is no fluff in God's Word. In narrative texts, especially, details are penned with purpose. God will use this insomnia event to be a major turning point in the story. Jobes contends,

> By making the pivot point of the peripety an insignificant
> event rather than the point of highest dramatic tension,

the author is taking the focus away from human action. Had the pivot point of the peripety been at the scene where Esther approaches the king uninvited or where Esther confronts Haman, the king and/or Esther would have been spotlighted as the actual cause of the reversal. By separating the pivot point of the peripety in Esther from the point of highest dramatic tension, the characters of the story are not spotlighted as the cause of the reversal. This reinforces the message that no one in the story, not even the most powerful person in the empire, is in control of what is about to happen. An unseen power is controlling the reversal of destiny. The Greek translation makes this implicit truth explicit with the statement, "The Lord took sleep from the king that night" (LXX of 6:1, pers. trans.). (*Esther*, 158)

She goes on to say, "In spite of having all the power of the Persian empire at his disposal, Haman's carefully laid plans were turned against him simply because the king had a sleepless night" (ibid.). Haman never saw it coming, and neither did Esther or Mordecai. The only one who anticipated it was the one making sure it was happening.

What do you do when sleep escapes you? When I cannot sleep, I try different methods to produce drowsiness. Sometimes I will listen to music, hoping it will be a praise-fueled lullaby. One of my favorite albums to listen to is Chris Rice's *Peace like a River: The Hymns Project*. The only problem is that because I love those tunes, I begin singing the songs instead of sleeping to them. I have been told that drinking a glass of warm milk helps. But since (1) getting the milk would involve getting out of bed, (2) I do not like warm milk, and (3) I am lactose intolerant, I have never given that suggestion a go. My best secret to falling asleep is counting LSU's mascot Mike the Tiger's jumping over a fence. I do not believe I have ever shared that confession before. I am not sure when I switched from sheep jumping over a fence to tigers, but this technique works for me every time. I wish I was super spiritual and could tell you that every time I am awake, I pray until the Lord's peace calms my heart and mind (and there have been those moments), but the tigers are my default means to dozing.

We are not told how many methods Ahasuerus attempted in trying to go to sleep, but the one that is revealed is certainly a title contender. Ordering the biggest, most boring book to be read to you (monotonously would be a bonus) could cajole the best of us to rest. Frankly, the king seems a little old for a bedtime story, but God works in mysterious ways.

Consider the Providential Investigation
ESTHER 6:3

We are not told at what point the servant started reading in the book of records, but he eventually recounted an event we know all about that occurred five years earlier. What do you think the chances are of that just happening? I recently read about a man who was bitten by a shark, attacked by a bear, and bitten by a rattlesnake—all in less than a four-year period (and he is still alive and leaves his house daily). The odds of that combo occurring are 893.35 quadrillion to one (Leahy, "Man Bitten by Shark, Bear, and Snake"). The odds of Ahasuerus "just happening" to have the record of Mordecai's actions read to him have got to be close to that range. But when God is factored into an equation, all percentages change! There was a 100 percent certainty Ahasuerus would hear whatever God wanted him to hear.

When the memory of being saved from assassination was brought to Ahasuerus's mind, he was no longer sleepy but stirred. It is as if a lightbulb turned on in his brain about what a big moment that was. One reason he was able to be awake at all was because Mordecai had helped him stay alive. When further inquiry was done, Ahasuerus realized Mordecai had never been recognized for his service.

What is the longest you have gone between doing something significant and being recognized for it publicly? Maybe you cut your neighbor's grass, and she still has not thanked you. Maybe you have done carpool for a sports team all year long, but none of the other parents have expressed any gratitude. Sometimes people can even do something heroic like thwarting an ambush and saving a fellow soldier from being captured, like Sgt. Salvatore Giunta did in 2007, but not be recognized for their efforts until years later (Shaughnessy, "Medal of Honor"). After five years Mordecai probably had not forgotten that he was not rewarded for helping save the king's life, but likely he had not given up hope of being recognized either. God oversees not just eternal rewards but also earthly recompenses and recognitions. In his sovereignty God made sure what had been ignored previously was addressed on this particular night.

Consider the Providential Interruption
ESTHER 6:4-5

The author does not tell us how long the book of record was read, but at the exact moment Ahasuerus realized nothing had been done for Mordecai, Haman was walking in to ask permission to kill him. Talk about timing. Talk about divine timing. Had Haman slept at all that night? Had his eagerness fueled an early dawn arrival to the palace? Wouldn't it be interesting if the construction of Haman's gallows made enough racket that it contributed to Ahasuerus's inability to sleep? Regardless, Haman's eagerness can be used for examination of our lives. What do we pursue with anticipation and haste? Do we ever pursue God in this way? Are we ever guilty of being like Haman and eagerly and hastily pursuing the detriment of those who like us the least? Do we eagerly and hastily pursue sin? Unfortunately for Haman, his "plans [were] about to run head on into the providence of God" (Bush, *Ruth/ Esther*, 418).

Did Ahasuerus ask who was in the court because he heard the ding of his security system letting him know a door had been opened? Or was the king asking who was in the court because he needed counsel? Duguid argues, "For all his impulsiveness, the king is helpless without his advisors. He counts on them constantly to tell him what to do" (*Esther and Ruth*, 76). The only one mentioned as being in the outer court was Haman who, though he wanted to take a life, was not about to rush into the king's presence without permission and lose his.

First Haman was summoned, and then he was surprised. Have you ever had something you wanted to ask someone, only to find that their initial engagement with you in conversation is so unexpected that you never get around to why you approached them in the first place? Haman was determined, but then he got distracted, unsurprisingly, at the thought of being honored by all.

Consider the Providential Irony
ESTHER 6:6-11

Haman was so prideful that there was no room in his mind for anyone other than himself to be the object of Ahasuerus's honor. He was narcissistic and foolish. Jason Meyer warns,

As finite creatures, we cannot fully grasp God's infinite
revulsion against pride's rebellion. God hates pride. What
makes pride so singularly repulsive to God is the way that
pride "contends for supremacy" with God himself. Pride sets
itself in opposition to God. The only fitting response is for
God to oppose the proud (Jas 4:6; 1 Pet 5:5). That is probably
why pride is not simply another sin among many, but a sin in
a category of its own. Other sins lead the sinner further away
from God, but pride is particularly heinous in that it attempts to
elevate the sinner *above God*. ("Pride," 9; emphasis in original)

I hope we, in our relationship with the King of kings, are never
like Haman in thinking, *Of course he wants to honor me. I am really impor-*
tant. He needs me. I am great. First of all, the only indispensable one is
God. We are born, we serve for a time, and then we die. But "from
eternity to eternity" (Ps 90:2), he is God. Second, we certainly can't
earn honor from the Lord or assume he owes us. After all, Jesus says,
"When you have done all that you were commanded, you should say,
'We are worthless servants; we've only done our duty'" (Luke 17:10).
Third, we should always be amazed by God's goodness to us and not
desensitized to it. May we never stop asking, "God, why are you so
good to us when we are often so bad?" Meyer contends the antidote
for our pride is to think more on God: "The rivers of self-forgetfulness flow down from the Godward heights of worship. . . . He, and he
alone, is worthy of all worship and praise" (ibid., 18). There was no
self-forgetfulness in Haman, and he was convinced he was worthy to
be honored and praised.

Haman's reply regarding what should be done for the one the king
wanted to honor revealed that it was not the first time Haman had considered the topic. Like a child who has his list ready to give to Santa at
the local mall, Haman did not need to conduct any research before
giving his answer. In fact, it rolled right out of his mind and mouth. We
can certainly deduce what he lay awake at night thinking about! And his
thoughts of personal exaltation were grand: a horse wearing a crown!
His craving for honor and significance was such a drive and passion
in his life that everything else would immediately be set to the side for
it—even killing an enemy.

What or whom do you desire more than anything or anyone else?
What takes priority over everything and everyone in your life? What is
it that, given the opportunity, you'd drop everything to pursue? There

is only one pursuit worthy of such passion and priority, but, unfortunately, we are too often ensnared and enslaved by lesser pursuits to acknowledge him faithfully. Let me ask the question one more time but in a different way: For Haman, the desire for glory and honor was apparent, but if God were to completely turn you over to depraved pursuits, what would most likely ensnare and destroy you first? As we have noted, without God's grace we are all Haman seeking only what cannot satisfy and what is to our detriment. We should, then, see Haman in this text and be absolutely terrified and beg God to save us from ourselves. Ask him to empower your true and consistent repentance from whatever sin repeatedly entices you. May he empower you to confess it to someone else for accountability and to help you make no provision for it in your life.

As with every plan proposed thus far in the book of Esther, the one receiving a recommendation was pleased by it. Can you imagine laying out so many specific details to express something you desired so passionately, only to then be commanded not just to let the person you dislike the most on the entire planet fully experience what you have longed for, but to lead them through it? For those of us who are striving to love our neighbors *as* ourselves, maybe it is not totally startling. What we want for ourselves we should also want for others. But if we are of the tribe that buys name-brand treats for its own pantry but generic brands for the church VBS, then we are probably horrified at what is transpiring, and we need to do a lot of study on the word *as.* The only person in Susa, however, who could be more surprised than Haman would be Mordecai.

My wife once had someone call her cell phone and tell her she had won a particular sweepstakes. The caller said he was on his way to our home to deliver our new 2015 minivan. Everything sounded great, except for the fact that we were living in 2017. And of course, the caller wanted to deposit the prize money she'd won directly into our bank. All he needed was our account number. As I got on the phone and began to ask questions, I was transferred to a manager (meaning one person in on the scheme handed the phone to another person in on the scheme). He did his best to convince me of the legitimacy of our victory, but I knew it was a sham, and he knew I knew. Eventually, he hung up on me, and strangely, that 2015 minivan that was on its way to our home ("a pretty blue color, sir") never showed up. Mordecai's sweepstakes win, however, was no sham.

What do you think it was like for both men when Haman approached the King's Gate seeking Mordecai with horses and one of the king's robes? I'm guessing Mordecai probably felt like most people did when Zacchaeus or Saul knocked on their doors prior to their conversions. I would not blame him at all if he tried to slink away. Maybe, though, Haman was immediately clear that his intention was for Mordecai's good. However it transpired, both men likely felt the events seemed surreal. And I am sure Haman and Mordecai were not the only ones who were in disbelief over what was happening.

Try to picture what the crew at the King's Gate was thinking as they saw and heard Haman declare the king's delight in honoring Mordecai. What a transformation! Instead of sackcloth Mordecai was wearing royal robes. Instead of crying through the city, Mordecai was led through the city with Haman crying out for all to honor him.

Consider the Providential Insult
ESTHER 6:12-13

After the city-square honor tour, Mordecai returned to work, but Haman had a different reaction. Specifically, the author describes Haman's hurry, mourning, and destination. It had not been long since Haman made haste to petition the king for Mordecai's death, but after his bad morning, his haste was homeward. The one who caused so many Jews to grieve over their possible elimination was suddenly mourning over his humiliation and Mordecai's exaltation.

When we seek to be honored rather than being honorable or rather than giving honor to the Lord, then we should not be surprised when God grants us humility rather than honor. At some point we have to believe and live it out.

- James 4:6: "But he gives greater grace. Therefore he says: God resists the proud, but gives grace to the humble."
- James 4:10: "Humble yourselves before the Lord, and he will exalt you."
- Psalm 18:27: "For you rescue an oppressed people, but you humble those with haughty eyes."
- Psalm 25:9: "He leads the humble in what is right and teaches them his way."
- Psalm 149:4: "For the LORD takes pleasure in his people; he adorns the humble with salvation."

- Romans 12:10: "Love one another deeply as brothers and sisters. Outdo one another in showing honor."

Note that Paul does not say, "Outdo one another in *seeking* honor," but "Outdo one another in *showing* honor."

In seeking unmitigated personal honor, Haman found ultimate humiliation. And that was not the worst of his problems. To lose our station or position in life is one thing, but to lose our lives eternally is another. For Haman, then, things were about to get a lot worse. As Duguid notes, "Even Haman's friends are not so dense as to write off this day's events as mere coincidence. . . . Haman will now surely fall to destruction" (*Esther & Ruth*, 79). In a matter of hours, Haman's confidants have switched from advocating for Mordecai's doom to acknowledging Haman's. They may not be so foolish after all.

Consider the Providential Invitation
ESTHER 6:14

Do you think Haman forgot he had been invited to a second feast with Esther and Ahasuerus when he headed home in such a hurry? Do you think he hoped they'd forget? In any case there was not an opportunity to ponder the words of his wife and friends for long. While Haman had been proclaiming Mordecai's honor, Esther had been preparing food. There is no doubt his head was spinning at all that had taken place, and in light of the reversal, Duguid offers a helpful warning: "Our fall could be just as sudden and as inescapable as Haman's, taking us from our present comforts to face a holy God in an instant. Are we ready for such an encounter?" (ibid., 82).

My cousin Mike was buried yesterday in West Colombia, Texas. He had congestive heart failure one night, and we received the phone call the next morning informing us of his death. In Vietnam he earned two purple hearts and a bronze star. In his later years he helped coach and shepherd troubled teens. But as he was taken to eternity, none of those accomplishments merited eternal life. His faith in Christ, which I pray was real and genuine, is the one and only hope he had. The same could be said for all of us.

None of Haman's plans had involved honoring Mordecai, and he certainly did not plan on being hanged on the very gallows he constructed. Life comes at us fast, but eternity even faster. The problem for many in our world is that death is not something for which they are prepared or are preparing. What Haman was most concerned about was not, in reality, most important. He bought into the lie that many fall for in our day—that life is all about making our own names great and being honored. But as he most likely is well aware of at this moment, life is not about our gaining honor but our giving honor, especially to the one to whom highest honor is due. The world does not revolve around us, but it does revolve just as the Lord tells it to because he is the center of all things. We should join with the psalmist who beckons us to . . .

> Sing a new song to the LORD;
> let the whole earth sing to the LORD.
> Sing to the LORD, bless his name;
> proclaim his salvation from day to day.
> Declare his glory among the nations,
> his wondrous works among all peoples.
>
> For the LORD is great and is highly praised;
> he is feared above all gods.
> For all the gods of the peoples are idols,
> but the LORD made the heavens.
> Splendor and majesty are before him;
> strength and beauty are in his sanctuary.
>
> Ascribe to the LORD, you families of the peoples,
> ascribe to the LORD glory and strength.
> Ascribe to the LORD the glory of his name;
> bring an offering and enter his courts.
> Worship the LORD in the splendor of his holiness;
> let the whole earth tremble before him.
>
> Say among the nations: "The LORD reigns.
> The world is firmly established; it cannot be shaken.
> He judges the peoples fairly."
> Let the heavens be glad and the earth rejoice;
> let the sea and all that fills it resound.
> Let the fields and everything in them celebrate.
> Then all the trees of the forest will shout for joy
> before the LORD, for he is coming—
> for he is coming to judge the earth.
> He will judge the world with righteousness
> and the peoples with his faithfulness. (Ps 96)

Conclude that There Is Nothing like God's Providence and God's Peripety; None Is Worthier of Glorious and Glad Praise

God's Providence

Did you notice in 6:1-14 that the only mention of Esther was in regard to the second feast she prepared? Did you also notice that what Mordecai experienced was not the result of some grand plan he designed or something he was working to achieve? So, if Esther was not leading the charge and Mordecai was not calling for change, who was in control? You know the answer, don't you? Prime asserts, "When it seems God is not active, he may be most at work. He may be most present when he seems most hidden" (*Unspoken Lessons*, 103). God always has perfect timing. While Esther and Mordecai were sleeping, God was working. How many things does the Lord do for us while we rest at night? Probably the same amount of things he does for us when we are awake but unaware. Esther 6 is such a great reminder that he is God and we are not. Jobes notes,

> Our God is so great, so powerful, that he can work without miracles through the ordinary events of billions of human lives through millennia of time to accomplish his eternal purposes and ancient promises. God delivered an entire race of people in Persia because the king had a sleepless night, because a man would not bow to his superior, because a woman found herself taken to the bedroom of a ruthless man for a night of pleasure. How inscrutable are the ways of the Lord! (*Esther*, 159)

God's Peripety

For those of us who grew up going to youth camps in the late nineties or working in them soon after, there is probably a good chance we have either performed or seen "The Champion" skit set to Carmen's song no less than a thousand times. I exaggerate, but only slightly. For years this skit was a staple option for youth groups hoping to be in the weekly camp variety show or who needed a dramatic presentation in the yearly Youth Night Service at a local church. Despite its overuse my favorite part of the song/skit never fails to move me each time I hear or see it. At what seems to be an incredible moment of defeat for Christ, his body is laid in a tomb. At this point a countdown is initiated beginning with the number ten. As the countdown decreases toward zero, the audience hears the panicked questions and anxiety from a voice representing Satan. His "victory" is short-lived as Christ triumphantly rises from death and renders it defeated. All this is marked in the song/skit with crescendo and celebration (and for those churches with fancy budgets, even special lighting).

Of course, the best we have to offer in way of portraying this monumental event in the history of the world and redemption pales in comparison to the actual resurrection of Christ. What a breathtaking moment indeed! All hope seemed lost. Satan, no doubt, was convinced that though he had failed to wipe out the messianic line, he had done something even greater and taken out the Messiah. Little did he know or understand that all of his schemes were simply accomplishing God's providential plan to save a people for his own name's sake. There is no greater reversal. Both Satan's and death's celebrations quickly turned to eternal defeat as Christ our Victor crushed the grave and rose victoriously. The irony is palpitating.

In Susa, as at the cross, the whole time Satan is carrying out the plans he believes will guarantee his dominion, he is ultimately contributing to his own destruction. Nothing went as Satan's minion Haman planned it or thought it would turn out but exactly as the Lord planned all along.

God's Praise

In Richie Duchon's article about an embarrassing pageant incident, he says, "I have to apologize. Those are the words Miss Universe host Steve Harvey was forced to utter—and may regret for years to come—after mistakenly crowning Miss Colombia . . . as the winner" of the Miss Universe pageant in 2015 ("Host Steve Harvey Botches"). Not unlike what would occur at the Oscars two years later, the wrong person was announced as the winner. Unlike Beatty and Dunaway, though, Harvey had left the stage and had to come back out to right the wrong. Also, unlike Beatty and Dunaway, Harvey had the right card but did not read the right name. To his credit, he owned up to his mistake. But that did not make it any less awkward when the crown was taken off of the head of Miss Colombia and put on that of Miss Philippines.

As we consider all the reversals in the book of Esther, I want to end this particular discussion by assuring you that Christ's crown will never be removed and his victory will never be reversed. Paul writes to the church at Corinth,

> Then comes the end, when he hands over the kingdom to God the Father, when he abolishes all rule and all authority and power. For he must reign until he puts all his enemies under his feet. The last enemy to be abolished is death. For God has put everything under his feet. Now when it says "everything" is put under him, it is obvious that he who puts everything under him is the exception. When everything is subject to Christ, then the Son himself will also be subject to the one who subjected everything to him, so that God may be all in all. (1 Cor 15:24-28)

Jesus reigns over all rule, all authority, and all power. He will one day abolish death forever. The only reversal coming is when sin's curse and the effects of the,fall are forever removed and the new heaven and new earth are revealed. All of this will be done so that God may be all in all. When every knee bows and every tongue confesses that Jesus is Lord, it will be "to the glory of God the Father" (Phil 2:11).

Because Christ is our Victor forever, we can know as well that his promises to us will never be reversed. As Jesus told a crowd one day in the temple,

> My sheep hear my voice, I know them, and they follow me. I give them eternal life, and they will never perish. No one will snatch them out of my hand. My Father, who has given them to me, is greater than all. No one is able to snatch them out of the Father's hand. I and the Father are one. (John 10:27-30)

As Jesus once told an anxious father, "Don't be afraid. Only believe" (Mark 5:36). Even when you cannot see him, hear him, or feel him, God is alive, awake, and accomplishing his purposes for your good and his glory.

Reflect and Discuss

1. Why is Esther 6 more about what God is doing than what Esther and Mordecai are doing? What can we learn or be reminded of about God from studying the chapter?
2. Why do we tend to doubt the Lord's perfect timing? Describe a time when you doubted the Lord's right timing only to be proven wrong.

3. How can we wait on the Lord joyfully rather than anxiously or angrily?

4. What are you currently pursuing with eagerness and haste? Would you say your life is more characterized by the pursuit of sin or a pursuit of Christ? Explain.

5. Have you, like Haman, ever eagerly and hastily pursued the detriment of someone else? How can the gospel help you keep this from occurring in the future?

6. Haman's desire for glory and honor is apparent. If God were to completely turn you over to depraved pursuits, what would ensnare and destroy you? What do you long for more than anything else?

7. We are often warned in the Bible to humble ourselves before the Lord, so why don't we consistently heed these exhortations? Why should we humble ourselves before the Lord?

8. Haman's fall happened so quickly in the text. Why should we remind ourselves often that in the blink of an eye we can be ushered into eternity and stand before the holy God?

9. Make a list of those you know who are not yet prepared to stand in the Lord's presence and give an account. How will you share the gospel with each of those people this week?

10. There is no one the Father wants to honor more than the Son. Why should we be just as eager to offer honor to Christ rather than seeking it for ourselves?

When What Was Concealed Is Revealed

ESTHER 7

Main Idea: May we be like Esther, confronting sin and calling for justice, rather than like Haman, who continued in sin and got caught in the consequences.

I.   **Esther's Revelation and Her Courageous Confrontation (7:1-6)**
    A.   In her confrontation she displayed great courage (7:1-2).
    B.   In her communication she used great cunning (7:3-4).
    C.   In her comparison she counted the cost (7:5-6).

II. **Ahasuerus's Realization and His Confusion (7:5,7-8)**
    A.   He was still easily swayed by others (7:5).
    B.   He was baffled by the betrayal (7:7).
    C.   He was perplexed about the punishment (7:8).

III. **Haman's Ruin and the Consequences (7:6-10)**
    A.   He was surprised by the consequences of sin (7:6).
    B.   We too want to avoid the consequences rather than offer a confession (7:7-8).
    C.   As he planned to do to another, it was done to him (7:9-10).

IV. **What Can We Learn from This Passage?**
    A.   Risk much for the gospel.
    B.   Confront evil rather than cooperating with it.
    C.   Identify with and intercede for God's people.
    D.   Live so that when what is concealed is revealed, it will be for your reward and not ruin.
    E.   Speak and work only for the good of others.

V.   **What Can We Learn about God from This Passage?**
    A.   God needs no counselors, and he always does what is right.
    B.   God will defeat all his enemies.
    C.   God's wrath has been satisfied in Christ.

Poor Wile E. Coyote. In so many Saturday mornings of cartoon watching, I witnessed his incessant and insane attempts to capture or kill the Roadrunner. He, however, was never able to dine on what he desired. Unbeknown to him, Wile E. would never be allowed to achieve his aim.

The cartoon's creator, Chuck Jones, had a list of nine rules to be applied to every episode. Among those rules were these: (1) The Roadrunner cannot harm the coyote except by going "beep-beep!" (And who did not go around the rest of the day making this sound to the annoyance of his or her parents?) (2) No outside force can harm the coyote—only his own ineptitude or the failure of the Acme products. (3) The coyote could stop anytime—if he were not a fanatic. (4) The coyote is always more humiliated than harmed by his failures ("The 9 Rules").

I find the similarities between Wile E. Coyote and Haman amazing. Since Mordecai only refused to bow to him, he posed no physical threat to Haman. But to Haman, Mordecai's refusal to honor him was like the Roadrunner's piercing "beep-beep" in Wile E.'s ears. Another similarity is that no outside force caused Haman more harm than himself. We are given no evidence that God was forcing Haman to act in the ways he did. Though, of course, the possibility exists that God delivered Haman "over to a corrupt mind so that" he did what was not right (Rom 1:28), the author does not tell us this. Haman was most responsible for his actions and their consequences. A third similarity is that neither Wile E. Coyote nor Haman chose to stop pursuing what they lacked. Day after day, Haman chose the temptations of pride and anger, ultimately to his own peril, which leads us to one difference between the coyote and the creep. In the cartoon Wile E. Coyote was more humiliated than harmed, but in Haman's case he would be humiliated and then hanged. The trap he had constructed for Mordecai was sprung on him. Apparently, art and life really do imitate each other.

Just as Wile E. Coyote could never eliminate the Roadrunner, God would never allow Haman (or anyone else) to eradicate his people. As Duguid notes,

> It was possible to be certain all along that Haman would never ultimately triumph, not because we have confidence in the greater cunning of Esther, but because we have confidence in God's covenant promise to Abraham and his seed. (*Esther and Ruth*, 92–93)

We only panic, in fact, when we forget God's promises, presence, and power. When the world around us seems to rage and evil seems triumphant, we need reminders like Esther 7:1-10 that in the end the wicked will not win. Even one of Israel's worship leaders had a crisis of faith and had to be reminded of this:

Indeed, you put them in slippery places;
you make them fall into ruin.
How suddenly they become a desolation!
They come to an end, swept away by terrors.
Like one waking from a dream,
Lord, when arising, you will despise their image.
. . .
Those far from you will certainly perish;
you destroy all who are unfaithful to you. (Ps 73:18-20,27)

Moses once asked the Israelites, "Who is on the Lord's side?" and all the sons of Levi gathered around him (Exod 32:26 KJV). Esther 7:1-10 is a great exhortation not to be on the side of the wicked, for their doom is as certain as gravity's constant victory over Wile E. Coyote.

In one twenty-four-hour period, Haman was feasting with the king and queen, bragging about his wealth and his sons and his power, and making plans to get rid of the one source of constant frustration in his life. Then, without warning, he was honoring the one from whom he wanted honor and his life was taken on the very device he hoped would kill Mordecai. What a turnaround. Haman had no idea when he was taken to the second feast that he would only return home to be hanged. Prime notes,

> Every day is like a fresh blank sheet of paper given us by God, and we can never tell what wonderful surprises he may choose to write upon it. So much can happen in just a few hours. Our lives may proceed at an ordinary pace, with nothing of great importance appearing to happen. Then, suddenly, without warning, dramatic and amazing events may crowd into the space of a single day. . . . On any particular day remarkable developments and answers to our prayers may take place as God chooses to unfold his will, and demonstrate his care. On any day God may be at work in ways that we are not in a position to perceive. He weaves into the pattern of his will the actions of all his creatures, whether wise or foolish. (*Unspoken Lessons*, 107–8)

With each day given to us, may we live for the Lord and, like Esther, confront sin and call for justice rather than being like Haman, continuing in sin until caught in its consequences.

Esther's Revelation and Her Courageous Confrontation
ESTHER 7:1-6

The moment of truth finally arrived (again, but for real this time). Esther would identify with and intercede for her people. We thought she was going to intercede on behalf of the Jews in the throne room or at the first feast, but instead she invited the king and Haman to this second feast. Of course, the Lord did some things during the night for which Esther had not planned and of which she may have been unaware. Regardless, Mordecai's one-man parade had not eliminated the Jews' problem. It was good for him to receive recognition, but God's people still needed to be released from the death edict. At the second feast Esther's fortitude was revealed as she confronted her enemy.

In Her Confrontation She Displayed Great Courage (7:1-2)

God never calls us to be courageous as an end in itself. Courage is always for believing or doing something for his kingdom. God is not asking any of us to walk around feeling courageous and fierce in ourselves but to take courage in him so that we may serve his purposes.

As a side note, I always need courage during confrontation, especially when I am confronting snakes. Two confessions: I hate snakes, and I am afraid of them. I always walk around "snake aware," scanning our yard and scanning piles of sticks and leaves. I am not sure when my apprehension started regarding these legless evils, but I have had it since my childhood of taking canoe trips with my family and seeing water moccasins sunning on logs. Earlier this week I decided to mow our grass. When I got to the end of the stone path that leads to our backyard, I stopped to get everything set for the mower. In the next second, however, I became very snake aware. Just off to my right was a big black snake. In the next moments my thought pattern went something like this:

- That's a snake.
- That's a really big snake.
- Is it poisonous? Look at its head.
- Does it really matter?
- Is there a chance it could bite the kids or our dogs?
- OK. I'm going to kill it.
- How am I going to kill it?
- I've got the push mower.

- Is using it on the snake going to turn out well?
- Do it—do it—your kids are counting on you.
- Go fast.

Next I turned the push mower, aimed, and went for it. I did not want to step too close to the creature so, as I maxed out my reach, the mower kind of came up a little and half the snake went flying off to the side. I pulled the mower back and then ran over that piece and then ran over all the grass around there in case I missed and the snake was on the run. I probably looked like I was doing the old dance move "The Cabbage Patch" but with a lawn mower.

This is where I should also say I had the bag connected to my mower; therefore, all I could think of in the next moments was that when I disconnected the bag, the snake's head would be waiting for me right at the top. I decided to delay dealing with it and cut the grass around there until the bag could not hold any more. Later, as I lifted the cover to unhook the bag, I was certain the snake was going to leap either out of the bag or out of the chute and get me. I prayed and asked God for courage and went for it. And when I did, there was no sign of the snake anywhere. I dumped the grass and reconnected the bag and continued to mow.

It wasn't long before I noticed, however, that no grass was going into the bag, which meant something was clogging the chute. So, I stopped the mower, slowly unhooked the bag, grabbed a stick, and started pulling what was in the chute toward the bag. And you won't believe what happened. Out shot the snake, striking at me! Thankfully, I knew what is recorded in Mark 16:18, so I knew I would be OK! Just kidding. The snake did come out of the chute but in pieces, for he had been vanquished.

I share this long story because I do not want you to miss that I am afraid of snakes, but in the moment of decision my sense of responsibility fueled my actions to take on the snake. There was something to be courageous for (my family, our pets), which fueled me in overcoming my fear. Above all, the Lord granted my prayer request and gave me courage. He can do that in whatever confrontation we face in which courage is required.

Speaking of snakes, Esther had her own to deal with, and her courage would be a means to an important end.

The real hero of the book of Esther is God, but that does not take away from Esther's role in the deliverance of her people. The second feast would mark the second time Esther risked her life. The first was entering the king's presence unsummoned (5:1). This later event would involve identifying with her people who had been sold to destruction, death, and extermination (7:4). Risking one's life requires courage (and selflessness). Esther also demonstrated courage not just by being around Haman but in calling him out to his face.

Did you know that with one exception every time the phrase "have courage" is used in the New Testament it is said by Jesus? In Matthew 9:2 he told a paralytic to have courage because his sins were forgiven. In Matthew 9:22 Jesus told a suffering woman, who had touched the hem of his garment, to have courage because her faith had made her well. In Matthew 14:27 he told his disciples in the boat to have courage because it was him walking on the water next to them. And in Acts 23:11 Jesus told Paul to have courage as he testified for the sake of the gospel in Rome. As Steven Cole notes, "We could sum up these instances by saying that we can be encouraged by our Lord's pardon (Matt. 9:2); His power (Matt. 9:22); His presence (Matt. 14:27); and His purpose (Acts 23:11)" ("Overcoming Spiritual Failure"). Courage is always fueled by something and for something. Esther's courage was fueled by her fasting (and faith) and for her people's freedom.

In Her Communication She Used Great Cunning (7:3-4)

As has been demonstrated numerous times in the history of the world, it is not just what we say that is important but how we say it. One famous example is Abraham Lincoln's Gettysburg Address. Utilizing 272 words and the length of three minutes, President Lincoln shared a message the world has not forgotten. The speech is remembered both for its content and for how its message was communicated. Another example is President Franklin D. Roosevelt's speech, which was delivered the day after Pearl Harbor was attacked. He began by saying, "Yesterday, December 7, 1941—a date which will live in infamy" ("A Date Which Will Live in Infamy"). He could have chosen to say, "We will never forget what happened yesterday," but probably no one would have remembered his speech. What is significant about Esther's conversation with Ahasuerus is not just its substance but also its style.

With her request Esther was not presumptuous, but she was personal. She never took the king's favor for granted or expected it to be guaranteed. She carefully petitioned for his grace. At the same time, she transitioned slightly from more formal to more familiar phraseology as she hoped to find favor in Ahasuerus's eyes specifically. After the preliminaries she finally revealed what she desired. She wanted to live and wanted life for her people as well. She used the exact wording from the edict: "destruction, death, and extermination" (7:4). The phrase, though, rang no bell with Ahasuerus—he had to ask Esther who was behind the threat against her. Whether what she was talking about registered with Haman at that exact moment is unknown, but how could it not, since he had so carefully drafted the decree of doom? Just when he thought things could not get worse than having to honor Mordecai, Haman was about to learn he was wrong about a lot.

Esther continued her request, carefully avoiding placing any blame on the king for the situation in which she and her people found themselves. Though Ahasuerus was responsible too, Esther knew Haman was the real culprit. If she had come in with communication guns blazing with blame, Ahasuerus would have immediately been defensive and may have denied her the opportunity to continue her request. After all, we tend to listen more when we think others are at fault than when we ourselves are accused.

In another strategic move, Esther noted she would not have burdened the king with the matter if her people had merely been sold to slavery. Her words express her acknowledgment that the king's time was valuable and her problem was not with suffering but with genocide. She masterfully framed her argument so that the king saw that what was threatened against Esther and her people would ultimately be detrimental to him. She communicated to Ahasuerus in a way that would bring him to a place similar to that in which David found himself during Nathan's visit (2 Sam 12:1-7): a place where he was moved to action and would seek to do the right thing before realizing the wrong he himself had committed. Duguid notes, "Esther's intricate plan was a necessary part of the process of bringing Haman to justice, a plan that required a combination of subtlety, boldness, and strength to carry it through" (*Esther and Ruth*, 91). One can be shrewd without being sinful, and Esther carefully walked that line.

In Her Comparison She Counted the Cost (7:5-6)

The author of Ecclesiastes contends there is "a time to be silent and a time to speak" (Eccl 3:7). At this point Esther was all in. For her (and her people), it was time for specificity rather than beating around the bush. The king listened to her situation and was sympathetic to her cause; he just needed to know on whom to exert his wrath. Finally, the moment of truth arrived. Esther called out Haman directly.

As I write this chapter, the #metoo movement is gaining a lot of traction in our culture. Those participating in the effort are seeking to take a stand against sexual harassment and assault. Survivors are finally bringing their pain to light and seeking to hold those who wronged them accountable. Opportunities are being given in court for those who have been wounded to confront and pursue the conviction of those who sought to take advantage of them. Like Esther they are getting to address their transgressors to their faces.

One of the most publicized examples of this involves a former USA gymnastics team doctor. Rachael Denhollander was the first to publicly make allegations against Larry Nassar. She and more than 150 other survivors of his abuse were given the opportunity to share impact statements in court. Denhollander not only used the opportunity to pursue justice but also to present the gospel. She courageously recounted to the court how, when she was fifteen, Nassar sexually assaulted her . . .

> under the guise of medical treatment for nearly a year, [and how] Larry's the most dangerous type of abuser. One who is capable of manipulating his victims through coldly calculated grooming methodologies, presenting the most wholesome, caring external persona as a deliberate means to insure a steady stream of children to assault. (Denhollander, "Read Rachael Denhollander's Full Victim Impact Statement about Larry Nassar")

With both conviction and compassion, Rachael would go on to speak these words directly to Nassar:

> Should you ever reach the point of truly facing what you have done, the guilt will be crushing. And that is what makes the gospel of Christ so sweet. Because it extends grace and hope and mercy where none should be found. And it will be there for you. I pray you experience the soul crushing weight of guilt so you may someday experience true repentance and true forgiveness from God, which you need far more than forgiveness from me—though I extend that to you as well. (Ibid.)

Confrontation is never easy, especially when the one we are facing has harmed us or, as in Esther's case, threatens our harm. I am thankful Denhollander chose to pursue both Nassar's conviction and his conversion. The courage it took to do so was tremendous. No less courage was needed when Esther broke her silence about Haman. She had no idea what the outcome would be, but she was obedient to seize the opportunity.

Ahasuerus's Realization and His Confusion
ESTHER 7:5,7-8

He Was Still Easily Swayed by Others (7:5)

Few of Ahasuerus's decisions presented in this book come without someone counseling him toward a specific action. He was convinced by others to banish Vashti, to gather virgins and find a new queen, and to help issue an edict that called for the annihilation of the Jews everywhere in his empire. Esther's opportunity to present her request is one more attempt to persuade the king to act. And again the author portrays Ahasuerus as tossed about by the whims of whoever has his attention.

One of the reasons God gave apostles, prophets, evangelists, pastors, and teachers to his church is to equip the saints, through his Spirit and Word, for ministry and maturity (Eph 4:11-13). When believers are equipped in the gospel, Paul contends they "will no longer be little children, tossed by the waves and blown around by every wind of teaching, by human cunning with cleverness in the techniques of deceit" (Eph 4:14). Ahasuerus was easily swayed by others because he lacked discernment and often lacked a desire for details. For those entrusted to our care, however, we must continually proclaim Christ, "warning and teaching everyone with all wisdom, so that we may present everyone mature in Christ" (Col 1:28). Thankfully the Lord provides his strength for this task (Col 1:29). Nothing is better for God's people than God's Word, and nothing will better protect them from being manipulated by the whims of the world more than their maturing in Christ.

He Was Baffled by the Betrayal (7:7)

Being betrayed by those we have trusted can be deeply wounding and confusing. My wife and I have experienced it in ministry, and I know firsthand that it can tempt you to be jaded and make you hesitant to trust anyone again. Prior to the revelation from Esther, Ahasuerus had trusted Haman. He even gave Haman his signet ring to put his stamp of approval on whatever Haman thought was best (3:10-11). As readers we have been aware for some time that this was a foolish and regrettable action: Haman was not acting in the best interests of the king but in accordance with his own desires for honor and vengeance. Nevertheless, Ahasuerus considered Haman a trusted deputy. And of all the names Ahasuerus might have expected Esther to mention, it is doubtful Haman's was on that list.

Gregory proposes one theory regarding why Ahasuerus was so confused and would have been enraged at Haman's betrayal. He contends that because the Hebrew word for "destroy" is a homophone for "enslave" that

> Haman solicited the king's permission to kill the Jews, but did
> so with an ambiguous word, such that when he followed the
> request with a payment of money, the king would naturally but
> mistakenly think that Haman was requesting merely to enslave
> a group of people. (*Inconspicuous Providence*, 132)

If this is indeed what happened, then at least the king was not guilty of genocide. Enslaving an entire ethnic group, though, is only slightly less repulsive than murdering them.

When I worked in the chancellor's office at LSU as a student, I saw firsthand how one man's actions could lead to the downfall of another. David "Sonny" DeVillier was an assistant to William "Bud" Davis, who was chancellor when I started at LSU. Through an audit it was brought to light that DeVillier had given white students 49 of 54 scholarships intended to help minority students. Chancellor Davis was never accused of wrongdoing in the matter, but he still resigned because of the scandal. As a student majoring in management, I learned a lot from that experience about leadership, responsibility, trust, and consequences. Ahasuerus was apparently learning as well.

He Was Perplexed about the Punishment (7:8)

Why did the king storm out of the room and head toward the garden? Perhaps he was processing everything he'd learned at Esther's second feast. When he offered to grant her request, he had no idea her life was in danger and that his closest counselor was to blame. Maybe there was no mistake with Hebrew homophones, and he had known that Haman wanted to annihilate an entire people group. If so, how could he punish Haman for something he'd signed off on? And how would he save face when the palace press crew caught wind of such a scandal? Ordinarily, at just this point he would ask Haman or another advisor what he should do.

We do not know why he went outside—about that we can only speculate—but what is clear is what happened when he reentered the room. When the king saw Haman falling on Esther's couch, he knew just what to do. If he thought Haman was begging for his life, then he did not reveal it. Perhaps Ahasuerus really believed Haman had decided to enact his plans against Esther, even in the palace. Regardless, the king saw what he wanted (or needed) to see when Haman was on the couch with Esther, and it provided just the excuse he needed to have Haman killed.

Haman's Ruin and the Consequences
ESTHER 7:6-10

He Was Surprised by the Consequences of Sin (7:6)

If Esther's use of the words "destruction, death, and extermination" were the dawn of concern for Haman, then Esther's naming him specifically would have been high noon. As surprised as Ahasuerus was about everything, Haman was certainly no less surprised. He had no idea Esther was a Jew. Sin often has surprising and unintended consequences. Would he have pursued the edict had he known of the queen's ethnicity? He was so self-absorbed that perhaps he would have, and conceivably he would have devised an assassination attempt on her life. Regardless, his pursuit of self-honor would be his undoing in the end. Like good ol' Wile E. Coyote, he was undone by his own fanaticism.

Sin never lets you know that it is leading you into a life-ending trap. Scripture, however, never ceases to sound the alarm. The father in Proverbs 5 informs his son, "A wicked man's iniquities will trap him; he will become tangled in the ropes of his own sin. He will die because there is no discipline, and be lost because of his great stupidity" (Prov 5:22-23). Haman was definitely tangled in the ropes of his own sin and was lost because of his stupidity! In Proverbs 6 the father asks, "Can a man embrace fire and his clothes not be burned? Can a man walk on burning coals without scorching his feet?" (Prov 6:27-28). The obvious answer to both questions is no.

Sin compels us to think only of ourselves and what we want, while sanctification compels us to think of others and what they need. As I have mentioned, we know it is "my sin but our consequences," but sometimes we have no idea how far reaching the "our" is in consequences. With my sin, for example, it is not just my family and immediate faith family that are impacted. Repercussions for it spill onto countless others who hear of my sin, both Christians and non-Christians alike. And the reality is that I may never know the full extent of what burdens others have borne because I chose sin. I may never know of the tears they shed, the questions they fielded, or other sacrifices made because I chose disobedience. Let us always remember that sin never leads anywhere good, beneficial, or holy. If we are to be surprised, let it be from the multiplied blessings of obedience rather than the multiplied burdens of disobedience. Haman was definitely experiencing the multiplied burdens of sin.

We Too Want to Avoid the Consequences Rather Than Offering a Confession (7:7-8)

I am not sure what I did to initiate the scene, but I can remember my mother dragging me out of one morning service at the church we attended when I was a child. As loudly as I could, I pleaded for my life and begged everyone near us to help me! Fortunately for my mother, we only sat four pews away from the back door. That's usually prime real estate for most Sunday morning gatherings, but as packed as the pews were that day, no help for me arose. I am sure the people who sat above us in the balcony wondered what in the world was going on below since they could hear the chaos but not see it. To his credit our pastor kept preaching.

Once confronted about his actions, Haman was terrified and in full-on survival mode (and I know all about that). He should have followed the king out of the room, but he already knew that would be useless. While he shouldn't have gotten so close to the queen (no one was allowed to be within a few steps of her), he was out of control and taking a risk—a risk that ultimately cost him his life.

Here's some wisdom for you: (1) We experience the consequences of sin because we get caught in sin. (2) We get caught in sin because we do not confess our sin. (3) We do not confess our sin because we think we can conceal our sin. (4) We conceal our sin because we do not want to confess our struggle to someone who cares for us. For some reason we always want people to think we are better than we really are, but in fact we are worse than they could ever think. Amazingly, God knows our absolute worst and still loves us and has atoned for our sins. So we are free to confess our struggles because our identity is not found in what anyone thinks of us but in what God says about us in Christ. So confess your struggles to someone who loves Jesus and you so you will not try to conceal something you will eventually get caught in anyway. Then you would end up having to confess and deal with the escalating consequences. Haman was caught and deeply concerned about the consequences speeding his way.

I see several ironies in what happened in the room after Ahasuerus stormed out. First, Haman was pleading for mercy, though he had been unwilling to extend any. Apparently he agreed that lives matter when his own was on the line. In all of his revealed thoughts and conversations about Mordecai, not a single syllable was shaded with mercy. Second, Haman was requesting help, but there was no evidence he was repenting. Regret for being caught is not the same as repenting from sin. You can know that you only regret sin (or maybe just getting caught in it) when you often repeat that sin. Repenting from a sin means doing all you can in the Lord's power not to return to it, and it means removing from your life anything that pushes you toward that sin rather than toward obedience. Third, he ultimately fell on one Jew (Esther) because another Jew (Mordecai) would not fall before him. His counselors' words to him thus proved to be prophetic. (6:13). If only they'd had such helpful foresight a little sooner!

As He Planned to Do to Another, It Was Done to Him (7:9-10)

Haman was hanged on the gallows he had constructed for Mordecai. This could have been a large stake that he was impaled by or a device he was suspended on. Either way, what he devised led to his own demise. Duguid notes,

> Haman's life was built around the pursuit of power and achievement, and he achieved both to the full extent that this was possible within the bounds of the empire. He had reached the top of his career path. No one apart from the emperor himself matched Haman's glory and status. Yet all that he had gained disappeared completely in the space of a few minutes, along with his life itself. At the end of his life, what did he have to show for all his striving after wealth and recognition? (*Esther and Ruth*, 95)

When the queen of England passes away, her nation will see that everything that happens thereafter has been planned down to the minutest detail. The communication provided to those in her circle will be that "London Bridge has fallen" (Wallace, "This Is the Plan"). The mourning process has already been prescribed, covering everything from colors to candles. I am not hoping this occurs anytime soon, but it will be something to see. Just a short time ago, at former First Lady Barbara Bush's funeral, hundreds of the Corps of Cadets at Texas A&M University lined the road. They stood at attention and saluted as the vehicle carrying her casket passed in front of them on its way to her final resting place near her husband's presidential library. There was, however, no fanfare for Haman at the end of his life in spite of his craving for it. There was no hero's send-off, no national mourning. When he'd boasted about being the only guest with the king and queen at the feasts, he certainly hadn't seen his own demise coming.

What Can We Learn from This Passage?

Risk Much for the Gospel

As we have noted, Esther courageously put her life on the line twice. Esther 6 is evidence that God can accomplish his plans without us, but chapters 5 and 7 are evidence that he chooses not to. God has placed us where we are for his purposes and not just for our worldly progress. Not a single risk of sin is worth what sin costs, but responding to and sharing the gospel are worth risking our all.

As you consider your life right now, what risks are you taking for the sake of the gospel? What actions are you taking because Jesus is your greatest treasure? Is there anything about your life that causes others to ask questions to which the only answer is Jesus?

What about gospel goals? Do you have any? Is there something you are praying God allows you to accomplish before coming to the end of your journey? Paul was always willing to endure and risk much for the sake of the gospel. He told the elders from Ephesus, "I consider my life of no value to myself; my purpose is to finish my course and the ministry I received from the Lord Jesus, to testify to the gospel of God's grace" (Acts 20:24). And ever planning, praying, and hoping, he told the church at Rome, "So when I have finished this and safely delivered the funds to them, I will visit you on the way to Spain" (Rom 15:28). Esther too risked her life for the sake of others. Jesus is worthy of whatever following him costs.

Confront Evil Rather Than Cooperating with It

Esther could have remained silent, but the problem for her people would not go away. Sin that is not confronted usually escalates rather than dissipates. The multiplication of sin, in fact, was one of Paul's concerns in 1 Corinthians 5. First of all, he could not believe that a brother was involved in blatant sin—the kind that not even the pagans put up with—and no one in the church was confronting him. He thus asked the congregation, "Don't you know that a little leaven leavens the whole batch of dough?" (1 Cor 5:6). In the strongest of terms, Paul then advocated for the church to be the church and exercise care for the sinning brother's soul.

Are you currently ignoring sin in someone's life? Are you ignoring sin in your life? We do not want to be better at dealing with the sins of others than we are at dealing with our own.

Are there injustices in your town about which you remain silent? Prime suggests, "Perhaps today may be a day for action. There may be key initiatives or actions we are to take today for the good of others, and for God's praise" (*Unspoken Lessons*, 115). We tend not to confront that with which we are comfortable. We also tend not to confront others if we lack courage or conviction. May the Lord grant us both.

Identify with and Intercede for God's People

In my senior year of college, I was the president of the Rotaract club, which is the college version of Rotary International. When I initially joined the club, I was interviewed by a former governor of Louisiana (not all of them are in prison). He asked where I saw myself in five years. I responded, "Hopefully, living in the center of God's will." Somehow, they still let me in, and I eventually was elected president.

At the beginning of each meeting, offering a prayer was customary. Often I would be the only one willing to do so. Without fail I would close each prayer in the name of Christ. After one meeting some of the members said they did not mind the prayers, but I should not mention Jesus because not everyone believed the same as I did. I responded by telling them that I saw everything the Lord entrusted to me as a stewardship and that one day I would give an account for my time as president of that organization. I then told them they were welcome to impeach me, but as long as I was president, we would be praying in Christ's name. If there were any lingering issues about the topic, I never heard of them.

Who in our spheres of influence have no clue that we are Christ followers? Is there anyone from whom we are hiding aspects of our Christianity intentionally? How long had Esther and Mordecai concealed their ethnicity? If it were not for the decree, would Mordecai have encouraged Esther to keep her identity as one of God's chosen people hidden the rest of her days?

If we deny Christ in front of others, he will deny us in front of his Father (Matt 10:33). Let us, then, stand and be counted among those who name Jesus as Lord. I hope if someone is taking a bold stand for Christ, we will never shrink back from and be embarrassed by them. May we instead strive to see how we can support them. Who knows how God may use your boldness to encourage other brothers and sisters in Christ?

Live so that When What Is Concealed Is Revealed, It Will Be for Your Reward and Not Ruin

Three weeks ago I received a text on a Saturday night from a friend in ministry who said his lead pastor had just been removed for sexual sin and their church would find out the next morning. He asked me to pray for him as a pastoral staff member and for their church. Two weeks ago on a Sunday morning, the largest congregation in my denomination found out its pastor had been removed from his position because of alcohol abuse. Last week I learned through social media that one of my pastor friends had been removed from his church because of confessing to some sexual sin he had hidden for many years, throughout the length of his marriage.

Hiding sin is exhausting physically, spiritually, mentally, and emotionally. Let David tell you about it: "When I kept silent, my bones became brittle from my groaning all day long. For day and night your hand was heavy on me; my strength was drained as in the summer's heat" (Ps 32:3-4). But if we like to keep our flaws hidden from one another, how much more do we desire to cover our failings?

One day we will be exposed for who we really are. The author of Ecclesiastes warns, "God will bring every act to judgment, including every hidden thing, whether good or evil" (Eccl 12:14). That is why Paul warns,

> So don't judge anything prematurely, before the Lord comes, who will both bring to light what is hidden in darkness and reveal the intentions of the hearts. And then praise will come to each one from God. (1 Cor 4:5)

Prime warns, "There may be evil schemes that God is going to bring out into the open today. Let us so live that we may have nothing secret of which to be ashamed" (*Unspoken Lessons*, 115). I hope we are living so that we will receive the Lord's commendation rather than his correction.

Haman would have never gotten so close to Esther had the king been in the room. He would have never acted the way he did if the king were present. Let us always remember our King is in the room. Let us also remember that our King not only expects our obedience but empowers it by his grace! The days God grants us will never be repeated. Let us waste none of them. Let us live each day for God's glory.

Speak and Work Only for the Good of Others

In almost every prayer time our elders have at Trace Crossing and in almost every service, we pray for the good of our sister churches in our city. We often specifically mention their pastors and congregations by name. No matter how they may treat us, we want to work, speak, pray, and serve for their good. I am thankful to share that the cooperative spirit for the sake of the gospel among many churches in our city has never been as evident as it is now. I believe the Lord has answered and continues answering the prayers we have been praying for these faith families and their prayers for us.

By contrast, Haman wanted nothing more for Mordecai than humiliation and death.

What do we typically want for others? What do we want more than anything else for those who wound us? What are we actually doing to and for others? Are we praying for them? Are we speaking well of them? Are we finding ways to serve them? Are we extending kindnesses to them that they do not deserve as a reflection of the grace we receive from the Lord?

Having grown up in an abusive home, I did not want to forgive my father. But the Holy Spirit would empower me not only to forgive him but also to lead him to Christ. As we have opportunity, let us do good to everyone because the gospel is fueling our concern for them.

What Can We Learn about God from This Passage?

God Needs No Counselors, and He Always Does What Is Right

Time after time we have seen Ahasuerus's need for the counsel of others. God, however, needs no counselors. As he asks,

> *Who has directed the Spirit of the* L ORD, *or who gave him counsel?*
> *Who did he consult? Who gave him understanding and taught him*
> *the paths of justice? Who taught him knowledge and showed him the*
> *way of understanding?* (Isa 40:13-14)

God is not only capable of making a decision, but he always makes the right one. As Duguid affirms, "Our King does what is right because he himself is righteous—he cannot do anything other than the right" (*Esther and Ruth*, 95).

God Will Defeat All His Enemies.

God is not just aware that all of his enemies will be defeated, but through the work of Christ, he is accomplishing their defeat. Paul says that in Christ, God "disarmed the rulers and authorities and disgraced them publicly; he triumphed over them in him" (Col 2:15). The humiliating turn of events in Haman's being hanged on his own gallows was just a foretaste of God's publicly disgracing his enemies. Haman's death is a reminder that one day all of God's enemies will be fully vanquished. John writes, "The devil who deceived them was thrown into the lake of fire and sulfur where the beast and the false prophet are, and they will be tormented day and night forever and ever" (Rev 20:10).

Importantly, death was no escape for Haman. In Revelation 6:15-17 John writes,

> *Then the kings of the earth, the nobles, the generals, the rich, the*
> *powerful, and every slave and free person hid in the caves and among*
> *the rocks of the mountains. And they said to the mountains and to the*
> *rocks, "Fall on us and hide us from the face of the one seated on the*
> *throne and from the wrath of the Lamb, because the great day of their*
> *wrath has come! And who is able to stand?"*

For Haman, Ahasuerus's wrath was satisfied toward him when he was hanged, but there will never be a moment in which God's wrath against Haman is satisfied. No, death is no escape for God's enemies. It only begins what will never end. As Paul exhorts us, "Friends, do not avenge yourselves; instead, leave room for God's wrath, because it is written, Vengeance belongs to me; I will repay, says the Lord" (Rom 12:19).

When giving place to God's wrath, we need to remember one more truth. John says, "The one who believes in the Son has eternal life, but the one who rejects the Son will not see life; instead, the wrath of God remains on him" (John 3:36). Not all those who are still under God's wrath are building gallows or plotting for total people groups to be destroyed. Some coach your children's sports teams or teach them ballet or how to play musical instruments. Some who are still under God's wrath say hello and wave to us when they see us checking our mailboxes. Though the evil inside them may not be as evident as Haman's, it is just as wretched and just as deserving of wrath. And you have the only answer to that bleak outlook that will suffice to save them. Do for them what you would want done for you: tell them about Jesus.

God's Wrath Has Been Satisfied in Christ

As noted, Ahasuerus's wrath toward Haman was satisfied when he was hanged. God's wrath toward individuals is only satisfied when they place faith in Christ. Duguid notes, "Our King's wrath was poured out in full upon his own Son on the cross. And if God's fury has been poured out in full upon Christ, now there is none left for us (see Gal 3:13)" (*Esther and Ruth*, 96). Paul says, "Therefore, since we have been declared righteous by faith, we have peace with God through our Lord Jesus Christ" (Rom 5:1). At great cost to himself, God covered all of our sin. He will not forsake believers because he has forsaken Christ in our place. Commenting on David's and Nathan's interaction in 2 Samuel 12, Jon Bloom exhorts,

> On this side of the cross we now know fully what David didn't: God put away our sin by placing them on himself. Only at the cross will we hear, "The Lord also has put away your sin; you shall not die." Ever. ("Success Can Be Perilous")

Is there any greater news? Who needs to hear this news from you today?

Conclusion

Sometimes we just need to be reminded that God will ultimately defeat all his enemies. We also need to be sure we are not among them any longer. As we have seen in Esther 7, God works out his plans, but he uses us in the process. I hope that we, like Esther, will be those who confront sin and call for justice rather than being like Haman, who continued in sin and got caught in its consequences.

If you are having problems confessing that you are a believer to someone, will you pray for the Lord to strengthen you? If you are avoiding confronting sin in your life or in the lives of others, will you pray for courage today? If you are concealing sin, will you repent from it right now? If you are not speaking and striving for the good of all others, will you ask the Lord to help you do so starting now? If you do not consider on a daily basis that God's wrath has been satisfied on your behalf in Christ, would you ask him to help you think on this often and move you to action with gospel gratitude and urgency?

Reflect and Discuss

1. What, if any, risks are you currently taking for the sake of the gospel? Is there anything that prevents you from risking much for Christ's sake? If so, explain.
2. Describe a time you had to confront evil or injustice. How did God sustain you through the process? What was the result? Is the Lord currently prompting you to confront evil or injustice, whether in your own life or in the life of someone else? If so, explain.
3. Why is it important to identify with and intercede for God's people? In what practical ways can we do this?
4. Is anything concealed in your life today that would bring shame or reproach on Christ if it were revealed? To whom can you confess this today and find accountability?
5. How have you seen the Lord reward obedience in your life?
6. Have you ever wanted "bad" for someone else, only to experience it yourself? Why is it important to continually speak and work for the good of others?
7. Why do we tend to forget that sin leads nowhere good, beneficial, or holy?
8. When, if ever, have the consequences of your sin impacted more people than you ever imagined possible? How can we consistently remember that it might be "my sin" but "our consequences"?
9. Why do we constantly need to be reminded that God will ultimately defeat all his enemies?
10. How often do you consider that God's wrath against your sin has been satisfied by Christ on the cross? Why should we ponder this truth more often?

Pleading on Behalf of Others

ESTHER 8

Main Idea: Much like Paul in Romans 9, Esther has unceasing pain and anguish at the thought of her people perishing; therefore, she pleads with Ahasuerus for their preservation.

I. **What's Going On in the Story (8)?**
   A. Esther's rewards and Mordecai's responsibilities (8:1-2).
      1. Esther received the estate of the enemy.
      2. Mordecai received a ring and responsibilities.
   B. Esther's repeated request (8:3-6)
      1. See her perseverance.
      2. See her passion.
      3. See her pleading.
   C. Ahasuerus's response (8:7-8)
      1. He was content.
      2. He lacked compassion.
   D. Mordecai's regulation (8:9-14)
      1. See the hope.
      2. See the horses.
   E. Jewish rejoicing (8:15-17)

II. **What Can We Learn from This Passage?**
   A. Let us not be so content with our own salvation that we lack compassion for those without it.
   B. Let us persevere in pleading to the Lord for others to come to salvation or to grow in sanctification.
   C. Let us announce the good news of the gospel for the joy of all peoples.
   D. Let us always remember our position of victory.
   E. Let us always remember our participation in the battle.
   F. Let our discipleship be our loudest declaration.

III. **What Can We Learn about God from This Passage?**
   A. God administers the power and placement of his people.
   B. Jesus is a better mediator than Esther.
   C. Our Father was contriving and completing our salvation.
   D. God's love transforms us.

The hymn "It Is Well with My Soul" has been a favorite of mine for a long time. It was not the first hymn I learned, though; that was "Trust and Obey." There are videos of me singing that hymn when I was three or four in our home in Port Arthur, Texas. My mom may have had several reasons for making sure I knew that song at such an early age.

As for "It Is Well," I can remember singing it frequently with the congregation in which I grew up. As I joined the adult choir in tenth grade, I particularly loved singing the bass part of the chorus and hearing the piano and organ compete. When I was a senior in high school, I sang "It Is Well" as a trio with my mom and sister in what some know as a Fifth Sunday Singing. When my father died during my senior year of college, the Spirit empowered me to sing the hymn while I prepared to preach his funeral—it was my first funeral to preach. Another powerful moment of God using "It Is Well with My Soul" in my life came at the end of the first Together for the Gospel gathering in 2006. As the room filled with mostly pastors belting out the truth of the gospel proclaimed in those lyrics, I was moved to tears, so I called my wife, put my cell phone on speaker, and let her join us in that moment.

If you have ever heard Brian Regan, the comedian, talk about snow-cones, you will know what I mean by saying I am thankful for each verse in the hymn, but these are my two favorites (and I am bolding my favorite parts of my favorite verses):

Though Satan should buffet, though trials should come,
Let this blest assurance control,
That Christ has regarded my helpless estate,
And hath shed His own blood for my soul.

My sin—oh, the bliss of this glorious thought:
My sin—not in part but the whole
Is nailed to the cross, and I bear it no more,
Praise the Lord, praise the Lord, O my soul! (Spafford, "It Is
    Well with My Soul")

I never grow tired of singing the gospel as recorded in this song. By God's grace I am not desensitized to Christ's substitutionary atonement when these lyrics appear on a screen, but I am moved afresh that I was helpless but Christ was not. I can also sing with confidence that all of my sin has been covered. No lurking transgression will prevent me from being reconciled to God because it is greater than Christ's finished work. No, I can lift my hands and my voice in praise because not just some of my sin has been paid for but all of it!

As much as I love the hymn, I did not know its history until my great aunt gave me a book about hymns and how they came to be written. She thought there might be some good illustrations for sermons in there. (Thanks, Sissie! Thanks also for knowing what should be an illustration and what should be a sermon.) What hymn do you think I turned to first to get its backstory? You guessed it. Only then did I learn the painful providence experienced by Horatio G. Spafford (1828–1888) that led to his penning my favorite hymn.

Spafford lived in Chicago, was happily married, had four daughters, was a successful attorney, held extensive real estate investments, was a supporter of D. L. Moody, and was an active member of a Presbyterian church (Osbeck, *Amazing Grace*, 202). In the Chicago fire of 1871, Spafford's real estate fortune was consumed. But that would not be the worst of Spafford's problems. Two years after the fire, and while D. L. Moody and Ira Sankey were leading evangelistic meetings in Great Britain, Spafford thought it would do his family good to vacation in Europe.

Due to a business matter, Spafford was unable to travel with his wife and four daughters but promised to join them as soon as he could. In November 1873, the Spafford women boarded the *S.S. Ville du Havre* and set sail. Four of the five of them would never make it to Europe. As they crossed the Atlantic, their ship was struck by another vessel. In the chaos that ensued, Anna Spafford led her four children on deck and prayed for the Lord to spare them if he was willing but, if not, to grant the grace they would need in their final moments. The *S.S. Ville du Havre* sank in twelve minutes. The four Spafford daughters were among the 226 passengers who drowned.

When the survivors arrived on shore, Anna Spafford sent Horatio a telegram that began with "Saved alone what shall I do" ("Telegram from Anna Spafford"). Spafford later framed the telegram and hung it in his office.

Osbeck says, "Horatio Spafford stood hour after hour on the deck of the ship carrying him to rejoin his sorrowing wife" (ibid.). When the ship passed the place where his daughters drowned, Spafford received such a measure of grace and peace from the Lord that he was led to write, "When sorrows like sea billows roll. . . . It is well with my soul" (ibid.). He had no idea in those moments how God would use what he was writing to help the generations who have come behind him to praise the Lord for his peace that passes understanding even in the deepest pain.

I have often considered Anna Spafford's telegram message of "saved alone." How difficult it must have been for her to send that message. I do not know the details of the twelve minutes it took for their ship to sink, but she was unable to save any of her daughters and was devastated by it. I assume she did everything in her power to rescue them, even pleading for others to help her, but there was no help.

At the beginning of Esther 8, we may find ourselves wondering whether "saved alone" will be all Esther can say as well. Will she have to report, "I was rescued, but not the rest of my people"? We will see in Esther 8 that "saved alone" is certainly not what she wants to say. Just as Anna Spafford most likely did in the icy waters of the Atlantic, Esther will plead for her people to be saved. Because though Haman is dead, his edict is not.

Esther's pleading will be reminiscent of other intercessions in the Old Testament. When the Lord determined to wipe out Sodom and Gomorrah because of their wickedness, Abraham pleaded for the righteous ones living in those places to be delivered (Gen 18:22-33). The Lord agreed that if there were ten righteous people in Sodom, then he would not destroy the city. As we know, there was not even half that number; nevertheless, the Lord rescued Lot and his daughters. Many years later Moses would intercede on behalf of Israel, asking the Lord to spare their lives (even after they wanted to end Moses's life) and not wipe them all out right at the edge of the promised land (Num 14:1-19). God would discipline the older ones as they wandered through the wilderness for forty more years, but he would deliver those nineteen years old and younger and lead them into the promised land. The Lord responded to Abraham's intercession, and he responded to Moses's intercession, but would Ahasuerus respond to Esther's?

This scene makes me wonder how much pleading we do on behalf of others. I hope we are not just content that we have been delivered but also care and are active for the sake of those still in darkness and death. Much like Paul in Romans 9, Esther had unceasing pain and anguish at the thought of her people perishing; therefore, she pleaded with Ahasuerus for their preservation.

What's Going On in the Story?
ESTHER 8

Esther's Rewards and Mordecai's Responsibilities (8:1-2)

Have you ever received a gift that was good, but it was not what you really wanted? (If you are reading this, Mom, I am still waiting on that four-wheeler!) Ironically, after the fireworks at the feast (7:1-6) and the eradication of the enemy (7:7-10), it would be Haman's possessions that were plundered (8:1-2). *Esther received the estate of the enemy*, which would have included all of his property, slaves, funds, and even family. Once his relationship with Esther was revealed, *Mordecai received a ring and responsibilities.* Ahasuerus's signet ring was probably still warm from being on Haman's finger when it was placed on Mordecai's for the first time. Esther then placed Haman's assets under Mordecai's charge. But while these rewards were amazing considering the situation, neither Esther nor Mordecai asked for them. There was, however, something Esther really wanted, something far more important than the king's ring or Haman's house. For what she desired, she was willing to put her life on the line one more time.

Esther's Repeated Request (8:3-6)

Esther did not want to be "saved alone." Despite the relief she must have felt when Haman was hanged and even some measure of vindication when she received his possessions, Esther remembered the plight of her people. She was not distracted, nor would she be deterred from seeking relief for the Jews from Haman's edict of death. *See her perseverance.* She had not received her full request, so she addressed the king once more.

When we do not see God moving or answering, we are often tempted to stop praying. For instance, there were plenty of times I was tempted to stop praying for my father's salvation, especially when he would say hateful things about my mother. Perhaps there's been a particular struggle in your journey, and you may be worried your prayers are not going past the ceiling. Keep praying (Luke 18:5). God hears our prayers, and he answers them according to his wisdom.

We can also *see her passion.* Esther's burden for her people could not be hidden, and she made no attempt to conceal it. Not caring what anyone else around might think, Esther fell before the king. Her tears saturated his feet. The full depth of her emotions was on display. This should make us think about what moves us to such emotion when we make our requests to the Lord. When do we cast off all restraints and let our full emotions out before him (and anyone else who might be around)?

God has never asked us to conceal our feelings. Perhaps your prayers have been filled with emotion as you've asked the Lord to save your marriage, to provide health for a loved one, or to help you fully repent of a sin. This morning our faith family prayed over a couple who is moving to another city. Before we even started praying, though, there were tears streaming down the cheek of the wife. We thanked God for the time he entrusted their family to our care and asked him to help them find a new faith family in the city to which they are relocating. Never fear being transparent before the Lord with the depths of your feelings. From whom do you think you received those emotions?

Besides Esther's perseverance and her passion, we can *see her pleading*. She was literally begging Ahasuerus to intercede and stop Haman's genocidal plan. There was nothing cold, distant, or reserved in Esther's actions. She was not ashamed to beg and plead with the king if that was necessary to help her people. Death was averted for her (once again) as Ahasuerus extended his golden scepter and allowed her to stand and make her request. But how would Ahasuerus respond?

Ahasuerus's Response (8:7-8)

Ahasuerus's response reveals *he was content*. He was not totally unsympathetic to her cause. After all, he had Haman killed and then gave Esther all of his stuff. Perhaps, though, he wondered why she was not satisfied. He had done his part, and his own wrath was settled with Haman's death. Haman did not manage to take Ahasuerus down with him, so the king felt good about how things stood. He was ready to shift back into passivity. On his own he would do nothing further, but he allowed Esther and Mordecai to write an edict of their own and sign it with his ring.

Ahasuerus's response also reveals *he lacked compassion*. Esther was pleading with Ahasuerus on the basis of what was morally right, but the king tended to do what was most advantageous rather than what was right (Smith, *Ezra, Nehemiah, Esther*, 274). His granting permission to write a new edict was based most on how he felt about Esther rather than how he felt about the Jews. For them Ahasuerus had no particular concern. I am thankful God grants our requests mostly because of how he feels about Christ, but this is not to suggest God lacks concern for us. Christ did not have to convince the Father to care about us; Christ was sent because the Father cared already.

Of course, even if the king did care, Haman's edict could not be revoked. So what was the next best option?

Mordecai's Regulation (8:9-14)

Because Haman's edict could not be changed, a new edict needed to be created. Where only death had been decreed, there was now opportunity for defense. Though the Jews throughout the empire may have felt all was lost, the new edict allowed them to *see the hope*. Smith notes,

> For all practical purposes, the effect was that the new decree gave the Jews legal protection to fight back, stripping any attackers of a favored legal position. Nevertheless, it did not remove the threat against the Jewish people. (*Ezra, Nehemiah, Esther*, 275)

The Jews still faced an uncertain outcome, but at least now their resistance would not be interpreted as rebellion.

Like Haman, Mordecai made sure the decree was written in every language and delivered as quickly as possible throughout the empire. In describing the method of delivery, the author lets us *see the horses*. Baldwin says, "These then were the equivalent of today's racehorses, bred from the royal stud (lit. 'sons of the royal mares')" (*Esther*, 96). If it were possible, Mordecai would have paid extra for same-day delivery. Good news was on the way for God's people. How beautiful were the hooves delivering it!

Jewish Rejoicing (8:15-17)

As I contrast Esther 4:1-3 with 8:15-17, Isaiah 61:3 comes to mind. There the prophet says the Lord's people will receive "a crown of beauty instead of ashes, festive oil instead of mourning, and splendid clothes instead of despair." Also the psalmist rejoices, "You turned my lament into dancing; you removed my sackcloth and clothed me with gladness" (Ps 30:11). Selfishly, where the author of Esther describes the reaction of the Jews throughout the empire, I wish what is written in Psalm 30:12 would have been added: "I can sing to you and not be silent. Lord my God, I will praise you forever." The author notes their gladness, but if they expressed gratitude to God specifically, it is not recorded.

Regardless, as the new edict advanced through the empire, so did joy among the Jews. For them fear was replaced with feasting, but for others feasting was replaced with fear. Professing to be a Jew became all the rage at that time in the empire, but that did not make such claims real.

Speaking of real, when Mordecai left the palace and walked among the people, my man was sporting some new threads. His new robes led to the entire city rejoicing. Talk about a transformation! It was a makeover he could never have imagined but one the Lord had completely planned.

What Can We Learn from This Passage?

Let Us Not Be So Content with Our Own Salvation that We Lack Compassion for Those Without It

If Anna Spafford had been given her preference, she never would have chosen to be "saved alone." We have seen in our text where Esther stood. She was not just concerned about her own survival but for the survival of her people as well. Our salvation is not just an end in itself. May God use our being reconciled to him as a means of advancing the gospel in and through us, and then God will receive great glory.

Do you have a genuine concern for non-Christians? Or are you content with having your own Willy Wonka-like golden ticket to heaven but feel no compassion for those who do not? Some people claim to be concerned about those who are outside of Christ, but Paul genuinely was, and he called on the Holy Spirit to be his witness:

> *I speak the truth in Christ—I am not lying; my conscience testifies to me through the Holy Spirit—that I have great sorrow and unceasing anguish in my heart. For I could wish that I myself were cursed and cut off from Christ for the benefit of my brothers and sisters, my own flesh and blood.* (Rom 9:1-3)

Now that is concern. If it were possible, Paul was willing to trade his own salvation so that none of his people, the Israelites (9:4), would perish. And Paul's burden never dissipated. His sorrow and anguish over their spiritual state was unceasing. Sometimes we have seasons of concern for the lost, but then something else captures our attention, and our regard for them wanes.

In Philippians 3:18, Paul told the believers in Philippi, "I have often told you, and now say again with tears, that many live as enemies of the cross of Christ." He added, "Their end is destruction" (Phil 3:19). Even as Paul wrote that, he was weeping for the many people who were living as Christ's enemies and, if they failed to repent and believe, would be destroyed. Paul wept for those who needed to be delivered. Esther wept for those who needed to be delivered. But do we weep for those who need to be delivered? Esther told Ahasuerus she could not "bear to see the disaster that would come on" or "the destruction of" her people (8:6). This should make us question whether we are living as if we can bear with people perishing. Like Paul and Esther, Adoniram Judson certainly could not.

Soon after he became a Christian, Judson felt burdened to serve the Lord as a foreign missionary. In the early 1800s in America, however, not only was there no missions-sending agency within his own Congregationalist denomination, but there was no other mission board from which he could seek support. In his passion for those who were perishing without Christ, Judson penned an article titled, "Concern for the Salvation of the Heathen," which was published in two magazines (Benge and Benge, *Adoniram Judson*, 52). In it Judson expressed his frustration with so many "Christians" who seemed unconcerned for those dying without having an opportunity to hear the gospel. He wrote,

> How do Christians discharge this trust committed to them?
> They let three-fourths of the world sleep the sleep of death,
> ignorant of the simple truth that a Savior died for them.
> Content if they can be useful in the little circle of their
> acquaintances, they quietly sit and see whole nations perish for
> lack of knowledge. (Anderson, *To the Golden Shore*, 63–64)

God would use Judson to help form one of the first missions organizations in America and then to serve as one of the first missionaries to be sent. Driven by deep concern for the souls of others, Adoniram and his wife, Ann, would sacrifice greatly for the sake of the gospel in Burma.

Are we in any way like those who aggravated and grieved Adoniram Judson, those who seemed so unconcerned that so many perish in our world without knowledge of Christ? How much does our concern for non-Christians impact our weekly agendas? May our attitude never be, "Chill on that evangelism topic; I'm good!" or, "I'm saved—that spreading the gospel thing is someone else's problem."

Referencing Jesus, Matthew says, "When he saw the crowds, he felt compassion for them, because they were distressed and dejected, like sheep without a shepherd" (Matt 9:36). If you currently lack compassion for the lost, I know who can help you. In fact, I often pray, "Jesus, please help me feel as much compassion for the lost as you felt for me." How awful it would have been that night in college when my apartment caught fire if I had just said, "I am safe," but then done nothing for my roommate sleeping upstairs. Esther could not have demonstrated her concern for others more clearly. Could the same be said about us?

Let Us Persevere in Pleading to the Lord for Others to Come to Salvation or to Grow in Sanctification

In light of Esther's perseverance in pleading to the king, I want to challenge you to keep praying in three ways. First, maybe you are close to giving up on praying for someone or about something today. Keep praying. Keep pleading. Keep travailing in prayer.

Second, keep asking "the Lord of the harvest to send out workers into his harvest" (Matt 9:38). One of the requests I bring before the Lord most often is that he will send believers out who love him, who love his Word, and who want to see all peoples have Scripture in their languages. Every youth/college event I preach, I ask those present to consider, as a possible career choice, immersing themselves with a people group and translating the Bible into their language. One of the families from our congregation, I am happy to report, will be coming home soon on furlough from where they have been serving with the Wycliffe Bible Translators. I am thankful for their obedience and sacrifice.

Third, like Paul, I hope we will not just pray passionately for people to come to Christ but also for them to grow in Christ. Paul prayed just as fervently for the sanctification of those he knew as he did for their justification. A great example of Paul's prayer for Christians postconversion is Colossians 1:9-14. He prays for new believers to know what God wants (1:9) so they will do it (1:10) in God's power (1:11) and because of the gospel (1:12-14). May the Lord empower us never to grow weary of praying and pleading for others.

Let Us Announce the Good News of the Gospel for the Joy of All Peoples

Wherever the proclamation written by Mordecai was read, joy followed, and that was just for an announcement that gave God's people the right to defend themselves. How much more joy will come from our announcing not just a victory that is possible but one that has already been won? Like the couriers we should carry this great news as far and as quickly as possible. As Jerry Bridges said,

> We are not to be a terminus point for the gospel, but rather a way station in its progress to the ends of the earth. God intends that everyone who has embraced the gospel become a part of the great enterprise of spreading the gospel. What our particular part in this great enterprise may be will vary from person to person, but all of us should be involved. (*The Gospel for Real Life*, 166)

May our prayer always be, "Let the peoples praise you, God; let all the peoples praise you. Let the nations rejoice and shout for joy" (Ps 67:3-4). Our High King has decreed deliverance from the curse of death. Joy spreads wherever this good news is announced. Who needs to hear it from you today?

Let Us Always Remember Our Position of Victory

The edict that Mordecai sent out informed the Jews the king granted them permission to defend themselves. If the Jews celebrated in hearing that they could at least fight for victory, how much greater should our rejoicing be since Christ has won ours? This great news has implications for our celebration. Our hope is certain. In fact, I often say our hope is not fingers crossed (hoping my team will win the game) but thumbs up (our hope is definite). We have no doubts Christ has already won the war and, in him, so will we.

The news of Christ's victory also has implications for our sanctification. We do not fight from a defeated position but from a delivered one. Christ has broken the power of our enemies. If we find ourselves feeling defeated, we need to consider two possibilities: We may be returning power where it has been relinquished (like those who still choose to obey a deposed leader). Or we may not be relying on Christ's power.

Let me give you even more good news. In John 15:5 Jesus says, "I am the vine; you are the branches. The one who remains in me and I in him produces much fruit, because you can do nothing without me." The fact we can do nothing without Christ is not all I want you to see here. The fact he never asks us to do anything without him is what I do not want you to miss. Christ does not expect us to obey a single command of his in our own strength. He knows we cannot. In him, however, we are not just hoping things will turn out for our good and God's glory. We know they will.

Let Us Always Remember Our Participation in the Battle

For the Jews in the Persian Empire, preservation would not come just from an announcement but from action. We will discuss more about this when we cover Esther 9:1–10:3, but it is worth noting here as well. If God's people were going to be saved, they would have to fight those who attacked them. While Jesus has done all of the fighting necessary for our atonement, it does not mean we are passive in our sanctification. Yes, we strive from a position of victory, but also yes, we have to strive and to put forth effort for our advance in what Christ has achieved.

Those to whom God in his power had given "everything required for life and godliness through the knowledge of him who called us by his own glory and goodness," Peter exhorted to

> make every effort to supplement your faith with goodness, goodness with knowledge, knowledge with self-control, self-control with endurance, endurance with godliness, godliness with brotherly affection, and brotherly affection with love. (2 Pet 1:3,5-7)

They were not to make every effort in hopes of having what they needed for life and godliness but because they already had it. For Paul the gospel did not produce passivity but a pressing on toward the "prize promised by God's heavenly call in Christ Jesus" (Phil 3:14). He pursued this goal not in hopes of Christ taking hold of his life but "because [he had] been taken hold of by Christ Jesus" (Phil 3:12). The Jews had permission to defend themselves, but they would still have to do their part. In Christ we do not just have permission; we have his power and his promises that fuel our progress in him.

Let Our Discipleship Be Our Loudest Declaration

In Esther 8:17 the author notes that after the new decree was distributed, "many of the ethnic groups . . . professed themselves to be Jews." Were these declarations genuine? Only God knows. We certainly see Rahab's conversion to the people of God when the fear of God seized the inhabitants of Canaan (Josh 2). But were the ethnic groups in Persia just switching to what seemed to be the winning team without experiencing true heart change? Again, we cannot know for certain. All we can know is what the biblical author tells us: fear of the Jews had seized them, and thus they declared themselves Jews.

I do not know where all those people are now, but I hope their declarations were real. Even more, I hope our discipleship is not just profession but practice. I once was at a special event at New Orleans Baptist Theological Seminary. Dr. Kelley, the NOBTS president, said our denomination had seen a lot of people make decisions about Christ, but we had not produced a lot of disciples for Christ. His words hit me like a lightning bolt that night, and I have never forgotten them. I hope your conversion is genuine and that you are not declaring yourself to be something you are not. May our discipleship be our loudest declaration.

What Can We Learn about God from This Passage?

God Administers the Power and Placement of His People

In the beginning of the book of Esther, the author informs us that Ahasuerus reigned over 127 provinces, and in the first chapter we get no news about any Jews at all. But when we arrive at Esther 8, two of the three most powerful people in the Persian Empire are God's people. No matter how perceptive any reader might claim to be, only God saw that coming because he was an active participant in making it happen.

But like the late-night salespeople who hawk their wares on television and continue to sweeten the deal, I have *even more* for you to consider. God does not just place his people in positions of power, but he places his enemies in their positions as well. As God told Pharaoh, "I have let you live for this purpose: to show you my power and to make my name known on the whole earth" (Exod 9:16). Jesus told Pilate, "You would have no authority over me at all if it hadn't been given you from above" (John 19:11). And consider this verse that I taught my oldest daughter, Arabella, one morning while we were having pancakes and Proverbs: "The LORD has prepared everything for his purpose—even the wicked for the day of disaster" (Prov 16:4). Take just a moment to bask in God's omnipotence and sovereignty. And be encouraged that no matter who is the "current ruler of the land" in any land and at any time, God not only brings a person up but also brings a person down and moves his people into positions of power for his purposes.

Jesus Is a Better Mediator than Esther

Without doubt Jesus is a better mediator than not just Esther but anyone. There is no one more qualified to plead on our behalf (Heb 4:14–5:10). And he longs to do this job instead of loathing it! Let that wash over you for a moment. His role as intercessor is full of delight for him rather than drudgery. Esther could barely gain access to the king for herself, but through Christ our access to the Father is never in doubt. His passion, however, is not just evidenced in his supplications on our behalf but also in his substitution. He does not just ask; he acts.

Our Father Was Contriving and Completing Our Salvation

Throughout the book Ahasuerus seems ambivalent about who lives and who dies except for when Esther's life was threatened. Were it not for Esther's persistence in interceding for her people, he most likely would not have had anything else written concerning the Jews. Unlike Ahasuerus, however, our heavenly Father is not in need of being convinced and is not merely contemplating our salvation; he is contriving and completing it. Our salvation was not only his idea but his achievement. Paul says,

> Everything is from God, who has reconciled us to himself through
> Christ and has given us the ministry of reconciliation. That is,
> in Christ, God was reconciling the world to himself, not counting
> their trespasses against them, and he has committed the message of
> reconciliation to us. (2 Cor 5:18-19)

As a matter of fact, it is not Jesus who is giving us to the Father but the Father who is giving us to Jesus (John 6:44). We come to Jesus because the Father gives us to him. How amazing is it that we do not have to try to persuade God to rescue us, but he is working to overcome all of our rebellion?

God's Love Transforms Us

The picture of Mordecai walking through town in his splendid new robes cannot contrast any more starkly than with the earlier image of Mordecai wearing sackcloth and mourning at the King's Gate. Change occurred, and Mordecai would never be the same again. In even more dramatic fashion, God's love transforms us. He comes to us when we are dead in our sin, but then he makes us alive in Christ and empowers us to go forth as his workmanship (Eph 2:1-10). In Ezekiel 16 God reminds his people that when they were abandoned (16:1-5), he adopted them (16:6-8), and then he adorned them with his extravagant and transforming love (16:9-14). He says, "Your fame spread among the nations because of your beauty, for it was perfect through my splendor, which I had bestowed on you. This is the declaration of the Lord God" (Ezek 16:14). Mordecai's transition was caused by another, and so is ours. May we always join Paul in saying, "But by the grace of God I am what I am, and his grace toward me was not in vain" (1 Cor 15:10).

Conclusion

What should we do in response to this text? Here are a few suggestions: (1) Plead to our King on behalf of someone or even on behalf of an entire ethnic group right now. (2) Persevere in your pleading. Do not be discouraged and do not quit. (3) Be positive you are in Christ. There could be no greater tragedy than to think you are in Christ only to find out in eternity that you were not. (4) Praise God for his power, his always doing what is right, and his desire to save you long before you even knew he existed. (5) Praise Jesus for his great intercession on our behalf.

Reflect and Discuss

1. Esther could not bear to see her people destroyed; Paul had unceasing pain and anguish at the thought of his people perishing. How would you describe your concern for those who are outside of Christ?
2. Why is it difficult to consider the needs of others as being more important than our own? Name someone you know who is particularly good at putting the needs of others before himself. Explain.
3. Esther was persistent in her request to the king to rescue her people. Why is perseverance in prayer often difficult for us?
4. Is there something or someone you are currently tempted to stop praying for? Why should you not quit interceding about that matter?
5. While the Jews in Persia gained the *hope* of victory with Mordecai's edict, in Christ we are *certain* of victory. What does it look like to engage in our sanctification from the position of his victory? Why do we sometimes struggle as if the battle were lost?

6. While Christ has won the victory for our atonement and reconciliation, we still have a role to play in our sanctification. Why isn't our sanctification just a "let go and let God" process?

7. Fear of the Jews prompted the conversion of some in Persia. What/whom did God use to bring you to Christ? Why is being certain we are genuinely converted so important?

8. God placed Esther and Mordecai in two of the three most powerful positions in the Persian Empire. What does this tell us about God? Are you ever prone to think his involvement in your current placement in life is less important to him? How can we steward well what he entrusts to us?

9. What makes Jesus a better mediator than Esther? How often do you express gratitude to him for his mediation on your behalf?

10. Esther had to plead with the king to do the right thing regarding her people. Why do we never have to convince God to do what is right? How can you show God how thankful you are that he did not have to be convinced to save you but was working for your conversion even before your birth?

Reversal, Relief, and Remembrance

ESTHER 9–10

Main Idea: In the final scenes of Esther, we see God reverse what the enemies of his people intended to achieve, and we see him grant rest and relief for his people. Moreover, we see his people rejoicing and seeking to remember their great deliverance.

I.   **May the Lord Find Us Faithful Where Others Have Failed (9:1-16).**
  A. Consider the reversal (9:1-5).
  B. Consider the retribution and rebellion (9:6-16).
  C. Consider their restraint (9:10,15-16).

II. **May the Celebration of the Lord's Deliverance Never Be Empty Ritual (9:17-28).**
  A. See their relief and rest (9:17-19).
  B. See their rejoicing (9:17-19).
  C. See the call for remembrance (9:20-28).
  D. Be grateful it has been recorded (9:20).

III. **May We Be Faithful Stewards of All God Entrusts to Us (9:29–10:3).**
  A. God accomplishes his perfect plan through imperfect people.
  B. God is in charge of our when, where, and what.
  C. The gospel fuels our how and our why.

IV. **May We Always Remember that God Is the Real Hero (9:29–10:3).**
  A. Consider their (limited) renown.
  B. What can we learn about Jesus from this text?
    1. In the battle for our deliverance, Christ alone has achieved victory.
    2. As Haman's sons' bodies were hanged in shame, so was Christ's.
    3. Christ brings eternal and true liberation.
  C. Consider the Lord's Supper.

Have you ever researched Armageddon on the internet? Of the first ten results of my search, six were referring to the movie, *Armageddon,* starring Bruce Willis. One was a page providing Jehovah's Witnesses' thoughts on the last battle. (Definitely not the most helpful resources.)

When I think of the word *Armageddon,* I have in mind a massive eschatological battle. And I suspect the topic fills the minds of some with anxious or fearful thoughts and great dread. But not unlike massive fireworks purchased at a pop-up tent that promised a lot of thunder and awe only to fizzle out at the Fourth of July celebration, Armageddon will be over before it even starts. Oh, there will definitely be a lot of awe and thunder in that day but just not as the world might be expecting.

In Revelation 19–20, the final two battles between evil and good are revealed. In Revelation 19:11-21, Jesus never even has to dismount but destroys his foes while sitting on a horse. (I hope the media have their cameras ready when the time comes because it will all go down really fast.) In Revelation 20:7-10 one last massive gathering of the forces of evil is described. John sums it up like this:

> They came up across the breadth of the earth and surrounded the encampment of the saints, the beloved city. Then fire came down from heaven and consumed them. The devil who deceived them was thrown into the lake of fire and sulfur where the beast and the false prophet are, and they will be tormented day and night forever and ever. (Rev 20:9-10)

I have no intention of swaying you to a particular eschatological camp here. I am simply pointing out that what the world thinks is going to be a massive war that rages on will really be the battle that never was. In Revelation 19, the enemies are gathered so the birds can become gorged on their flesh. And in Revelation 20, the enemies surround the saints just to be scorched. To the glory of God, the saints will go on to dwell with Jesus after these events, which will be for our eternal joy. That is the way the Bible says God's people will live happily ever after.

In the months between the twenty-third day of the third month, when Mordecai's edict was dispersed (Esth 8:9), and the thirteenth day of the twelfth month, when the purge had been decreed by Haman, it's possible that the enemies of God's people psyched themselves up for an epic battle. Maybe they were making plans about gathering together and surrounding the homes of the Jews and calling dibs on what would be plundered. But just as in Revelation 19–20, there would be no victory for the forces of evil. Those among the Jews who had been filled with dread as the date drew near found that the day of doom turned out better than they could have imagined.

Importantly, just as the Lord takes "no pleasure in the death of the wicked" (Ezek 33:11), neither should we. While we glorify God by saying, "Hallelujah! Salvation, glory, and power belong to our God, because his judgments are true and righteous" (Rev 19:1-2), we should also be grieved that there are those who perish because they foolishly rage against God and his people. Esther 9:1–10:3 is one last reminder that God's people will always be preserved, but God's enemies will perish and be punished forever. In the final scenes of Esther, we see God reverse what the enemies of his people intended to achieve, and we see him grant rest and relief for his people. Moreover, we see his people rejoicing and seeking to remember their great deliverance.

May the Lord Find Us Faithful Where Others Have Failed
ESTHER 9:1-16

In J. R. R. Tolkien's *The Fellowship of the Ring*, the ring-bearing hobbit, Frodo, bemoans to Gandalf, "I wish it need not have happened in my time."

Gandalf responds: "So do I and so do all who live to see such times. But that is not for them to decide. All we have to decide is what to do with the time that is given us" (*The Fellowship of the Ring*, 50).

We cannot control circumstances passed to us or what we inherit from previous generations, but we can control what we do with them. Sometimes previous generations leave messes for those who come behind to clean up. For example, Saul's refusal to kill Agag and to ban all of his plunder left ramifications for Samuel and the generations that followed, possibly including Esther's generation. If Haman, the Agagite, was indeed linked to Agag, then after all this time God's people were finally going to do what previous generations had failed to accomplish. If, as I noted earlier in this book, Haman was called an Agagite simply because of his hatred of the Jews, then Esther's generation would eliminate all those who in the spirit of Agag are enemies of God's people. Either way, the Jews in Persia were given an opportunity to stand and fight together for their preservation. They were not passing the problem to anyone else!

Consider the Reversal (9:1-5)

It turns out luck was not as much of a lady as Haman thought she would be on the thirteenth day of Adar. Of course, we know luck had nothing to do with the Pur that was cast (3:7); the matter was under the complete control of the Lord. What Haman had thought would be a day of dancing over his enemies turned out to be absolutely devastating for his family and many other foes of God's people.

In our faith family we often sing songs that reflect the truth of Romans 8:28: "We know that all things work together for the good of those who love God, who are called according to his purpose." One of the reasons we can sing this truth is because we see it appear over and over in the Lord's Word. We see God working for Joseph's good what his brothers meant for evil. We see God working for Shadrach's, Meshach's, and Abednego's good what Nebuchadnezzar meant for their harm. We see God working for Daniel's good what those jealous of him intended for his demise before they became brunch for the lions! We also can see in Esther 9:1–10:3 that God is working for the good of his people what Haman and his group intended for evil. Of course, we see God's working for our good most clearly in Christ's death and resurrection, though Pilate, Herod, and the religious leaders acted with evil motives. Included in the "all things" of Romans 8:28 are not just our own actions but what all others might do to us as well.

As familiar as this verse is to me, I still need grace in "relearning" to believe it. There are just so many times when we are tempted to say something like this: "I know you said you would work all things for our good, Lord, but I can see no way in which this situation can be worked for good." When you are tempted to doubt similarly, just reread the book of Esther and be reminded that God truly can work all things for the good of his people—even if that means dealing with drunk kings, defiant queens, harem life, and an edict of death.

In Esther 9:1-5 those who hated God's people hoped to conquer them, but God's people would prevail because of God's provisions. First, *God provided unity among his people.* When there is a war to be waged on the battlefield, we tend not to fight in the barracks. God used the threat of destruction to eliminate any divisions there might have been among the Jews. As Paul would say to the believers in Corinth, "If one member suffers, all the members suffer with it; if one member is honored, all the members rejoice with it" (1 Cor 12:26). On the thirteenth day of Adar, if one Jew suffered, all would suffer; if one Jew fought against his enemies, all would join him; and if one Jew triumphed, all would triumph. I hope our battles against the flesh, the world, and the devil will unite us as well.

I currently receive accountability reports via email from a software program that one of my friends is using to strive for godliness as he uses technology. My friend knows he is not in the battle alone. God gives the gifts of his Spirit, his Word, and his people to stir us to Christ each day. We can and should remind one another not to choose sin. When people ask me how our church is doing, one of my responses is that we are not fighting one another but are fighting for one another. Indeed, one of the greatest ways we can serve those in our faith family is to help them fight for joy in the Lord while the battle with the flesh, the world, and the devil rages.

Second, *God provided so that, of the adversaries who attacked the Jews, not a single one of them could successfully stand against his people* (Smith, *Ezra, Nehemiah, Esther*, 279). As the Jews defended themselves, God made sure they would not be conquered but would be conquerors.

Third, *God provided so that every ethnic group was afraid of the Jews.* The enemies were not just thwarted physically but also psychologically. Baldwin notes,

> The fear of God's people was explicable only in terms of fear of their God, who vindicated their righteous cause by convicting their enemies in the whole Persian empire of having backed the losing side. (*Esther*, 103)

The situation was similar to the time about which Rahab confessed,

> *I know that the LORD has given you this land and that the terror of you has fallen on us, and everyone who lives in the land is panicking because of you. For we have heard how the LORD dried up the water of the Red Sea before you when you came out of Egypt, and what you did to Sihon and Og, the two Amorite kings you completely destroyed across the Jordan. When we heard this, we lost heart, and everyone's courage failed because of you, for the LORD your God is God in heaven above and on earth below.* (Josh 2:9-11)

Fourth, another place God provided help for his people was probably one from which they least expected it when everything began. *God provided support for the Jews from the Persian officials.* All of them. None of God's enemies could stand against his people, but every government official stood with them. Pagan people were used by the Lord to protect and preserve his people. I have tried to point this truth out to you clearly throughout this book: God does not just reign over those who know and love him. He reigns over all. He does not just use those who comply with his will but even those who do not know it.

Consider the Retribution and Rebellion (9:6-16)

In both Susa and all the provinces, God empowered the Jews to strike down those who hated them and attacked them. At least 75,500 foes lost their lives on the thirteenth day of Adar, ten of whom were Haman's sons. An additional 300 enemies were killed on the fourteenth day, as Ahasuerus allowed another day of fighting in Susa. I want to point out three aspects of the fighting.

First, *consider the act of defense*. God's people were defending themselves against those who attacked them. They were not launching preventive attacks. They did not initiate the action by raiding the homes of their foes. Rather, the Jews followed what was prescribed in Mordecai's decree and offered a vigorous defense.

Though the Jews had every right to annihilate anyone who attacked regardless of gender or age, Esther 9 does not record any specific instances of women and children being killed. If they were, then it serves as a reminder of the consequences of poor male headship in the home. May we never lead our families to fight against God. And may we who are husbands and fathers always remember that our rebellion against God produces painful consequences for our wives and kids. Look at Haman and his sons and learn.

Second, *consider the issue of divine justice*. When God's people entered Canaan, God used them as instruments of divine justice against the sins of those who were living in the land. As Paul says in Romans 6:23, "The wages of sin is death." In Numbers 25 God instructed his people to put to death all those who had led his people astray in worship of the Baal of Peor. It seems harsh, but in reality it is about holiness. God alone deserves worship, and he does not want anything to pull us away from him. His command was to put away those who were luring his people away, and none of those killed in Numbers 25 were innocent. All who were killed were worshiping a false god, Baal.

An attack on God's people is an attack on God. While he "was still breathing threats and murder against the disciples of the Lord," Saul encountered the Lord who asked him, "Saul, Saul, why are you persecuting me?" (Acts 9:1,4). Jesus identified so strongly with the suffering Saul was inflicting on *his people* that he could ask why Saul was persecuting *him*. Do not rush past that thought.

When Helen Roseveare, who served as a medical missionary in Africa, was beaten and abused by rebel soldiers, she said the Lord brought to her mind that those were his beatings. What they were doing to her, they were really doing to him. She counted it a privilege, then, to suffer for the cause of Christ. The soldiers had no idea Christ was identifying with Helen's suffering, just as Saul had no clue his persecution of the church was really a persecution of Christ. Nevertheless, that did not excuse what he or the soldiers did.

None who died in Susa or the provinces on the thirteenth or fourteenth days of the month of Adar were innocent. All were guilty. Here again is a visible picture of what we all deserve: death for our sin and rebellion against God. I am sure we each want to see ourselves as standing on the Lord's side, but do not miss that without Christ we would all continually strive against the Lord. Left to our own resources, we are all "alienated and hostile" in our minds and express evil through our actions (Col 1:21). This is why our only hope for change is being reconciled by Christ (Col 1:22).

Was Esther wrong for asking for another day of killing, especially since Haman's original edict called for attacking the Jews on one day only? The biblical author neither condemns nor vindicates her. Unlike so much of our contemporary news that is filled with commentary, here we get only the facts. Ahasuerus asked her what she wanted, and she wanted one more day of routing the enemies of her people. Some say she was vindictive and bloodthirsty and that this was how she got the name *Esther*—after Ishtar the Persian goddess of love and war. Others say she was completely in the right as she sought to wipe out all of those who wanted to harm God's people. Like many other aspects of the book of Esther, however, we cannot make a definite call on her motive or her innocence or guilt. We can just affirm that on that second day three hundred more enemies of God's people were put to death and that none of those were innocent. We can also affirm their stupidity: After seeing what happened the previous day and hearing reports from the provinces, did they really think their ongoing efforts against the Jews would turn out differently?

What a prime example of sin's foolishness this provides! We can clearly see its consequences one day yet assume that dabbling in it will lead to benign consequences the next. Sin will never lead you to anything good, and sin will not give you a pass. When will we learn? Probably not soon enough. So let us consider the three hundred rebels who fought on day two and learn from their foolish and fatal decision.

Third, *consider the deadly passion of Haman's household.* Certainly Haman's ten sons wanted to vindicate their father. They were probably among the leaders of those in the citadel who were more than likely seeking Mordecai's death, and maybe Esther's too if they could get to her. Passion and courage were not lacking among them, but unfortunately godliness was. The sons are reminders of two important things.

First, we can be passionate and still perish. Strong feelings and even sacrifice are noble qualities but not when used for the wrong purposes. People can have intense convictions about atheism, for example, but that does not make that way of thinking any more beneficial or true than it is for those who hold mild views of atheism. If we are wrong on an issue, we are wrong, and it does not matter how much passion we feel or exert toward whatever it is.

Second, reading about Haman's sons should prompt us to ask what we are leading those who come behind us to be passionate and sacrificial about? Haman's sons followed their father's footsteps right up to the point of joining him in eternal death. So where will our steps lead those we disciple? How many in our congregations are leading their children to be passionate about their favorite sports teams or leisure activities? How many in our congregations are leading those they are "discipling" to be passionate about things of the world? Where are the moms and dads who are passing down a legacy of making every effort to grow in godliness or making every effort to go with the gospel? Read these names and consider that Parshandatha, Dalphon, Aspatha, Poratha, Adalia, Aridatha, Parmashta, Arisai, Aridai, and Vaizatha each had an eternal soul. Their father led them to be passionate not about their Creator but about what perishes. What are the names of those entrusted to your care? What passions do they foster because of you?

Consider Their Restraint (9:10,15-16)

If a biblical author writes something multiple times, we should pay attention to it. For instance, Luke notes twice that Barabbas "had been thrown into prison for a rebellion that had taken place in the city, and for murder" (Luke 23:19,25). He does not want you to miss that Christ, the innocent one, will be killed, while Barabbas, the guilty one, will go free. Of course, there could not be a clearer picture of Jesus's substitution in our place. He is innocent, but we are guilty. He was punished; we are pardoned. Luke wants to be sure we get it.

No biblical author ever repeats something because his memory failed while he was writing! (That's certainly a possibility in this volume though. Have I mentioned that I hate snakes?) Three times in Esther 9 the author points out that the Jews had the opportunity to plunder the goods of those they killed, but they refused to do so. For the Jews this battle was about preservation and not economic advancement. As instruments of God's divine justice, their focus was on punishment, not plunder.

Years before, Abraham refused to take money from the king of Sodom (though he earned it with his victory in battle) because he did not want anyone to think he had advanced economically because of a pagan (Gen 14:22-23). And where Achan failed in the battle of Jericho (Josh 7:10-26), Esther's generation proved faithful. Strain notes,

> We do need to understand that in conducting holy war, the people of God were engaged in something quite different than a modern program of ethnic cleansing or geopolitical land grabbing. They were prosecuting the judicial decree of God in his wrath upon his enemies. It was, in fact, a graphic picture and expression of a deeper conflict, we've seen this before, that has raged, really, since Genesis 3:15 when God declared that the seed of the woman and the seed of the serpent would live in perpetual enmity, one with another, 'til one would come who'd crush the serpent's head. ("Holy War")

Had they lost, the Jews would have certainly been plundered. As a matter of fact, it was the main motivation Haman provided in his edict. But God's people exercised restraint. Their primary aim was life, not loot.

May the Celebration of the Lord's Deliverance Never Be Empty Ritual
ESTHER 9:17-28

See Their Relief and Rest (9:17-19)

The completion of a final exam always served as a highlight for me, both in college and in seminary. I wanted to run through the middle of the quad and shout "FREEDOM!" at the top of my lungs. There was

nothing like the feeling of relief that came after the flurry of preparation and perspiration. When I completed and defended my dissertation,
that feeling was multiplied many times over. I might have even cried. I
teared up at my graduation for sure. Relief!

After their battles God's people had relief from their enemies and
rest from striving, both of which came only after resolution to their
problem (Smith, *Ezra, Nehemiah, Esther*, 284). There is often little rest
and relief while a battle rages, though we long for it desperately. Rest
typically follows resolution. Suddenly, where they had first expected
ruin, there was an opportunity for reflection. The emotional toll of waiting for months to see how everything would turn out, the preparations
for defending their children and property, and the fatigue from fighting could all be released. It was time for recovery.

In Christ we too have relief from our enemies and rest from our
striving, but what we experience now in part we will know one day in
full. What a glorious day it will be when we are forever free from anxiety,
fear, and even striving in our sanctification! While we will still have work
in heaven, it will be free from toil and exhaustion, and it will always be
fruitful and done joyfully. What a glorious day it will be when we no
longer have a need for internet filters or must put away good gifts that
we have turned into terrible gods. Through Christ we will experience
full rest and relief, and we are one day closer to it today than we were
yesterday.

See Their Rejoicing (9:17-19)

Relief and rest are not ends in themselves, though, but means to rejoicing. The Jews' fasting was important, but now it was time for feasting. As
I mentioned earlier, the rejoicing was not in the deaths of the enemies
but in deliverance. Wherever they were, the Jews celebrated with a day
of good food and joy. Can't you picture the hugs, the smiles, children
being lifted into the air, hands raised in victory, and even dancing that
surely filled the streets? Breathing in oxygen and knowing they were
alive must have felt so good! In God's strength and with his provisions,
they had fought for one another, for life, for the ones who would come
behind them, and they had won. I am sure the celebration had to be
similar to the one that occurred on the banks of the Red Sea as the
last waves crashed over the charging Egyptian army and the Israelites
knew their enemy was vanquished and they were free! It is no wonder a

spontaneous worship service erupted on that shore (Exod 15). If I had a tambourine that day, I would have shaken it too (Exod 15:20)!

Every Sunday we gather and celebrate Christ's victory and the rest and relief he's granted us from sin and wrath. We celebrate life! We celebrate that one day all our enemies of the flesh, the world, and the devil will be put away forever. But rejoicing is not just for Sundays or holidays. I hope that rejoicing is one of your daily practices. Much as the Jews did after the battle, we can celebrate with certainty. Christ is our Victor. We have won because he has won!

See the Call for Remembrance (9:20-28)

For some reason we are prone to forget God's goodness to us. We see this tendency throughout the Bible. God does something great for his people. They are glad for a time. Then they forget. Esther and Mordecai did not want those in any generation to forget God's deliverance. They therefore instituted Purim as a yearly reminder and commanded every generation in perpetuity to observe it. Jews in the modern world, in fact, just observed Purim not long before I sat down to write this chapter.

This feast was not instituted by the Lord but by others as a means to celebrate something that should not be forgotten. In the Old Testament, God's people were often instructed to raise an *ebenezer* or a cairn so they would not forget something God had done and could teach future generations about God's goodness. Every time a child or grandchild would ask why a particular stone of remembering had been placed or why God's laws were so important, parents and grandparents had an opportunity to share the truth that

> *We were slaves of Pharaoh in Egypt, but the LORD brought us out of Egypt with a strong hand. Before our eyes the LORD inflicted great and devastating signs and wonders on Egypt, on Pharaoh, and on all his household, but he brought us from there in order to lead us in and give us the land that he swore to our fathers. The LORD commanded us to follow these statutes and to fear the LORD our God for our prosperity always and for our preservation, as it is today.* (Deut 6:21-24)

As the psalmist says, "We will not hide them from their children, but will tell a future generation the praiseworthy acts of the LORD, his might, and the wondrous works he has performed" (Ps 78:4).

With regard to Purim, Gregory offers some helpful thoughts:

By naming the festival "Purim," attention is focused on
something deeper. And it is this: the lot, or destiny, of God's
people is not left up to chance and it is not determined by
someone like Haman casting lots before his gods. No, only
God determines the lot of his people. The name reminds the
people that it is God and God alone who determines how
things turn out in the world. (*Inconspicuous Providence*, 166)

Relief for the Jews was not just gained, it was given. With the establish-
ment of a yearly reminder, God's people were encouraged to always
remember the Giver!

Whatever it takes, may we never forget God's goodness to us through
the gospel of Christ. Set reminders. Set alarms on your phone. Leave
yourself notes posted where you will see them each day. Keep lists of
the daily graces he extends to you. Participate in corporate singing with
your faith family and in hearing God's Word preached. Celebrate each
baptism and each time the Lord's Supper is observed. These are all aids
in helping us remember and rejoice in who he is and what he has done
for us.

One additional note about Purim. Gregory points out,

In the Jewish calendar, the year begins and ends around
March. It begins with a celebration of the Passover and
ends with a celebration of Purim. That is, it begins with
a celebration of how God delivered his people from the
oppression of Pharaoh in a foreign land, and it ends with
a celebration of how God delivered his people from the
oppression of Haman in a foreign land. (Ibid., 169)

Even when the Jews were far from home, God was not far from them.
This should be a great comfort to us, who are also "strangers and exiles"
(1 Pet 2:11).

Be Grateful It Has Been Recorded (9:20)

Nothing helps us remember and rejoice more than things we record.
No doubt realizing this, Mordecai wanted things written down so that
there would be a physical reminder of what occurred. How grateful we
should be for the written Word of God, and how passionate we should
be to see that all peoples have it in their languages! Consider these
thoughts from David Strain:

In many ways, the application of the whole book of Esther is right here in this section of Esther chapter 9. The answer to the question, "What is the book of Esther intended to do in the hearts of its readers?" is here. Here is the "So what?" question answered regarding Esther. The whole thing is designed to explain why the Jews observe Purim, that is, why do we rejoice and celebrate? Here's what you do with the truths of the book of Esther—you remember grace and you rejoice. The Jews did it at Purim; it's what we do every Lord's Day. . . . Part of our task, as we seek to remember the Sabbath day to keep it holy, is to do what the Jews do here at Purim, to remember to rehearse again the "old, old story of Jesus and his Cross," that we might reignite the flames of rejoicing in our hearts. A Sunday that is morbid and dark is not a godly Sabbath. Today is the day when life and immortality were brought to light, the day in which light was created, when the Light of the world broke through the darkness of death for us and our salvation. Today, brothers and sisters, of all days, we have reason for joy. Jesus Christ lives and reigns and has won a victory for us. ("Holy War")

Aren't you grateful the gospel has not just been proclaimed to you but preserved for you to read again and again in God's Word? Read, remember, rejoice, and then repeat.

In considering all that Mordecai recorded and the letters he and Esther sent, there is a bit of irony concerning where the book of Esther begins and ends. Remember when Ahasuerus's counselors had him send out a decree so that women would be kept in their place in their homes (1:22)? "At the end of the book of Esther, a letter goes out to the entire empire, with the king's own wife issuing the final command" (Gregory, *Inconspicuous Providence*, 167).

May We Be Faithful Stewards of All God Entrusts to Us
ESTHER 9:29–10:3

God Accomplishes His Perfect Plan through Imperfect People

At the beginning of this book, we did not even know Mordecai and Esther existed. Once we did, we were introduced to them and to their compromises and their initial lack of public identification with God's people. But as the story progressed, so did Esther's and Mordecai's understanding of what was entrusted to them, not just for their sake but for the sake of God's people scattered throughout the empire. Both displayed great courage and, above all, good stewardship of the positions of influence the Lord gave them. Recorded in the closing verses of the book is their power, influence, and making the most of their lives not just for Ahasuerus's kingdom but for the Lord's.

God accomplishes his perfect plan through imperfect people. This is good news for those who often have to admit, "I am conscious of my rebellion, and my sin is always before me" (Ps 51:3). Though we will still have moments of disobedience until glorification, God can and will still use us for his name's sake. Our plea is Christ's perfection and not ours. As Esther and Mordecai progressed in their understanding and usefulness, may we as well.

God Is in Charge of Our When, Where, and What

As we have noted, God is no less in charge of our *when, where*, and *what* than he was for Esther and Mordecai. Nothing is accidental or arbitrary about our skills, circumstances, or opportunities. For such a time as this, you and I have been entrusted to make disciples as we go to the nations and to our neighbors.

I often stress to high school and college students that we are not living a trial run. Life is not like a video game in which you can just go back to the last saved checkpoint and start over after a mess up. Your freshman year in high school or in college could not be more real. And while you may repeat a grade, you will never repeat a year.

As I write, Senator John McCain is serving his last term in the United States Senate. He was diagnosed with brain cancer in July 2017. Now that he does not have to run for reelection, he feels more freedom than ever to vote his conscience. In considering his time winding down both in political service and life in general, McCain referenced

> a line from *For Whom the Bell Tolls*: "The world is a fine place and worth the fighting for and I hate very much to leave it." McCain wrote: "I hate to leave it. But I don't have a complaint. Not one. It's been quite a ride. I've known great passions, seen amazing wonders, fought in a war, and helped make a peace. I made a small place for myself in the story of America and the history of my times." (Cooney, "I Hate to Leave")

Two phrases from McCain's response struck me. The first one was "I hate to leave it," and the second one was "the history of my times." If we would only consider both of these phrases more often, perhaps we would be gripped with gospel urgency. The days the Lord gives us are the history of our times. They are our *only* days. And soon we will no longer be in the positions in which we serve or even on this planet.

Even if you've worked for years with the same company and make many sacrifices, do not be surprised if the day after you retire they give your office to the next person to serve in your old position. The author of Ecclesiastes reminds us, "A generation goes and a generation comes, but the earth remains forever," and "There is no remembrance of those who came before; and of those who will come after there will also be no remembrance by those who follow them" (Eccl 1:4,11). Do you know the names of your great-great grandparents? Without looking at records, I do not. Since those who came before us did not know us and those who come behind us will not remember us, we should maximize our striving to reach those who are with us here and now. These are the only days of our lives.

The Gospel Fuels Our How and Our Why

I have made this point many times over in this book, so I will not belabor it here. All God expects from us, he provides for us in Jesus. He does not expect us to be strong in our strength but in his. He does not expect us to persevere in our power but in his. He does not expect us to contend for the gospel so that he will keep us; rather, we contend for the gospel because we are kept. We seek to know what he wants and do it in his power because we have been delivered, redeemed, and forgiven. The resources and the reasons for what we do arise from the gospel. May we who have put our hope in Christ "bring praise to his glory" (Eph 1:12).

May We Always Remember that God Is the Real Hero
ESTHER 9:29–10:3

Consider Their (Limited) Renown

As powerful as Mordecai became, he was not in command of the empire. His was definitely a significant position (ask Joseph), but he still served under a pagan king. And even though it might have been all the world they knew, Persia was not all the world there was, and certainly not all the planets in our galaxy or every star in existence belonged to it. As great as the deliverance was for the Jews, they were still in Persia, and they were still under Ahasuerus's reign. Neither Esther nor Mordecai was ultimate liberator of God's people. He was still to come! And he is "KING OF KINGS AND LORD OF LORDS" (Rev 19:16).

In the book of Esther, a significant issue was resolved for God's people, but it wasn't the ultimate issue. Even though they were granted victory over the edict of doom, the Jews were still under the domain of darkness with sin and death. They did not die on the day they battled, but eventually death came for them all and the children they fought for as well as the grandchildren they never met. A greater victory was needed.

The recording of their renown is also a reminder that we can be faithful and God can bless that faithfulness, but history does not revolve around us. Twice in high school my first name was misspelled on our baseball team's calendars and once on an award I received for football. I learned early on, then, that only one name matters. Be faithful. Be a good steward. But remember that any good that comes through us is a work of God's grace; therefore, he should receive the glory.

What Can We Learn about Jesus from This Text?

First, *in the battle for our deliverance, Christ alone has achieved victory.* Unlike the Jews who worked together, no one gathered to help Jesus be our substitute. His closest friends abandoned him, and some blatantly betrayed him. Unlike the Jews who had every Persian official standing with them, Jesus had no political person intervening on his behalf. Pilate washed his hands of the issue, and he and Herod bonded in their opposition. Christ alone stood against our enemies and defeated them with his death.

Second, *as Haman's sons' bodies were hanged in shame, so was Christ's.* He was hung on the tree because in our place he was cursed. He received the full punishment of divine wrath, but he also experienced the full brunt of our shame. Haman's sons' bodies hung in defeat, and they deserved it. They are an example of what happens to all who come against the Lord. And the shame and defeat they experienced should be what we experience. But look! There is Christ, crucified in our place.

Third, *Christ brings eternal and true liberation.* The Jews in Esther's and Mordecai's day experienced rest and relief from their enemies in a particular instance, but Christ provides rest and relief from our enemies forever. An example of the temporary nature of the Jews' relief can be seen in Ahasuerus's taxation on the land (10:1). Nothing dispels relief and rest like getting a letter from the IRS in your mailbox! Whom the Son has set free, however, will be free forever! No more taxation and no more trouble.

Consider the Lord's Supper

Though few of us observe Purim, we have been given a celebration feast as well. The Lord's Supper is a reminder of God's greatest reversal and his greatest goodness to us. The Jews celebrated Purim with rejoicing in relief, but how much more should the resurrection fuel our praise? At Purim they gave gifts to the poor, but at the Lord's Supper we celebrate what Jesus gave to the poorest. He says to us, "Blessed are the poor in spirit, for the kingdom of heaven is theirs" (Matt 5:3).

At Purim they would look backward and remember, which we do with the Lord's Supper. However, we also look forward. We know Christ is coming again, and we will drink the cup together with him. The Lord's Supper provides us a time to remember the cost paid for us to be able to participate in a future Table. All the feasts combined in the book of Esther cannot compare with the feast we will experience one day. As John was told to write, "'Blessed are those invited to the marriage feast of the Lamb!'" (Rev 19:9). John Frame notes, "We eat only little bits of bread and drink little cups of wine, for we know that our fellowship with Christ in this life cannot begin to compare with the glory that awaits us in him" (*Systematic Theology*, 1069).

Conclusion

Through his providence and in keeping with his promises, God placed Esther and Mordecai in positions of power to preserve his people and punish his enemies. Somewhere in the empire were those who would one day be recorded in the messianic genealogies listed in the Gospels. We do not know where they were, but God did. He kept them alive so that "when the time came to completion, God sent his Son, born of a woman, born under the law, to redeem those under the law, so that we might receive adoption as sons" (Gal 4:4-5). God kept them alive so that through them his Son might be sent. And through his death, we are granted life. As Paul declares, "He has rescued us from the domain of darkness and transferred us into the kingdom of the Son he loves. In him we have redemption, the forgiveness of sins" (Col 1:13-14). The decree of death has been destroyed!

In the book of Esther, God does not have to be named for us to notice his work. But it certainly was his work, so let us join the psalmist in declaring, "Not to us, LORD, not to us, but to your name give glory because of your faithful love, because of your truth" (Ps 115:1).

Reflect and Discuss

1. In what ways, if any, are you striving for faithfulness where your parents or those who discipled you failed?

2. What reversals, if any, have you seen the Lord bring about in your journey? How have you seen him turn to good what others intended for your harm?

3. Though the striking down of God's enemies seems harsh, why is it ultimately about holiness? How do we reconcile a text like Esther with Christ's call to love our enemies and pray for them?

4. The fate of Haman's sons should be a warning to all of us. How can we train those who come behind us to be passionate about and sacrificial for the things of God and not just our own agendas?

5. The struggle against enemies produced unity among God's people. How should our struggles against the flesh, the world, and the devil produce the same in us? What things prevent us from uniting in these battles?

6. How often do you rejoice in the rest and relief Christ provides? How and why should you do so more?

7. In what ways are you intentional about reminding yourself of what God has done for us in Jesus? Why do we have to be intentional about this?

8. How grateful are you to have God's Word recorded? How do you demonstrate this gratitude? What can we do so that all may have his Word?

9. In what ways has our journey through the book of Esther and seeing how God uses imperfect people to accomplish his perfect plans encouraged you? How has it been helpful?

10. What is something you have learned through your study of Esther? How will it impact how you live?

WORKS CITED

Associated Press. "Senior North Korean Defector Says His Sons Were Reason He Fled." Accessed April 16, 2018, http://www.latimes .com/world/la-fg-korean-defector-20170125-story.html.

Anderson, Courtney. *To the Golden Shore*. Valley Forge, PA: Judson, 1989.

Babcock, Maltbie D. "This Is My Father's World." Accessed April 14, 2018, https://hymnary.org/text/this_is_my_fathers_world_and_to_my.

Baldwin, Joyce G. *Esther: An Introduction and Commentary*. Downers Grove, IL: InterVarsity Press, 1984.

Benge, Janet, and Geoff Benge. *Adoniram Judson: Bound for Burma*. Seattle, WA: YWAM Publishing, 2000.

Bloom, Jon. "Success Can Be Perilous." *Desiring God*. January 13, 2010. Accessed April 28, 2018, https://www.desiringgod.org/articles /success-can-be-perilous.

Bratt, James D., ed. *Abraham Kuyper: A Centennial Reader*. Grand Rapids, MI: Eerdmans, 1998.

Breneman, Mervin. *Ezra, Nehemiah, and Esther*. The New American Commentary 10. Nashville, TN: B&H, 1993.

Bridges, Jerry. *The Gospel for Real Life: Turn to the Liberating Power of the Cross . . . Every Day*. Colorado Springs, CO: NavPress, 2003.

"Brer Rabbit and the Tar Baby." Accessed May 1, 2018, http://american folklore.net/folklore/2010/07/brer_rabbit_meets_a_tar_baby.html.

Bush, Frederic. *Ruth/Esther*. Word Biblical Commentary 9. Grand Rapids, MI: Zondervan, 1996.

Charles, H. B. *On Pastoring: A Short Guide to Living, Leading, and Ministering as a Pastor*. Chicago, IL: Moody, 2016.

Cole, Steven J. "Overcoming Spiritual Failure" Accessed April 28, 2018, http://www.fcfonline.org/content/1/sermons/032215m.pdf.

Cooney, Samantha. "'I Hate to Leave.' John McCain *Opens* Up about His Brain Cancer Diagnosis and the Future of Politics." *Time*. April

30, 2018. Accessed April 30, 2018, http://time.com/5260113/john
-mccain-health-book.

"Corvette Cave In Exhibit Opens on Two Year Anniversary of Museum
Sinkhole." Accessed April 14, 2018, https://www.corvettemuseum
.org/corvette-cave-in-exhibit-opens-on-two-year-anniversary-of
-museum-sinkhole.

Denhollander, Rachael. "Read Rachael Denhollander's Full Victim
Impact Statement about Larry Nassar." *CNN.com.* January 30, 2018.
Accessed April 28, 2018, https://www.cnn.com/2018/01/24/us
/rachael-denhollander-full-statement.

Dever, Mark. *The Message of the Old Testament: Promises Made.* Wheaton,
IL: Crossway, 2006.

Dowden, Landon. *Exalting Jesus in Ezekiel.* Christ-Centered Exposition
Commentary. Nashville, TN: Holman Reference, 2015.

Duchon, Richie. "Host Steve Harvey Botches Miss Universe Announcement." *NBCNews.com.* December 20, 2015. Accessed April 28, 2018,
https://www.nbcnews.com/pop-culture/pop-culture-news/host
-steve-harvey-botches-miss-universe-announcement-n483586.

Duguid, Iain M. *Esther and Ruth.* Phillipsburg, NJ: P&R Publishing, 2005.

Firth, David G. *The Message of Esther: God Present but Unseen.* Downers
Grove, IL: IVP Academic, 2010.

Fitzpatrick, Elyse. "Introduction to Esther." Pages 599–600 in *Gospel
Transformation Bible.* Wheaton, IL: Crossway, 2013.

Fox, Michael V. *Character and Ideology in the Book of Esther.* 2nd ed. Grand
Rapids, MI: Eerdmans, 2001.

Frame, John M. *Systematic Theology: An Introduction to Christian Belief.*
Phillipsburg, NJ: P & R Publishing, 2013.

Gilbert, Mathew. "The Greatest Treasure." Accessed April 24, 2018,
http://tracecrossing.org/#/resources/sermons.

Goldsworthy, Graeme. *According to Plan.* Downers Grove, IL: IVP
Academic, 1991.

———. *Gospel and Kingdom.* Exeter: Paternoster, 2012.

Gregory, Bryan R. *Inconspicuous Providence: The Gospel according to Esther.*
Phillipsburg, NJ: P & R Publishing, 2014.

Hallo, William W. "The First Purim." *Biblical Archaeologist* 46, no. 1
(Winter 1983): 19–26.

Hautman, Nicholas. "Oscars 2017 Best Picture Mix-up: Everything
We Know So Far, Plus What Went Wrong." *US Weekly,* February
27, 2017. Accessed April 27, 2018, https://www.usmagazine.com

/entertainment/news/oscars-2017-best-picture-mix-up-everything
-we-know-w469304.

Henley, William Ernest. "Invictus." Accessed April 14, 2018, https://
www.poets.org/poetsorg/poem/invictus.

Henry, Matthew. *Commentary on the Whole Bible*. Grand Rapids, MI:
Zondervan, 1970.

Herodotus. *The Histories*. Translated by Aubrey De Sélincourt. Revised
with introduction and notes by John Marincola. London: Penguin,
2003.

Ironside, H. A. *Ezra, Nehemiah, and Esther*. Grand Rapids, MI: Kregel, 2008.

Jenkins, Bethany. "Esther and the Silent Sovereignty of God." *The Gospel
Coalition*. July 16, 2015. Accessed April 9, 2018, https://www.thegos-
pelcoalition.org/article/esther-the-silent-sovereignty-of-god.

Jobes, Karen H. *Esther*. NIV Application Commentary. Grand Rapids,
MI: Zondervan, 1999.

"John D. Rockefeller." August 25, 2016. Accessed April 12, 2018, http://
www.newworldencyclopedia.org/entry/John_D._Rockefeller.

Kaiser, Walter C., Jr. *Preaching and Teaching from the Old Testament: A Guide
for the Church*. Grand Rapids, MI: Baker Academic, 2003.

Kell, Garrett. "I Was a Pastor Hooked on Porn." *The Gospel Coalition*.
August 27, 2017. Accessed April 25, 2018, https://www.thegospel
coalition.org/article/i-was-pastor-hooked-on-porn.

Keller, Timothy J. "Esther and the Hiddenness of God." Accessed
January 20, 2017, https://gospelinlife.com/downloads/esther
-and-the-hiddenness-of-god.

———. "If I Perish, I Perish." Accessed January 27, 2017, https://gospel
inlife.com/downloads/if-i-perish-i-perish-5528.

———. "Preaching Christ in a Postmodern World." Unpublished Doctor
of Ministry class notes presented though Reformed Theological
Seminary, January, 2002. Accessed April 6, 2018, http://servant
ofmessiah.org/wp-content/uploads/2015/09/Timothy-Keller
-Preaching-the-Gospel-in-a-Post-Modern-World-Rev-2002.pdf.

Kuruvilla, Abraham. *Privilege the Text!* Chicago, IL: Moody, 2013.

LaSor, William Sanford, David Allan Hubbard, and Frederic William
Bush. *Old Testament Survey*. Grand Rapids, MI: Eerdmans, 1996.

Leahy, Stephen. "Man Bitten by Shark, Bear, and Snake Had Odds of 893
Quadrillion to One." *National Geographic*. April 24, 2018. Accessed
April 27, 2018, https://news.nationalgeographic.com/2018/04
/odds-of-man-bit-shark-bear-snake-dylan-mcwilliams-animals-spd.

Longenecker, Richard N. *Biblical Exegesis in the Apostolic Period.* Grand Rapids, MI: Eerdmans, 1975.

Mahaney, C. J. *Humility: True Greatness.* Sisters, OR: Multnomah, 2005.

Mathis, David. *Habits of Grace: Enjoying Jesus through the Spiritual Disciplines.* Wheaton, IL: Crossway, 2016.

Metaxas, Eric. *Bonhoeffer: Pastor, Martyr, Prophet, Spy.* Nashville, TN: Thomas Nelson, 2010.

Meyer, Jason. "Modern Era Genocides." Accessed April 24, 2018, https://genocideeducation.org/resources/modern-era-genocides.

———. "Pride." Pages 9–19 in *Killjoys: The Seven Deadly Sins.* Edited by Marshall Segal. Minneapolis, MN: Desiring God, 2015.

Mohler, R. Albert. *He Is Not Silent.* Chicago, IL: Moody, 2008.

Mohr, Jon. "Find Us Faithful." Accessed April 20, 2018, http://steve greenministries.org/product/find-us-faithful-5.

Muller, Roland. *Honor and Shame: Unlocking the Door.* Bloomington, IN: Xlibris, 2000.

"The 9 Rules of Every Wile E. Coyote and Road Runner Cartoon." *Time,* March 6, 2015. Accessed April 28, 2018, http://time.com/3735089 /wile-e-coyote-road-runner.

Osbeck, Kenneth W. *Amazing Grace: 366 Inspiring Hymn Stories for Daily Devotions.* Grand Rapids, MI: Kregel, 1990.

Owen, John. "Of Communion with God the Father, Son, and Holy Ghost." In *The Works of John Owen,* vol. 2. Johnstone and Hunter, 1850–1853. Reprint, Carlisle, PA: Banner of Truth, 2004.

Paton, Lewis B. *A Critical and Exegetical Commentary on the Book of Esther.* International Critical Commentary. New York, NY: Charles Scribner's Sons, 1908.

Piper, John. "Be Strong and Courageous in Jesus." *Desiring God.* February 20, 2017. Accessed April 26, 2018, https://www.desiringgod.org/be -strong-and-courageous-in-jesus.

———. *The Dawning of Indestructible Joy: Daily Readings for Advent.* Wheaton, IL: Crossway, 2014.

———. *A Hunger for God: Desiring God through Fasting and Prayer.* Wheaton, IL: Crossway, 1997.

———. "Was Dietrich Bonhoeffer Wrong to Plot against Hitler's Life?" *Desiring God.* March 28, 2008. Accessed April 23, 2018, https://www.desiringgod.org/interviews/was-dietrich-bonhoeffer -wrong-to-plot-against-hitlers-life.

Platt, David. "Let Justice Roll Down like Waters: Racism and Our Need for Repentance." Accessed April 24, 2018, http://t4g.org/media /2018/04/let-justice-roll-like-waters-racism-need-repentance.

Prime, Derek. *Unspoken Lessons about the Unseen God: Esther Simply Explained.* Auburn, MA: Evangelical Press, 2001.

Prime, Derek J., and Alistair Begg. *On Being a Pastor: Understanding Our Calling and Work.* Chicago, IL: Moody, 2004.

Purves, Carol. *Chinese Whispers: The Gladys Aylward Story.* Leominster, UK: Day One, 2005.

Roberts, Vaughan. *God's Big Picture.* Downers Grove, IL: InterVarsity, 2002.

Roosevelt, Franklin D. "A Date Which Will Live in Infamy." Accessed April 28, 2018, http://historymatters.gmu.edu/d/5166.

Ryle, J. C. *Expository Thoughts on the Gospels.* London, UK: Wertheim and Macintosh, 1856. Accessed April 20, 2018, https://www.monergism .com/thethreshold/sdg/expository_web.html#markc14.

Schwartz, John, and Matthew L. Wald. "The Nation: NASA's Curse? 'Groupthink' Is 30 Years Old and Still Going Strong." *New York Times.* March, 9, 2003. Accessed April 16, 2018, https://www .nytimes.com/2003/03/09/weekinreview/the-nation-nasa-s-curse -groupthink-is-30-years-old-and-still-going-strong.html.

Segal, Marshall. "Introduction." Pages v–xiii in *Killjoys: The Seven Deadly Sins.* Edited by Marshall Segal. Minneapolis, MN: Desiring God, 2015.

Shaughnessy, Larry. "Medal of Honor Takes Moment to Earn, Years to Receive." *CNN.com.* November 16, 2010. http://www.cnn.com/2010 /US/11/16/medal.of.honor.giunta.process/index.html.

Smith, Gary V. "Esther." Pages 421–27 in *What the Old Testament Authors Really Cared About: A Survey of Jesus' Bible.* Edited by Jason S. DeRouchie. Grand Rapids, MI: Kregel, 2013.

———. *Ezra, Nehemiah, Esther.* Cornerstone Biblical Commentary 5B. Carol Stream, IL: Tyndale House, 2010.

Spafford, Anna. "Telegram from Anna Spafford to Horatio Gates Spafford re being 'saved alone' among her traveling party in the shipwreck of the Ville du Havre." Accessed April 29, 2018, https:// www.loc.gov/item/mamcol000006.

Spafford, Horatio G. "It Is Well with My Soul." Accessed April 29, 2018, http://library.timelesstruths.org/music/It_Is_Well_with_My_Soul.

Strain, David. "Beauty and the Beast." Accessed January 27, 2017, https://www.fpcjackson.org/resource-library/sermons/beauty-and -the-beast.

———. "Holy War." Accessed April 30, 2018, https://www.fpcjackson .org/resource-library/sermons/holy-war.

———. "The Lord Reigns." Accessed January 20, 2017, https://www. fpcjackson.org/resource-library/sermons/the-lord-reigns.

Teitel, Amy Shira. "How Groupthink Led to 7 Lives Lost in the Challenger Explosion." *History.com.* January 25, 2018. Accessed April 16, 2018, https://www.history.com/news/how-the-challenger -disaster-changed-nasa.

Tolkien, J. R. R. *The Fellowship of the Ring.* Boston, MA: Mariner Books, 1994.

Tripp, Paul David. *Instruments in the Redeemer's Hands.* Phillipsburg, NJ: P&R Publishing, 2002.

———. *Parenting: 14 Gospel Principles That Can Radically Change Your Family.* Wheaton, IL: Crossway, 2016.

Vines, Jerry, and Jim Shaddix. *Progress in the Pulpit: How to Grow in Your Preaching.* Chicago, IL: Moody, 2017.

Wakely, Robin. "רעב". Pages 683–90 in vol. 1 of *New International Dictionary of Old Testament Theology and Exegesis.* Edited by Willem A. VanGemeren. Grand Rapids, MI: Zondervan, 1997.

Wallace, Francesca. "This Is the Plan in Place for When the Queen Passes Away." *Vogue.* March 17, 2017. Accessed May 1, 2018, https:// www.vogue.com.au/culture/features/this-is-the-plan-in-place-for -when-the-queen-passes-away/news-story/908b31bb1fcfd569bc6a25 8307c1b1a8?.

Watson, Thomas. *A Body of Divinity.* Carlisle, PA: Banner of Truth, 1957.

White, E. B. *Charlotte's Web.* New York, NY: HarperCollins, 1952.

Whitney, Donald S. *Spiritual Disciplines for the Christian Life.* Colorado Springs, CO: NavPress, 1991.

Wilson, Jared. "The Church and Idolatry." *Ligonier Ministries.* June 1, 2012. Accessed April 26, 2018, https://www.ligonier.org/learn /articles/the-church-and-idolatry.

SCRIPTURE INDEX